Y0-BRV-536

MANAGING THE CATALOG DEPARTMENT

third edition

by
Donald L. Foster

The Scarecrow Press, Inc.
Metuchen, N.J., & London
1987

Library of Congress Cataloging-in-Publication Data

Foster, Donald LeRoy, 1928–
    Managing the catalog department.

    Bibliography: p.
    Includes index.
    1. Cataloging--Management. I. Title.
Z693.F67 1987   025.3'068'4   86-33884
ISBN 0-8108-1973-2

Copyright © 1987 by Donald L. Foster
Manufactured in the United States of America

025.30684
P754 m
1987

CONTENTS

PREFACE TO THE THIRD EDITION

Once again, the opportunity to revise this book has been a welcome one. First, because of the warm reception given the first two editions; second, because of the advances made in recent years in management tools, techniques, and philosophies.

Expanding and updating in the previous edition focused mainly on department communications and on various technological issues that confronted department heads in the early 1980s. Much of the updating in this, the third edition, continues to center on technology. Other revision includes new sections on career development, performance standards, problem solving, time management, attitude surveys, and workshop training, among others.

I would also like, once again, to emphasize the purpose of this book, which is to offer readers an introduction to "managing the catalog department." This is not a book on cataloging. Another point that should be underscored is that the examples used to illustrate management principles continue to center on manual cataloging. Although computer-based cataloging, especially networking, is fast becoming the norm, few libraries are fully automated or are as yet able to support online catalogs. At any rate, the management principles and practices discussed in this book will apply to just about any cataloging operation, regardless of whether the end product is a card, book, COM, or online catalog.

Throughout the book, I have followed grammatical convention and used the male pronoun "he" in referring to the department head and, depending on the context, "he," "she," or "they" in referring to catalogers and support staff. No sexual bias is intended. But until the English language creates a singular pronoun that refers to both sexes, I prefer to avoid the cumbersome repetition of double pronouns.

Finally, let me here again thank the many librarians who have offered comments and suggestions for this third edition. Their continued interest is appreciated and their advice seriously taken.

D.L.F.

INTRODUCTION

The purpose of this book is to introduce the reader to the theory and, especially, to the practice of managing a catalog department. It is not a how-to catalog, but a how-to-manage-it book. It does not, in other words, cover hanging indentions, see-also references, corporate entries, and the like; rather, it deals with management. Where a specific cataloging routine is detailed it is either because a management principle needs clarifying or because an understanding of the activity is considered by the author to be essential to successful bibliographic administration.

The book is therefore written for the librarian (or the prospective librarian) who is already familiar with the fundamentals of cataloging and classification and who now seeks an understanding of their application in a typical library environment. Acquiring the knowledge necessary to construct a department manual, close a card catalog, and recruit and train staff is just as essential to the organization and control of library materials as is the ability to assign subject headings. Nor are we concerned here with the theoretical and historical aspects of bibliographic organization. Theory is discussed, but only as it relates to day-to-day management.

One more point must be stressed. Many of the terms used will denote in the minds of many readers a fairly large organizational structure; however, these terms can be easily translated to fit the smaller library setting, as can the management principles to which they relate. The principles and practices discussed pertain as much to the one- and two-person cataloging operation as to the large catalog department. Thus, where appropriate, the reader may wish to substitute "branch librarian" for "department head," "student assistant" for "marking chief," and so on.

For the purpose of our investigation, however, and as a convenient frame of reference, we will be discussing management as it applies to a traditional catalog department, one that may or may not belong to a computer-based network, but one that has not as yet developed on online catalog as part of an institution-wide, fully integrated automated system. Our traditional department, along with a serials department, acquisition (or monograph) department, and perhaps one or two other processing units, will constitute what is called in most libraries the technical services division. The technical services division plus the readers' service division will, in turn, make up the two main branches of our hypothetical library. Many libraries do not, of course, operate on a divisional plan. Others have three or four divisions instead of the traditional two. In still other libraries a good deal of the original cataloging will be decentralized, performed by subject specialists, reference librarians, and bibliographers in branch and departmental libraries. Generally, though, no matter how the library is organized administratively, it will have one unit, usually called the "catalog department," whose main purpose will be to catalog and classify all or most of the materials entering the library, and whose management we will study in the following chapters.

Chapter 1

THE DEPARTMENT

Neither an ideal nor a typical catalog department exists, either on paper or in reality. The variables that dictate the structures of real-life departments make it impossible to construct a composite of any sort. Factors such as type of library, number of titles processed, size of professional and support staff, use of outside processing services, membership in a bibliographic network, manual or automated cataloging, and managerial philosophies (or lack of philosophies) of the library administration have made standardization impossible. Yet most departments, no matter how large or how small, do seek similar goals, perform similar functions, and confront similar management problems. Even a small library that receives the vast majority of its books preprocessed will have at least some in-house cataloging responsibilities. Therefore, before exploring the theory and practice of cataloging management, it is best to define the various functions of a typical (or, better, an atypical) catalog department. To begin with, we will follow the progress of a book (it could be a nonbook, of course) as it moves through the various pre-cataloging, cataloging, and post-cataloging operations. Although more and more libraries are automating their cataloging, acquisition, and other bibliographic operations, we will be examining here mainly manual functions, since the majority of libraries still maintain traditional card catalogs.

Pre-cataloging. Many operations related to the cataloging and classification of books and other materials are, in most libraries, actually performed before the materials arrive in the catalog department. Such tasks as ordering cards and verifying entries are, for example, quite often the responsibility of acquisition personnel. At any rate, it is important to understand something of the acquisition operations if we hope to fit the cataloging and classification of books into the total processing operation.

First, the book must be selected by a librarian, patron, selection committee, or other individual or group for inclusion in the library's collection. After selection and before the actual ordering, the author, title, edition, and imprint are verified. That is to say, the item must be checked against Publishers Weekly, Books in Print, dealers' catalogs, or other standard bibliographic tools to establish information necessary for purchasing the book. In order not to duplicate efforts, it is important that during this initial verification, the searcher find and record as much bibliographic information as possible, including whether or not catalog cards or other cataloging data are available. The point is, no one in the catalog department should have to re-search the same tools for the same bibliographic information. Also, the searcher must estimate the book's cost and select the appropriate dealer or vendor. Although this verification is usually done by the acquisition department, in many larger libraries a special bibliographic or searching unit would be responsible for this as well as all other library searching. In smaller libraries, it is possible that the entire operation would be performed by one individual (perhaps the same person who will catalog the book after it arrives), while in larger libraries these various steps (selecting, verification, typing forms, ordering, and so on) might be performed by different staff members.

During the verification procedure a multiple order form is typed, usually in standard 3 x 5 size. The number of carbons will depend on the uses to which each is put. One part will be the dealer's copy; another will be filed into an orders-outstanding file; perhaps another will go into an encumbrance file; another might be used as a bibliographic or catalog department work slip; still another might be a notification slip for the person or branch library that ordered the book; perhaps another will be filed into the public card catalog as a notice to patrons and librarians that the book has been ordered and will soon be available for use; and finally, another can be used to order catalog cards. Conceivably the library will use its slips for all these purposes, although most institutions will be satisfied with three or four copies. A library can, and usually does, use at least one or two slips for more than one purpose.

After the bibliographic search and the typing of order slips, the book is ordered and one slip dated and filed into an orders-out file. When the book is received it is checked against the order slips, and the invoice is paid. The book, with the remaining slips, is then sent to the catalog department.

In many larger libraries, not only is much of the bibliographic searching done before the book reaches the catalog department, but quite often catalog cards are ordered, perhaps even sent along with the book to the catalog department. Acquisition personnel may also search and photocopy from the National Union Catalog (NUC), retrieve cataloging copy from a microfiche file, or produce a printout on a network terminal. In some libraries, even the cataloging of books with Library of Congress or other cards is performed in the acquisition department or special searching section. In this case, the materials by-pass the catalogers.

Depending on the organization of the technical services division, materials can enter the catalog department not only from the acquisition department but through various other routes. Usually the form of the material and how it is received in the library will dictate the route. A magazine, for instance, will probably be ordered and sent to the catalog department from the serials department and a gift will come from the gifts and exchange librarian. But each item--whether purchased or a gift, a book, magazine, or microfilm--should arrive in the catalog department with multiple order forms attached and at least some preliminary searching performed, perhaps even with catalog cards or other bibliographic copy included.

Cataloging and classification. The book has now arrived in the catalog department. As indicated earlier, at some point before its arrival it will have received at least some preliminary searching either before or after it was ordered. Also, if the responsibility for retrieving cataloging copy lies in the acquisition department, a set of cards, computer printout, or other hard copy will accompany the book and multiple order forms.

Upon the book's arrival, a staff member will check for handling and disposition. Is it a serial, added copy, reference book, or rare book? Will it need original cataloging or can it be cataloged with LC (Library of Congress) or other copy? If it goes to a specific location or must receive special treatment (binding, for instance) it will be flagged. Also at this point, one or more of the following might be done: 1) the book is matched with catalog cards or other cataloging information; 2) cards are ordered; 3) the book searched on a computer terminal; and/or 4) the book is set aside to await cards.

If original cataloging is necessary because of the unavailability of catalog cards or other cataloging copy (and it has been decided not to wait for the possible future availability of cataloging information), the book then passes on to a professional cataloger. In a small department of one or two professionals there will be little choice as to who will do the cataloging. In larger departments, however, the choice will depend upon the subject matter, type of material, or language. Generally, most catalog departments divide the original cataloging by subject specialty, one cataloger processing science books, another art books, and so on. Exactly how finely the work is divided will depend on the number of catalogers and the amount of material the library acquires in each subject field. The department head may also want to divide by form, language, or location. In a larger department, for example, there will be at least one cataloger who handles only serials and another who catalogs all phonograph records (division by form), perhaps another who catalogs all Russian language books regardless of subject (division by language), and still another who catalogs only books going to the law library (division by branch library).

If necessary, the cataloger will search the card catalog, NUC, computer database, and other tools to verify the author and title. Perhaps he will find an earlier edition or even another book on the same subject from which he can pull a call number or subject heading. However, if this verification has already been done before the book arrived in the department--and it should have been--no further searching is necessary. After verification, the cataloger will do the descriptive cataloging, select subject headings, and assign a call number. In larger libraries these three operations might actually be performed by two or three different catalogers.

The cataloger will then either fill out a special worksheet indicating all the descriptive cataloging information he wants included on the master card, or he will type a 3 x 5 scratch card ("p-slip") formatted similarly to the final catalog card. The former method is becoming more and more popular in larger libraries and is definitely the most convenient for computer input. In either case, the professional cataloger should not spend time typing the final, clean copy nor bother with computer input. His time is too valuable for what are essentially clerical routines.

The cataloger then sends the copy to a clerk who will type a unit card for duplication, or, in the case of an automated system, input the information into the computer. The unit card will be duplicated by Xerox, multilith, computer printer, or other means, and the card set returned to the typist. If the duplication method does not provide for the subject headings and added entries, a clerk must type the necessary headings.

If catalog cards, computer printout, Cataloging in Publication data, or other bibliographic information are available, the book need not, and should not, go to a professional cataloger. If the library is willing to accept, as is, cataloging from the Library of Congress, a book vendor, or a central processing service, the book can then be handled by a clerk. The clerk merely compares the LC or other copy with the book, makes necessary adjustments, types headings and call number if necessary, checks against the shelflist for possible call number duplication, and processes the book. The typist may also type the book plate and book pocket, although this can be done later when the piece is marked. The book and catalog cards are then revised for clerical and typing errors, the book sent to the preparation section for marking and labeling, and the cards filed into the shelflist and the main card catalog.

Post-cataloging. After the book has been cataloged and classified, a good deal still remains to be done before it is ready for use. If not already accomplished somewhere along its journey through the catalog department, the book must be marked, book pocket or date due slip affixed, ownership markings stamped or embossed, and, finally, the catalog cards filed. If the library subscribes to a processing service or belongs to a regional network that furnishes shelf-ready books, much of the post-cataloging processing may be provided by the service. If not, it is usually the responsibility of the catalog department to make the book ready for the shelf.

Organizing the Department

For an in-depth look at the modern catalog department, we must examine more closely the specific cataloging activities. In smaller libraries, many of these activities will be combined; perhaps all will be performed by one full- or part-time professional with some clerical help. In larger libraries, each activity would represent a separate unit within the catalog department, staffed by several professionals and/or nonprofessionals. How a specific catalog department is organized will, therefore, depend a great deal on its size. If we examine the organizational charts of libraries of various sizes and types we find obvious similarities as well as some marked differences, depending on the exact state of development and the organizational philosophy of each library. Within a matter of a few years, a department could, for example, grow from one or two people to, say, twenty or twenty-five full-time professionals and clerks. Conversely, because of the growing popularity (and necessity!) of centralized processing, many departments will experience cuts in personnel, and thus reductions in the size of their operations. The point is, changes occur and are continually occurring. While catalog departments were considered as static in the past, today they are dynamic organizations subject to constant change.

Thus, despite similarities in the goals of all catalog departments, their structures can differ greatly. An organizational plan that will work well in one department may not work at all in another. Nor is it clear exactly what kind of structure will work best in any given situation, particularly in times of change. Simply to keep abreast of changing technology, the department head must continually examine, experiment, and adjust. And after he has evolved the structure that best meets local needs, circumstances will force him to re-examine, re-experiment, and re-adjust.

If a department becomes large enough (approximately ten or more full-time staff) the department head will want to organize it into sections. The nature of this sectioning will depend on the size of the department, the processing flow-patterns, and, of course, the specific activities performed by the department. Several of these activities may, in fact, have little to do with the cataloging and classification of books and other materials, yet they will be assigned to the catalog department simply because they must go somewhere. Converse-

ly, certain functions that have traditionally been assigned to
the catalog department (LC cataloging, for instance) are, in
some libraries, now found in acquisition or other departments.

Bibliographic searching. Of all the functions related
to the cataloging and classification of library materials, bibliographic searching is perhaps the least standardized. Some
libraries search before the materials are ordered (pre-order
searching); others search after the materials have been received (post-order searching); still others search immediately
before the materials are cataloged (pre-cataloging searching);
and many libraries search at all three points. Thus, staff
responsible for the bibliographic searching will also vary from
library to library. In one library, all searching will be performed by a searching section in the acquisition or bibliography department; in another, searching will be part of the
catalog department's responsibilities; in still another, it will
be centralized in a separate searching or bibliographic verification department in the technical services division; however
in most libraries, bibliographic searching will be performed in
all departments of the library, each search done for a specific, immediate purpose. The person who orders a book will
search for necessary ordering information; whoever receives
it will search again to clear acquisition records and perhaps
determine whether to order catalog cards or send the piece
on for original cataloging; and, finally, after it reaches the
catalog department it will be searched again for cataloging information.

Clearly, multiple searching leads to duplication of effort; and in most libraries duplication is evident. Yet different library units require different kinds of bibliographic information for different reasons; and each requires this information at a different time. The lag between when the book is
first searched for ordering information and when it is cataloged
can be many months (years?), making the pre-order search
of a new title of little value to the catalog department. It is
often not until a book arrives in the department, or even several months later, that the Library of Congress, library network, or central processing service will have catalog cards
available.

In any case, if the searching procedure is well organized,
much or most of the pre-cataloging searching will have been
accomplished before the book arrives in the catalog department.

The author and title will have been verified and the availability of cards or LC copy determined. The tools used would be the public card catalog, order files and other internal records, NUC, computer terminals, and such standard bibliographic tools as Publishers Weekly (PW) and Books in Print (BIP). Specifically, which tools are searched will depend on the nature of the material (is it a foreign publication, microfilm, periodical, etc.?) and the source from whom the library orders its catalog cards. If, for example, the library buys cards from a commercial processing firm, the company's monthly and annual listings of newly-published cards will have been checked.

If cards or Cataloging in Publication information are indeed available, then no further searching is necessary. Cards can be ordered and the book set aside to await the cards. If the book arrives with cataloging copy, it, along with the copy, is sent to the LC cataloging personnel for processing. But if the item has not been fully searched, the responsibility lies with the catalog department. Depending on local needs and the size of the department, this pre-cataloging search can be part of the initial screening process performed when the book arrives in the department, or it can be part of the duties of a special pre-cataloging person or section handling all cataloging with LC cards. If cards are unavailable at that time, most libraries will set the book aside for a specified period (usually three to six months) and then search again for cards. If nothing is found after the second (or third, fourth, etc.) search, the book can be sent on for original cataloging.

Maintaining the "backlog" of materials awaiting possible cataloging copy can be a complex problem in itself. Control is usually provided by filing one of the multiple order forms in a special holding file. Slips are filed either by author or title, depending on how the acquisition records are filed. A backlog number (i.e., accession or order number) is stamped on a second slip which is placed in the book and the book is shelved in numerical order. When cards arrive, the title is checked in the order file and the book retrieved and sent to be processed.

To facilitate communications between those searching for bibliographic information and those using it, the library must develop a work slip (often the back of an order slip) and establish a coding system to indicate the tools searched and the information found. For example, the letter "PC" might stand for the library's public card catalog, "SO" for standing order file, "PS" for proof sheet drawers, "NUC" for the National Union Catalog, and so on. To save time, the most common symbols should be printed on the work slip with enough space after each to indicate the exact volume, page, or drawer where the information was found. Also there should be space to record the degree of success in locating the information. Traditionally this is done with a series of checks and zeros. A zero (0) after an index, computer file, or other tool would mean that it was searched but no information was found; a check (√) means that the author's name was listed; two checks (√√) that both author and title were located; and three checks (√√√) that exact copy was found. Each library must, of course, develop its own coding system to meet local requirements.

LC cataloging. Most catalog departments now have a full- or part-time staff member (or, in large libraries, a separate section of personnel) who catalogs books with catalog cards and LC copy. In a library receiving most of its books pre-processed from a book vendor, this may mean simply matching incoming cards with books, and checking for clerical errors. In larger libraries this operation might include the following steps:

1. Searching for cards, NUC copy, network database copy, or other cataloging copy.
2. Production of cataloging copy (for example, typing from CIP data, photocopying from NUC, producing cards at the network terminal from MARC (Machine-Readable Cataloging) tapes, or simply recording LC card numbers for ordering card sets.
3. Editing copy (for example, deleting imprint on a computer printout and indicating the correct imprint).
4. Either ordering cards or duplicating a master by Xerox or other method.
5. Matching cards with books.
6. Typing headings and call numbers.
7. Revision of work.

If cards and books are ordered in the acquisition department the chief task is simply the mechanical matching of cards with books as they arrive in the department, a task that can be performed by a clerk or student assistant. If a good deal of searching and editing is required, a professional or paraprofessional must at least supervise. No matter how complex or how routine the operation, or whether it is handled by a part-time student assistant or by an experienced professional, the vast majority of books the library receives will be processed in this way. The growing importance of centralized processing and the continuing reliance on services of outside organizations and bibliographic networks make this a vital operation in every library.

Original cataloging. The original cataloging and classification of books and other materials is the responsibility of the professional members of the department. Although professionals will be assigned to other duties--including the supervision, revision, and training of clerical staff--their primary responsibility will always be original cataloging. In a small library that relies heavily on a central processing service, original cataloging may be done only for the occasional locally published item not processed by the service. But in larger libraries, original cataloging can be a major concern, often the responsibility of a specially organized unit within the catalog department and consisting of several catalogers each specializing in a specific subject field, language, or type of material. Each professional cataloger would be responsible for the descriptive cataloging, classification, and subject cataloging (i.e., assigning subject headings) of materials in his area of specialty, and in some libraries each function might be performed by a different cataloger.

The first of these functions, descriptive cataloging, is the standardized description of a book or other material. This description is usually printed on catalog cards, although in some libraries the information is produced by computer in book form or on microfiche or microfilm. The rules used by most libraries for this standard description are the second edition of the Anglo-American Cataloging Rules (AACR2). However, because of their complexity, small libraries usually simplify the Rules to fit local needs. Libraries following AACR2 will include in their descriptions: author or main entry, title, edition, imprint, collation, series, and any notes considered necessary to identify the book or explain its bibliographic history. Libraries taking short cuts might omit such items as edition statement, place of publication, size of book, series statement, and notes.

Besides describing the book the cataloger must assign a classification number. Following the classification system used in the library (in U.S. libraries, either the Library of Congress classification or Dewey Decimal system), the cataloger will fit the book into its proper subject class in the schedule. The LC system is most often found in academic libraries and large public libraries and Dewey (the abridged edition for small libraries) in school and most public libraries. Finally, the cataloger must analyze the subject content of the book. Using a standard subject heading list, either the Sears List of Subject Headings or the LC subject heading list, the cataloger assigns appropriate subject headings to the book. The Sears list is used mainly in small and medium-size libraries and the LC list in academic and larger public libraries.

To select subject headings, assign a call number, and describe the book, the cataloger naturally relies heavily on the descriptive cataloging rules, subject heading list, and classification schedule used by the library. But he has other aids, too. Certainly he will build on the order searching done in the acquisition department. Also, he can look in either the LC subject heading list or an earlier edition of Sears for suggested call numbers which are printed after many of the headings. After he has assigned a call number he can consult the shelflist for subject headings used for other books under that number. He may also want to look in such tools as NUC, PW, and the American Book Publishing Record (ABPR), which list not only full entries but suggested classification numbers and subject headings. Certainly he will search the card catalog, NUC, and, if available, a bibliographic computer file for earlier editions from which he can cull call numbers, subject headings, and appropriate notes. He may also want to compare classification numbers and headings used for similar books in the library. The sequence of steps and how the cataloger batches the work will depend on the materials being cataloged (language, degree of difficulty, subject matter, whether book or nonbook, and so on), the location of the card catalog and other tools in relation to his work area, and, most important, his own work habits. Each cataloger must develop his own routine, of course.

Besides cataloging and classifying the book, the cataloger should make appropriate name and subject cross-references. And if in his search he uncovers out-dated subject headings or books with incorrect call numbers he must see that neces-

sary corrections are made. It is just as important to keep
alert to housekeeping needs and uncover and correct errors
as it is to catalog a new item.

Periodicals, newspapers, and other serial publications
are usually assigned to a cataloger specializing in serials; or
in larger catalog departments a separate section will be established to deal with the processing of serials. In many libraries, serial cataloging is performed in the serials department or in the serials section of the acquisition department
along with the ordering, claiming, check-listing, and other
serial functions.

The main reason for separating serials from monographic
cataloging is that, over the years, the publication idiosyncra-
sies, complex entries, and unique cataloging codes of serial
publications have made their processing an extremely involved
operation. The cataloger not only must know the special cataloging rules that apply to serials, he must be familiar with
serial publishing in general and with the unique internal serials records and routines maintained by the library. These
internal records usually include check-in files on which are
recorded the daily, weekly, and monthly receipt of individual
issues of periodical subscriptions. These check-in files are
usually kept in special card cabinets or index files located in
the acquisition or serials department. Each card will contain
the title, publisher, frequency of publication, space for
checking-in single issues, plus room for such in-house information as binding and routing data, costs, and name of the
agent. Annuals and other less frequently issued serials are
often noted on special cards filed in the public card catalog
or in the shelflist. If the library's serials records have been
automated, serial record-keeping and updating procedures will
have been integrated into one machine-readable file.

Card preparation. After the cataloger has typed a
p-slip containing all information to appear on the finished set
of cards he sends the slip to a typist who will produce a
clean master. The master will be the basis for duplicating
the complete card set to which the typist will later add the
headings. If the library purchases cards from the Library
of Congress or elsewhere, someone may still have to type
headings and call numbers. Even if the library belongs to
a computer-based network and receives its cards complete with
headings and call numbers, some cards may still have to be

typed for materials not cataloged by the service and corrections and additions made and cross-references and information cards produced. In a school library this typing might be done by a clerk or student assistant who devotes only part time to such in-house tasks, whereas in a large public or academic library the volume of work may require a special typing pool supervised by a paraprofessional. If the library belongs to a bibliographic network or otherwise has automated its cataloging, the major part of card preparation would consist of typing cataloging data into computer terminals and then having card sets sent from network headquarters or producing cards on a terminal printer.

In any case, the typing of catalog cards (or inputting copy at a terminal) is an exacting job that requires trained personnel. The typist must know the card format used by the library, including exact spacing, punctuation, indention, and capitalization; and should understand at least something about the cataloging rules followed by the institution. Terminal operators must also know tagging and MARC formating procedures.

A typical manual card production routine would go something like this: type the master from the p-slip furnished by the cataloger; return the p-slip and master to the cataloger (or to the typing supervisor) who checks for typing errors; send the master to the card reproduction section to reproduce card set; return cards to the clerk to type headings and complete any other activities performed at this point, such as typing book plate, penciling the call number in the book, filling out bindery slip, and typing circulation card. After revision, the cards are filed and the book is sent to the marking section. Still other activities performed at this point might be typing cross-references and adding information to the shelflist card, including cost of book, copy and volume numbers, and date received. Whether these activities and the final revision occur at this point will depend on local requirements and the flow-patterns developed.

Terminal operations. In an automated cataloging system, cataloging copy that has been prepared by a cataloger is sent to a terminal operator to be keyed into the computer, but instead of typing a p-slip the cataloger fills out a work-form. The cataloger can code the various data elements himself or the terminal operator will assign the necessary codes either before inputting or at the terminal as the copy is being added to the data base. In some departments, the terminal operator transfers the cataloging data onto a work-form from a p-slip prepared by the cataloger, noting the appropriate tags and indicators. Also at this point, the terminal operator must prepare necessary cross-references and if an on-line authority file has been built into the system the headings must be checked against the computer file.

After the record has been typed onto the terminal screen but before it is entered into the data base, it should be proofread. A signal is then sent to the computer and the record enters the data base and catalog cards (or, in the case of a microform catalog, microforms) are produced at the computer center and sent to the department for filing into the card catalog.

In libraries that belong to a computer-based network, terminal operations begin at the point of searching. The book upon entering the catalog department goes directly to the terminals for searching in the data base. If a matching record contributed by a participating library is found, the operator can either produce cards or, perhaps more likely, send the book and a printout containing the cataloging information to a professional or paraprofessional who verifies the cataloging, checks the call number against the shelflist, and consults the appropriate authority files. If no record is found in the data base, the book is searched in NUC and the department's other bibliographic tools and sent to a cataloger for original cataloging. Or if there is a likelihood that a participating library will soon catalog the title and enter it into the network's data base, the book can be set aside for a later search (or searches).

Card reproduction. In libraries subscribing to a central processing service or belonging to a computer-based network, card reproduction may mean occasionally typing an extra card for local use; while in libraries doing their own processing, card reproduction will call for an elaborate printing plant able to reproduce thousands of cards each week. Every library will need to duplicate at least some cards (various card duplication methods will be discussed in Chapter 3). The department may, of course, have its cards reproduced outside the library. This would mean simply sending the typed masters, batched according to the number of cards in each set, to the printing firm.

Catalog maintenance. The card catalog (or in a few libraries, the microform or book catalog) is the primary product of the catalog department. It is the bibliographic tool that results from all the department's cataloging and classification activities. The maintenance of this tool is an important function of every catalog department. Yet when a department is short-handed, as many are, catalog maintenance is the function most often neglected. The results are filing backlogs, outdated cross-references, and worn and torn cards. In a smaller library, catalog maintenance might be the part-time responsibility of a clerk or student assistant under the direct supervision of the head librarian. In a larger institution, catalog maintenance could be performed by a separate unit within the catalog department consisting of several full-time clerks plus additional student help.

In most libraries, the public card catalog is a "dictionary catalog" in which all cards (author, title, subject added entries, series, and guide and cross-reference cards) are filed together in one alphabetical sequence. A less common arrangement is to divide the catalog into two separate sections (author-title and subject) or even three separate sections (author, title, and subject) with the cards arranged alphabetically within each catalog. Besides the main card catalog, every library has a shelflist in which cards are filed in call number order--in other words, in the same order as the books appear on the shelves. Some libraries maintain separate shelflists for various collections, particularly if materials in these collections are arranged by different numbering or classification systems. There may be a separate shelflist for juvenile books, one for biographies arranged alphabetically by biographee, another for microfilms arranged by accession numbers, and so on.

To better understand what is involved in maintaining both the main card catalog and the shelflist, we must look at the individual maintenance functions. In a small department, all functions would be performed by one clerk with perhaps some student help. Many functions would, in fact, be performed simultaneously. In larger departments, each would be separate and distinct, perhaps performed by different individuals or even different units within the department.

1. Filing cards. The primary function of the catalog maintenance personnel is the continual filing of catalog cards

in the public card catalog and shelflist. The routine followed in most libraries is to divide the operation into three distinct steps: 1) preliminary sorting; 2) filing; and, 3) revision. First, the new cards are put in preliminary alphabetical order, or, in the case of shelflist cards, in numerical order. Usually this is done in the catalog department by clerks or student assistants. After sorting, the cards can be filed either in card catalogs in the department or in special drawers near the public catalog. The latter arrangement makes them accessible to patrons even when there are filing delays.

In step two the filers take a section of preliminarily filed cards and interfile them into the main catalog. Although cards should not remain in the preliminary files too long, there should, nonetheless, be enough cards so that filers do not have to file only one or two cards into each drawer.

The third step is revision. For easy revision the filer should have placed the cards above the rods where they will remain until a revisor, either a professional or an experienced paraprofessional, checks for errors. After the cards are checked, the revisor pulls the rods, drops the cards in place, and replaces the rods. If the revisor does not follow immediately behind the filer, then the filer should drop the cards into their permanent position with the rods through the holes, placing a notched colored slip, called a filing flag, in front of each new card. Later, as the cards are checked, the revisor removes the slips. In this way revision can be done whenever convenient.

Filing cards into the card catalog is an important operation in which errors should not be tolerated; yet it is a tedious task that invites mistakes from the most experienced filers. The revisor is, therefore, in an important and sensitive position. The revisor must not only check the work of the filers but is also responsible for interpreting the filing rules for others, organizing routines, training filers, and setting and maintaining standards.

Strict adherence to the filing rules is essential. No matter how small the library, it is important to follow an established set of filing rules, namely the ALA Filing Rules or LC's Filing Rules. Clerks must never simply file cards alphabetically or numerically into the catalogs without regard for established rules; nor should they try to make up their

own rules, as simple as this may seem. The LC and ALA
rules are difficult enough to interpret without attempting to
develop one's own system. For this reason, the department
head must tolerate few exceptions to the established rules.

2. Shifting cards. To prevent drawers from becoming
overcrowded, the catalog department must, from time to time,
shift the cards. As with many maintenance operations, this
is a relatively minor task in a small library, but with a large
public catalog it can take a good deal of time to plan and exe-
cute. To allow for expansion and to prevent shifts more than
every two years, the drawers should not initially be more
than two-thirds full. If possible, a row of empty drawers
should be left to allow for expansion; thus, when crowding
occurs in an area, cards can be expanded into the empty
drawers in the row. In expanding the catalog, not only must
cards be shifted but labels must be changed.

3. Preparation and maintenance of labels on catalog
drawers. The preparation of labels is, of course, closely
linked to the expansion of the catalog. Each time the catalog
is expanded new tags must be made. Even if a library buys
ready-made labels from a library supplier, the need for constant expansion will sooner or later force the maintenance
staff to begin making its own to fit expanding needs. To
make labels as neat and legible as possible it is best to type
them on a typewriter with oversize type, perhaps the marking typewriter.

As an aid in helping users replace drawers in their
proper locations, many libraries code individual drawers. The
most common coding method is to number each drawer consecutively. In addition, the labels for each section or row can be
color coded.

4. Handling temporary slips. Whenever a member of
the catalog department removes either a main entry or shelflist card (although usually not an added entry) he should replace it with a temporary card. The "temp," made of colored
stock for quick identification, should include the call number,
author, brief title, and, if considered necessary for identification, the imprint and series statement. The initials of the
person removing the card and the date of removal should also
appear somewhere on the card, plus a clearly stamped or printed
statement indicating that the colored card is temporary.

Temps are used in libraries to keep the catalog, the primary record of the library's holdings, as complete as possible. A staff member, by removing a card to make corrections or changes, is, in effect, making this record incomplete and inaccurate. Anyone searching the catalog for that particular title will be misled by the absence of a card. The patron will think the library does not have the book, the acquisition librarian may unwittingly order a second copy, and the cataloger may assign a call number already assigned to that title. The temp not only helps keep bibliographic control of items in the collection but it is an aid to filers in refiling cards. For this reason it is important that whoever removes a card in order to change either a call number or the main entry makes sure that the temp is removed when the card is eventually refiled.

The catalog maintenance section should, first of all, see that other staff members properly use the temps, and secondly, develop a formal or informal program to keep the catalog clear of old cards. This means that every three or four months someone should quickly scan the drawers for colored temporary cards, checking the dates to see how long each has been in the catalog. Those that have been in the catalog for a relatively long time should be checked for problems and misfiled cards. Department heads who feel they cannot spare the time to search the catalog for out-dated slips must at least keep filers and revisors on the lookout for old slips.

5. <u>Maintenance of authority files</u>. Every catalog department must somehow maintain uniformity of main entries, subject headings, and cross-references. In the past, most libraries sustained this uniformity through what is called authority files. The authority file is a record on catalog cards of past decisions on the correct form of entries and headings used in the main card catalog. Each card in the file lists the correct entry, heading, cross-reference, or series, the authority on which the decision was based (NUC, for example), plus any cross-references in the card catalog pertaining to that particular entry.

To maintain consistency in their catalogs but to prevent duplication of work, most libraries have been using their main card catalogs and other working tools as their authority files. Uniformity of subject headings, for instance, is maintained through the standard subject heading list, either LC or Sears. The person in charge of authority maintenance, usually a paraprofessional, places checks in the subject heading list beside those headings and cross-references used in the catalog. Also, any additions not listed in the subject heading list are written in the margins. Additions and exceptions to the standard subject heading list should, however, be kept to a minimum.

If a library chooses to use its public card catalog and NUC in place of a name authority file, the cataloger need not create and update separate cards for name authorities. If an entry appears in the card catalog, the cataloger can assume it to be correct; but if no entry is found, either in the card catalog or in NUC, he applies the "no conflict" principle; that is, if no conflict exists with other entries in the catalog the entry is accepted as it appears on the title page, following, of course, the latest edition of AACR.

With the publication of AACR2 and the subsequent changes in entry headings made by the Library of Congress there is developing a need in many libraries for stricter authority control methods. Also, the growth of computer-based networks and the increased sharing of cataloging records are requiring more rigorous standards, at least among networking libraries. Yet networking can also make authority work easier. The flexibility of the computer allows extensive heading changes with relative ease and, when programmed to do so, the computer is able to correct errors that develop during the inputting of original headings. Another aid in authority work has been the publication of the Library of Congress' Name Authorities, a cumulative microform edition of its authority file, and the publication of LC's authority data in MARC format. Both are providing libraries with direct access to LC's authority records.

But whether a library maintains conventional authority files, an online authority file, or uses its card catalog, LC's authority file, NUC, subject heading list, and other working tools as its authorities, someone must assume the responsibility for their maintenance. One person, for example, should be responsible for seeing to it that entries are made and cross-references updated. Although it is the catalogers who usually select cross-references as they catalog the materials, the total operation should be coordinated through one staff member who can see that references are updated, and who will periodically check for additions and changes. A tedious and time-consuming task, it is nonetheless one that catalog departments can not afford to neglect. Such housekeeping chores must be done if a library expects to have a viable card catalog that will answer patron queries satisfactorily.

6. Maintenance of guide cards. It is important that typed or printed guide cards be placed in the main card catalog (usually an inch, or not more than two inches, apart) to highlight names, topics, and subdivisions. The department can purchase either printed guides, guides with printed inserts, or blank guides. It is perhaps best to use guides that will accept both printed and locally typed inserts. Most library suppliers sell sets of guide cards designed specifically for school, public, and academic card catalogs of various sizes.

Maintenance personnel should also see that information and reference cards are developed and updated. These cards direct patrons to special collections and explain the use of the catalog. Like guide cards, information cards can be purchased from library supply houses; others, however, will have to be typed locally to fit individual needs. Each drawer should, for example, have a printed guide explaining how to locate authors, titles, and subjects. The catalog should also contain cards calling the user's attention to vertical file, government document, archive, slide, and other special collections.

7. Replacement of worn and missing cards. Patrons and staff will be constantly reporting torn and misfiled cards, damaged drawers, and misspelled headings. Although it is annoying to have to drop everything to search the catalog for a misfiled card or to retype a heading, this is still another housekeeping chore that must be done by someone at sometime, and preferably promptly. Unless the department is large enough to have a typist on call to take care of such emergencies, it is best to maintain a file of card catalog problems. When the file becomes large enough, a clerk can spend a day or two retyping cards and searching (and re-searching) for misfiled cards. If a card cannot be found, it is best to type a temp; then, if and when the original appears, the temp can be replaced by the original.

8. <u>Withdrawals</u>. Not only are libraries constantly adding books to their collections, but they must, from time to time, withdraw them. Books become outdated, worn, lost, damaged, or mutilated, and must be officially withdrawn from the collection. Although the decision to withdraw usually comes from outside the department, changing the records is part of the catalog department's maintenance responsibilities.

The withdrawal procedure starts when the catalog department is notified that a book has been lost, stolen, or damaged, and must therefore be officially withdrawn. To the catalog department this means one of two things. Either all the records (in most cases, the catalog cards) must be removed, or, if there are other copies or volumes of the same title still in the collection, the shelflist must be changed to reflect the new status. In the first instance, all catalog cards are removed; if a replacement has been ordered, the cards are filed together by author or title in a special "withdrawn file" where they can later be pulled and reused when the replacement arrives. If there are other copies or volumes of the title still in the collection, the clerk merely adds after the copy, volume, or accession number the word "withdrawn" or its equivalent, the date, and for statistical purposes the reason for withdrawal: "missing," "worn," "replaced," etc. If all cards are removed it is important also to remove any name or subject cross-references in the card catalog and authority files that apply to the particular title.

9. <u>Added copies and added volumes</u>. Once a book is cataloged, all additional copies and volumes received by the library need only be added to existing library records. No additional cataloging is necessary. When volume ten of a set or a second copy of a monograph arrives in the department, it automatically goes to the added copy shelf. The added copy clerk pulls the shelflist card and makes the necessary notation on the card. In the case of an added volume, some libraries will also indicate this on the main entry and even on added entries. If an added copy has been received for a department or branch library, most libraries note this on a special location card filed behind the main entry. Or, if the library stamps locations on the cards, the added location will be stamped on the main entry. If the added copy is going to a branch library or other location is will be necessary to make an extra set of cards for that library. This should be the responsibility of the added copy clerk.

In most libraries, issues of newspapers, periodicals, and other serial publications are added daily, weekly, monthly, and yearly to special checklist cards located in the serials department. Or the department can use special form cards which are filed immediately behind the main entries. On each form card are printed appropriate dates with space for checking off individual items as they arrive in the library.

10. Maintenance of location stamps, cards, and sleeves. As mentioned above, to indicate the locations of books housed outside the main library collection, libraries 1) stamp locations above or below the call numbers on catalog cards, 2) check off locations on specially printed location cards filed behind the main entries, or 3) slip appropriately-labeled transparent card protectors over the catalog cards. The library can have stamps prepared by a local stationery store, have location cards printed by a local printer, or purchase transparent slip-on sleeves, with appropriate locations ("Reserve Book," "Reference Department," etc.) imprinted across the top, from a library supply house. It is the responsibility of maintenance personnel to update locations not only when a volume or copy is added or withdrawn but whenever an item is transferred from one location to another.

Book preparation. Although a post-cataloging function, book preparation is, nonetheless, usually assigned to the catalog department. Book preparation consists mainly of marking and labeling the books and other materials cataloged and classified in the department. In many libraries it also includes stamping, pasting, or otherwise affixing book plates, card pockets, date-due slips, identification markings, and accession numbers. In addition, those responsible for the preparation activities will cut pages, slip on book jackets, tip in errata slips, and make minor repairs. A typical book preparation sequence would be: apply ownership markings; accession book; cut pages; paste book plate, pocket, and date-due slip; type marking label (or mark by hand on spine); apply label to spine; separate book and cards and sort cards (if accompanying the book); revise. In many libraries, much of this, including applying ownership markings, pasting book plates, and accessioning is done before the book is cataloged; in still other libraries these operations are now considered unnecessary and are omitted altogether. If the library subscribes to a central processing service, much of this work will be furnished by the service.

Although the marking of books is clerical in nature, it is important that the specific activities be organized by a professional or paraprofessional who understands not only each of the steps involved, but their relationship to the library's cataloging, reference, and circulation operations. The placement of book pockets and date-due slips, for instance, must have the approval of the circulation department. Above all, the routines must be carefully outlined and efficiently carried out. Unfortunately, like many other cataloging routines, the various marking, typing, labeling, pasting, and stamping tasks lend themselves to error and inefficiency. It is essential, therefore, that the work be accurately performed and carefully revised. It is important, too, that materials flow uninterrupted through the various operations. Yet, for maximum efficiency the work must be batched; books must not be allowed to dribble through the marking section. If the marker is forced constantly to switch jobs, over-all production will suffer. Also important is the elimination of unnecessary tasks. The supervisor must omit any operation which no longer serves a purpose. Is it, for example, necessary for the library to accession books? Is it perhaps redundant both to stamp ownership markings and to paste book plates? Outdated, unnecessary, redundant steps should be discovered and eliminated.

Whoever is in charge of book preparation activities must also select necessary supplies including labels, book plates, date-due slips, circulation cards, and plastic jackets, as well as recommend the equipment most suitable for the volume and type of materials processed. A periodic review of library supply catalogs will help keep the department up-to-date on new supplies and equipment coming on the market.

Chapter 2

THE DEPARTMENT HEAD

What makes a successful department head? Characteristically,
writers on management are quick to offer lists of leadership
traits they consider important. These listings can range anywhere from five to a hundred-and-five words and phrases.
Unfortunately, they raise more questions than they answer.
This may be because the terms used are nearly always vague,
ambiguous, and overlapping. Certainly, it is difficult (impossible?) to list mutually exclusive traits that can apply to
all department heads in every possible library situation. Most
lists, in fact, tell more about their enumerators than about
management. It is indeed difficult to arrive at a consensus
except to say that the terms found on most of these computa-
tions seem to center on the three broad areas of intelligence,
personality, and supervisory ability. Clearly, intelligence
(that is to say, judgment, scholarship, verbal facility, and so
on) has much to do with a department head's ability to manage. The more intelligent he is the better administrator he
will make--but only to a point. Most behavioral scientists
have also found that an administrator's I.Q. is an accurate
indicator of success only up to a certain level of intelligence.
Recent studies indicate that those with extremely high intelligence scores are less likely to be successful administrators
than those with average or slightly above average intelligence.
As for personality traits, most researchers do seem to find
certain traits more desirable than others, including self-
confidence, initiative, individuality, and perceptiveness. According to these researchers, the department head who believes in himself, who is innovative, who places the stamp of
individuality on his department, and, most important, who can
readily differentiate values will tend to be the more successful administrator. Finally, the successful department head
must have the ability to supervise others. He may be a

recognized authority in the field of bibliographic organization and have a winning personality, but if he does not understand and effectively employ the basic principles of management, he will not supervise others effectively.

Areas of Responsibility

To better understand exactly what makes a successful department head we must examine the way he performs in his day-to-day areas of responsibility. Namely, how does the department head relate to 1) his supervisor, 2) members of the department, 3) the job, 4) library users, 5) the profession, and 6) himself? Anyone expecting to manage effectively must score well in these six areas.

Administration. The primary responsibility of the department head is to carry out the goals, objectives, and policies established by the library director. With the goals of the library in mind, the department head must organize department resources to carry through the library's missions. Unfortunately, he must also at times work under uncomfortable restrictions. The effectiveness of the department depends not only on the authority and responsibility delegated to the head of the department but on how he operates within the limits of this delegation. This is the real test of his ability to manage. Can he get the job done not only when the resources are provided but despite a lack of resources? To keep books moving through the department or to maintain high department morale, there may be times when he will have to overlook or circumvent certain policies or procedures. Yet he also has the obligation to keep the administration informed on department progress, or lack of it. This means progress not only with respect to the number of books cataloged, but personnel development as well. He must be able to analyze the department's growth and interpret it clearly to the library director.

The department head must, therefore, keep the administration informed on exactly how the department is performing. Communication lines must be kept open, and, when appropriate, problems, progress reports, ideas, and complaints passed on to the administration. If, for example, the department head or someone else in the department discovers a more efficient way to do a particular job, the idea must be passed

along. If there are personnel problems that cannot be solved
at the department level they must be taken to the division
head or, if necessary, to the director. They want to know,
and should know. More importantly, they can help.

Staff. While the department head is responsible to the
library administration, he is also responsible to his staff. By
the very nature of his position, he is dependent upon the
professionals and support staff (paraprofessionals, clerks, and
student assistants) working in the department. He must,
therefore, know their strengths, weaknesses, capabilities, motivations, and backgrounds. Certainly he does not have to
"like" them all, but he must understand them. He is expected
to delegate authority, motivate others, maximize skills, and
upgrade performance standards. To get the most out of his
people, he must give them a feeling that they can make significant contributions to the library--in other words, inspire
them. He must, at all times, relate to the members of his
department, both professionals and nonprofessionals. Yet
everyone, in and outside the department, must realize who is
in charge. This, above all other qualities, is hardest to define, hardest to acquire. The head of the department must
be warm and friendly, while still leaving no question of who
is boss. This is particularly difficult in a democratic or participatory management situation.

Regardless of how democratic the management, the department head is the one entrusted with the responsibility of
running the department. He must, however, be willing and
able to take the counsel of others; that is, listen to the opinions of members of his department, be quick to adapt their
ideas, and give full credit. Another important trait is flexibility. The department head whose ideas are set in concrete
cannot work well with ideas, things, or, especially, people.
The flexible person is the one who gets the most out of and
gives the most to his staff. He cannot do this by insisting
that "We've always done things this way around here and
that's the way we're going to continue to do them."

The job. As head of a catalog department, nothing
commands more confidence and respect than knowledge of the
field. Nothing is more difficult to conceal than lack of knowledge. In certain library management positions a pleasing personality with a minimum understanding of the job can often
get a librarian through--but not in the catalog department.

Beyond a thorough knowledge of the basic principles of bibliographic organization and control, the department head should
have a working knowledge of two or more foreign languages
and be able to translate others with a dictionary. A strong
subject field is important too, even for the department head
who is seldom called upon to use it. An understanding of
one subject will provide an appreciation of others. Also important is an understanding of the principles of library automation, even if the department is not as yet online. Finally,
the department head must keep abreast of new developments
in the field. He cannot expect others in the department to
be knowledgeable in the cataloging and classification of library materials, subject fields, languages, and automation, if
he is not.

The patrons. Everyone in the catalog department is
there to serve the library patron. Although the head of the
department may consider himself safely hidden from library
users, their needs should, nonetheless, influence his day-to-
day decisions and actions. The fact that staff members seldom contact those who consult the catalogs they produce or
read the books they process does not mean that user needs
can be ignored. If the needs of patrons, as conceived by the
department head, conflict with the duties prescribed by the
library administration, as they often will, some hard realities
must be faced and undoubtedly some compromises made. Such
compromises will in some degree reflect the quality of service
the department provides.

The profession. The department head, like every other
librarian, has a responsibility to the profession. This means
keeping up with the profession through reading, educational
travel, attendance at seminars and short courses, and active
membership in professional organizations. This also means
doing the "extra" expected of professionals. The department
head must be constantly working for the profession, and must
speak out when necessary. As a part of middle management,
he must be a professional leader. He must, for example, encourage others to take an active interest in librarianship. He
must be continually seeking opportunities to assist others in
solving problems, planning improvements, and evaluating progress. This is the way to ensure professional growth.

Himself. The department head has a responsibility to
himself, too. This means knowing himself. Can he take both

victories and defeats? Does he have a high tolerance for
frustration? Can he ask himself embarrassing questions--and
get straight answers? Can he meet crises with calmness?
Can he recognize his own mistakes, admit them, and avoid
repeating them? Here is where the list of management traits
becomes inexhaustible: self-control, self-confidence, objec-
tivity, sensitivity, dependability, and so on--and on.

Management as Leadership

To manage a catalog department successfully is to lead
successfully. More often than not, the one quality above all
others that determines the selection of a department head is
his potential to lead. No matter how much technical knowledge he may possess, if the head of the catalog department
cannot lead, encourage, and develop staff he is a poor manager. This is not to say that there is only one way to lead.
There are several. Management experts have been attempting,
ever since World War II, to identify these various leadership
styles. So far at least, those styles most often identified in
the literature have been: autocratic leadership, democratic
leadership, laissez-faire leadership, and charismatic leadership.
Nobody, of course, fits precisely into any one category. Yet
most department heads do seem to exhibit traits identifiable
with one style more than another. A person labeled as an
autocratic department head, for example, administers by di-
rective. He bases his leadership on the hierarchical structure
of the library, passing down orders to the staff, taking his
authority from the division head and library director. He is
usually intolerant of the opinions of staff, and seeks obedience
rather than cooperation. In contrast, the democratic leader
seeks the advice of others and encourages group participation.
He draws ideas and suggestions from the staff, consults on
all important matters, and, in some cases, allows both professionals and nonprofessionals in the department to determine
policy. The democratic head is more of a moderator than a
director.

The laissez-faire leader (often called the free-rein leader) maintains an even lower profile than the democratic leader.
He plays down his role as administrator, exerting minimum
control, functioning primarily as an information-source. He
advises, at most suggests, never orders. The fourth category,
and the one that has most recently been identified in the lit-

erature, is the charismatic leader. While he often exhibits characteristics of one of the other styles, his ability to lead is based primarily on the force of his personality, specifically on his self-assurance and his compelling magnetism. He is the leader with whom people easily identify. But while the charismatic leader draws fierce loyalty from most members of the department, from others he may encourage repulsion.

Which leadership style is most effective? All things being equal, most would say the democratic leader. Today it seems self-evident that just about any catalog department would function best in a democratic, participatory atmosphere. Actually, though, which style (or more realistically, which combination of styles) best suits a department depends largely on staff needs, library needs, situation needs, and of course personal needs. And the leadership style of the library directory will, for better or worse, imply the style his department heads will follow.

Ideally, though, leadership styles should vary with the situation. For example, the group-minded typing pool is best directed by democratic techniques. The individualistic cataloger thrives best under a laissez-faire personality; so would the creative individual. The cataloger with a rigid personality, who lives a structured life and is somewhat autocratic himself, will feel most comfortable under an autocratic department head. Likewise, the autocratic department head who needs to dominate others will find it difficult to supervise someone who operates best in a free-rein atmosphere, who likes to develop his own rules, and who must work at his own pace.

But while, theoretically, the department head should vary his leadership style with the situation, this is seldom possible. Most feel more comfortable in one style than another. Anyone who is basically an authoritarian leader must work within an authoritarian frame-work. A "good guy," who is most comfortable as a democratic leader, will find it difficult, if not impossible, to operate otherwise. If a department head can comfortably switch styles when the occasion arises, he should take advantage of this. He is one of the truly fortunate administrators.

Whatever the style adopted, the department head must be consistent. Staff must know where they stand and be able to predict actions and reactions of the boss. Whatever the style, it must be identifiable, and it must be known. If the department head has the ability to vary with circumstances, they must know this, too. Perhaps even more important, the department head himself must be aware of his own leadership style. Unless he is he will be unable to adjust and, where necessary, switch styles to fit changing administrative situations and organizational structures.

Functions of the Department Head

Behavioral scientists often define management in terms of basic managerial functions. For the most part, these functions remain valid regardless of whether we are considering the management of a catalog department or an automotive assembly line. Granted, it is not easy to divide activities into neat categories. Nor is it easy to relate theoretical functions to day-to-day activities. Yet to gain still more of a feeling for what management is all about, it is well to examine these basic functions as they apply to the head of a catalog department.

Planning. Planning is invariably first on everyone's list, and in actual practice it usually precedes all other functions. But while planning is a primary function, it is perhaps not as vital at the department level as on higher administrative levels. At any rate, the planning function will differ according to its place in the hierarchical structure. Department planning, for instance, is usually short-range compared to the longer-range planning of the library director or the division head. At the department level, planning consists primarily of developing the means of implementing the plans and objectives of the library administration. To put it another way, short-range department planning is the who, what, where, and how of long-range planning.

But at whatever level, the planning function is dependent upon the planner's ability to understand the present and predict the future. It is based, first, on research and, secondly, on forecasting. To plan effectively, the department head must study and then predict such things as funds, personnel, library programs, cataloging output, user needs, and the type and quantity of materials entering the department. Department planning does not mean planning by the head of the department alone. It must involve everyone in the department, just as long-range administrative planning must involve all department heads.

Directing. Another basic function of the department head--and the one that is perhaps the most difficult to develop--is that of directing. To direct effectively the department head must know his people--and know himself, as well. Perhaps more to the point, he must know and appreciate the relationships between himself and his staff. It is by means of the directing function that the other functions are put into practice. And while much of the department's planning is initiated and even carried out at the division level, directing the department must be done exclusively at the department level--and by the head of the department.

Controlling. It is through the controlling function that the department's objectives are accomplished. These objectives must be established and executed, results measured against objectives, and necessary adjustments made. The department head controls department activities by controlling what people do, how materials flow through the department, and the use of equipment and supplies. The controlling function, like most other management functions, is one that the department head must constantly apply to cataloging activities.

Organizing. In organizing his department the department head identifies and groups activities essential to the accomplishment of library objectives. He assigns certain responsibilities to this clerk, other responsibilities to that one. Certain books go to this cataloger, other books to another. A section in the department is organized to operate the computer terminals, another to mark and label books. Working within the limitations imposed by department personnel, resources, and environment, the department head organizes the department into operative units; within these units he delegates assignments.

Coordinating. As the chief administrative officer of the department, the department head is responsible for coordinating activities within the department. In addition, he must coordinate department activities with those of other library units. This is a particularly difficult function because it cannot be dictated. It is achieved only through effective interpersonal relationships. Understandably, then, much of the department head's success as coordinator will be dependent upon good communications.

Managerial Authority

For still another view of cataloging management, we should look briefly at authority, defined in its simplest terms as the straightforward right to manage others. No one can successfully run a catalog department without authority. Unfortunately, this right does not come automatically; nor does it come from any one source but from several--some obvious, others not so obvious. Most apparent is formal authority. Until quite recently, formal authority was considered the only possibility. Formal authority, delegated through the organizational structure, originates from the top: the library director has authority over the technical services librarian who, in turn, has authority over the department heads, who supervise the members of their respective departments. Among other forms of administrative power one of the least obvious yet most important is informal authority. Informal authority comes from the personal qualities and abilities of the individual. A cataloger, for example, might be an authority figure not because of his formal position in the department but because of his recognized knowledge of cataloging. Others may look to him for advice and guidance rather than to their formal leader, the head of the department.

Related to informal authority is authority acquired through acceptance by members of the department. For leadership to be really effective, a staff member must accept the authority of his supervisor; if a cataloger rejects the authority of the department head, authority does not exist. If suggestions or commands are not "accepted," the department head must determine why, and do something about it. If he does not, he is, in effect, no longer in authority.

Another source of authority is based on the circumstances of a situation at a given time. The cataloger who has seniority, who presently has the director's ear, or who controls the lines of communication (the editor of the staff newsletter, for instance) may also exert a certain amount of authority.

The origins of authority are, therefore, not always

obvious. This is certainly true in departments containing a large number of professional librarians whose backgrounds, education, experience, and personalities vary widely. Anyone managing a catalog department certainly must gain the formal authority due the position; but just as important, he must possess the personal qualities and technical competence that will assure complete authority.

To understand fully what authority is all about, we must examine a few of the basic principles which writers in the field have so far identified.

Span of authority. The span of authority principle states that no department head can successfully supervise more than six subordinates. Actually, though, while there are clearly limits to the number of people one person can effectively manage, it is difficult to state an exact number. Perhaps a more realistic principle would be: the more subordinates reporting to a supervisor, the less effectively he can supervise. The exact number depends on several variables, perhaps the most important being the uniqueness of the assignments. Although a department head might not be able to successfully train and directly supervise a six-member staff consisting of, say, one cataloger, a searcher, two typists, a marker, and a filer, he could certainly directly supervise more than six catalogers, especially if all were doing the same type of work. Likewise, one paraprofessional could supervise eight or more terminal operators if all were experienced and inputting essentially the same copy.

Thus the span of authority of either the department head or one of the unit chiefs will depend upon:

1. Experience of the supervisor.
2. Experience of the staff.
3. The variety, complexity, and importance of the activities being supervised.
4. The repetitiveness of activities.
5. The amount of time available for direct supervision.
6. The amount of assistance staff members can expect from co-workers.
7. The degree of decentralization in the department.

Unity of authority. The unity of authority principle states that no one can have more than one boss. This is not to say that the director of the library, technical services librarian, and the head of the catalog department are not hierarchically above the cataloger, but that the cataloger should have only one immediate supervisor to whom he is directly responsible. Nor does this mean that others in the department cannot assist, make suggestions, or give advice to the newcomer. It does mean that no one should be torn between two or more supervisors. In other words, the department head should never place a member of his staff in a position of having to decide which conflicting order to follow. If he places a new cataloger under the supervision of a senior cataloger, all training should then be channeled only through that person.

Equalization of authority. This principle states that all staff who report to a supervisor should have approximately the same status and authority. Thus all division heads who report to the library director should have equal status, as should all department heads who report to a division chief. Likewise, all section heads reporting to the head of the catalog department should be equal in rank, and all typists reporting to the chief typist should have equal status. While theoretically sound, this concept is not too practical in most cataloging operations. To say that a professional cataloger, chief typist, and marking section supervisor who report to the head of the catalog department all have equal status is simply not reasonable. When a department head does deviate from this rule, however, as he must, he should use titles that will distinguish clearly the major and minor status divisions. To avoid possible confusion and misunderstandings, everyone in the department must understand the authority and status of everyone else.

Delegation of authority. The principle of delegation states that to manage effectively, department authority must be divided and delegated. The supervisor of an active catalog department cannot possibly control all internal operations directly, unless, of course, the department is a relatively small one. Like other authority principles, this one, too, is not always followed. Many department heads, while giving lip-service to the delegation principle, lack confidence in their people or simply will not take a chance on them. Still others just do not have the ability to delegate. Likewise, members of a department, instead of making decisions or carrying through assigned tasks, may find it easier to "ask the boss." They may be afraid of being criticized for making mistakes, or lack the necessary self-confidence to go-it-alone. Perhaps they just do not want to make the effort. Despite the obstacles, effective operation of a department requires delegation of authority.

Decentralization of authority. Similarly to the delegation principle is the principle of decentralization. While delegation is based on the division of authority among individuals in the department, decentralization is the transfer of authority (as well the transfer of activities, functions, operations, and responsibilities) to the units within the department. Each unit, then, is relatively independent of the others, being held together through the authority of the department head. There are disadvantages as well as advantages to decentralization. It is the obligation of the department head to avoid the limitations while emphasizing the advantages. Among the advantages of decentralization are that it does the following:

1. Shortens lines of communication.
2. Places decision-making responsibilities in the hands of those immediately in charge of the operation.
3. Distributes the supervisory load.
4. Develops supervisory capabilities in staff.
5. Creates an effective chain of promotion.
6. Provides opportunities for staff to demonstrate initiative.
7. Promotes department flexibility.
8. Challenges department members.

Disadvantages of decentralization include these:

1. Possible lack of uniformity in procedures.
2. Possible loss of coordination and communication between units.
3. Possible duplication of activities.
4. Possible lack of qualified personnel to assume supervisory responsibilities.
5. Possible loss of control by department head.

In a decentralized department, professionals and support staff responsible for the various units must be well qualified. Also, the department head who is serious about decentralizing his department must delegate real authority. If he insists that section chiefs clear every decision before they can take any action, decentralization will not work. Consequently he must be prepared to face occasional mistakes, and when they occur he must resist the tendency to curtail the authority he has delegated. Staff will learn by their mistakes, just as the department head does. This means that he must maintain a hands-off policy, and give his people a chance to work out their problems. He must not be continually looking over their shoulders, or feel obliged to step in and solve every little problem that arises. Finally, he must be alert to faulty communication lines, duplication of effort, and loss of control. Decentralization is necessary for an effectively run department--but it will succeed only if everyone is aware of possible breakdowns.

Decision-Making

One thing that distinguishes the catalog department head of today from a decade ago is the amount and variety of decisions he must make. Managing a catalog department is no longer a matter of simply deciding which cataloger should process which books. The modern department head is confronted with innumerable day-to-day decisions centering around personnel, finances, materials, and cataloging methods.

What exactly is the decision-making process? What steps can be taken to assure a sound decision? As with all aspects of library administration, opinions differ on specifics. Nevertheless, writers on management do agree that to reach sound decisions, the decision-maker must take a systematic approach. He can use a highly formalized pen-and-paper or computer-based systems approach, or, if he is like most library administrators, he will prefer to develop his own less formal approach to solving day-to-day problems. The following system is typical.

1. Define the problem: The department head must be sure he is dealing with a genuine problem, not with a symptom. He must uncover basic causes and origins. If, for example, a cataloger requests a different subject field to catalog, it may not be the subject but the revisor who is causing problems; or perhaps a language associated with the subject field is giving him trouble. Although it sounds obvious, the fact is, a problem must be understood before it can be solved. This means that the known must be separated from the un-

known, the important from the unimportant, the fact from the bias, and the concrete from the vague. If there seems to be difficulty in formulating the problem it should be written down in one or two sentences. The more completely the problem can be stated and yet kept precise, the easier the other steps will be. If the total problem is not defined or if only part of it is attacked, someone will eventually have to backtrack and do a proper job. The department head must resist the temptation to give a traditional response to a problem. If an automatic solution is available, no problem exists.

2. Analyze the problem: Analysis is best done by dividing the problem into workable facets. Depending on the nature of the problem, the department head may want to separate it by elements, time sequences, stages of difficulty, or degrees of urgency. If a part of the problem can wait for a few days, weeks, months, or at least until the more immediate aspects are worked out, then he should put that portion aside and concentrate on the more urgent matters. Yet he must consider not only an immediate solution but future ramifications, and recognize the relationship of possible solutions to other problems.

3. Examine alternatives: After a careful analysis the department head should come up with one or more hypotheses. These hypotheses are, then, the alternatives for consideration. Each should be listed, no matter how fragmentary, impractical, or farfetched. If, for example, the library is examining the best way to duplicate catalog cards, all possible methods should be listed--stencil, Xerox, computer printer, and so on--no matter how expensive or how seemingly inadequate the process. What might seem impractical at first may be, after the process of elimination, the best alternative.

Each alternative should then be carefully weighed, and the advantages, disadvantages, and consequences of each listed. What are the pros and cons? What are the costs? Finally, the obviously impractical choices should be weeded. The initial process can then be repeated and the few choices selected that best fit the situation and match department goals and objectives.

4. Reach a decision: Theoretically, a decision should automatically appear, if only through the process of elimination. Yet it seldom does. This does not mean that an or-

ganized step-by-step approach is a waste of time. All it means is that although a logical approach is best, what usually evolves are possibilities and compromises, not ideal solutions.

Plainly, then, this and similar formulas do not always work as neatly as one might hope, at least not for the kinds of problems that arise in the catalog department of today. Although the above formula is a logical one to follow, there is much more to decision-making than following predetermined steps and miraculously emerging with a pat solution. More often than not, decision-making in the catalog department is a matter of compromise and risk-taking. To compound the frustration, the department head will be expected to make more policy decisions in a day than the library director will make in a week. Granted, the decisions may not be as critical as those faced by the director, but they will be more numerous, varied, and urgent. Moreover, decision-making in most catalog departments is not simply a matter of sitting down quietly to think out a clear-cut problem according to some predetermined formula, with the expectation of automatically arriving at a solution. It is usually a complicated process involving many people and situations which add to, instead of alleviating, the confusion. A cataloger may suggest, for example, that a special information card be placed in the card catalog to aid users looking for information found only in the library's government document collection. The department head might talk over the suggestion with the head of catalog maintenance, who suggests a wording which will conform with the library's other information cards; the department head would then show the proposed card to the government publications librarian who might suggest changing the emphasis of the card; the government publications librarian might talk it over with the reference librarian; in turn, the reference librarian might suggest using a sign instead of an information card; next, the reference librarian, readers services librarian, and technical services librarian might meet to discuss other approaches; and so on, until a collective decision is worked out.

Most decisions evolve gradually and painfully after suggestions, doubts, and objectives are heard from all quarters. Yet in spite of (or because of) the confused atmosphere engulfing most decision-making situations, a systematic approach is still the preferred method, even for the individual able to organize alternatives rapidly. To supplement the department head's decision-making formula, here are a few more points to consider when confronted with a cataloging problem:

1. Determine if it is an emergency or not. The urgency of the decision will dictate, more than anything else, the course of action.

2. Concentrate on the important alternatives. Focus on those policies and procedures that are critical and have some hope of being initiated.

3. Do not try to anticipate all eventualities--that is simply impossible. Concentrate only on major eventualities, and the minor problems will take care of themselves.

4. Do not be afraid to make a decision even though it is inadequate. As long as provision is made for modifying or completely changing the decision, an informative error, if it is the best that can be achieved, will provide necessary feedback to help in selecting the ideal solution.

5. If necessary, make a temporary or remedial decision. There are times when a stop-gap decision will be made with the understanding that its only purpose is to take care of the immediate crisis. However, do not allow a remedial decision to become permanent.

6. Do not make a decision that boxes the department in, prevents staff from making corrections, or restricts them from selecting other alternatives. Whatever the ultimate decision, chances are that at least some modifications will have to be made later.

7. Whether the decision is temporary or permanent (relatively speaking, that is), be decisive. Indecision causes tensions and cultivates loss of confidence.

8. Therefore, decide something, even if the ultimate decision is not to decide or to make a tentative decision. In many cases, the decisiveness will be just as important as the decision itself.

9. Do not put off a decision. While a spur-of-the-moment decision is usually not advisable (unless, of course, it is unavoidable), neither is it wise to put

off until tomorrow what must be decided today.
Take enough time to decide--but only enough time.

10. Do not expect all decisions to be right all the time.
     No one is infallible, and no one is expected to be.
     All anyone expects is that the decision-maker do
     his best.

11. When necessary, be subjective, be political, be
     partisan. Theoretically, decisions must be made
     objectively. Yet in real life such subjective factors
     as politics, personalities, emotions, and interdepart-
     mental relationships must be considered.

12. Plan ahead. Keep in mind alternative solutions in
     case the first solution does not work out. Be pre-
     pared to amend or completely change the original
     solution.

Time Management

Besides managing people, places, and things, managers
manage time. The problem is that although most department
heads seem to put a good deal of effort into managing the working hours of employees, they often take a haphazard approach
to managing their own time. The department head, to be a
successful manager, must carefully organize his working hours,
which includes following a few simple time-saving techniques.

Delegate. One of the best ways for a department head
to save time is to delegate. Besides being a time-saver, delegation is an excellent in-service training technique. By allowing staff members to take on new responsibilities the department head helps them grow in their jobs. But for delegation
to work, the department head must trust his staff, be recep-
tive to their ideas, and encourage them to learn by doing and
by making mistakes.

The first step in the art of delegation is to insist that
everyone in the department do his or her own work. Staff
members cannot be expected to take on new responsibilities if
supervisors continually perform their jobs for them. This
often happens when an employee has just been promoted to a
new supervisory position. Because the new supervisory re-

sponsibilities are unfamiliar and perhaps a bit more difficult
to perform than the previous duties, there is the tendency for
the new supervisor to continue performing his or her more
familiar assignments.

Set priorities. Many department heads waste time because they don't know where they are going. They make
false starts, get sidetracked, become discouraged, and end
up doing half-a-job in twice the time. The answer is to establish priorities and then to set a deadline for each priority.
This puts pressure on to get started and to get finished.

In most libraries the head of a catalog department cannot possibly do everything he wants to do, at least not do
everything all at once. Some tasks are more important than
others, other tasks can be delegated or combined, and still
others will solve themselves or be forgotten if no action is
taken. If the department head's attention is directed toward
the wrong action at the wrong time he will be ineffectual and
waste time. Unless he sets priorities he runs the risk of
spending time in work unrelated to the department's present
goals; the result is management-by-crises.

Establish routines. Whether a librarian is cataloging
books or managing people, an excellent time-saving technique
is to carve out a set of routines, especially for the more
repetitive tasks. Many cataloging activities are routine and
can be grouped into a small number of categories. Many, in
fact, can be done routinely by others in the department, some
by an office machine or computer.

But for routines to be effective, they must be personalized. Everyone is different. Some people work best in the
mornings, others in the afternoons. If the department head
is at his best in the morning he should set aside that time
for activities that require the most concentration. He cannot,
of course, reorganize his department to fit his personal desires. But he should at least try to schedule his most demanding tasks during those hours when he is at his best. Conversely he should not waste his prime-time hours doing routine things of low priority, even if this means taking material
home to work on at night when he is at his best.

Don't procrastinate. Many department heads tend to
put off until tomorrow what they should do today. Even if

there is only enough time to do part of a job, a start should
be made. This provides a psychological edge for later on
when the department head can pick up where he left off.
It's too easy to find reasons to delay a decision: more details are needed, a committee has to be formed, a report written, a meeting called. Even if an action or decision turns
out to be wrong, chances are that the time saved by avoiding
procrastination can be used to correct any damage that might
have been done. Postponing an unpleasant task usually means
doing what the department head likes to do rather than what
he should do, which, in turn, results in a backlog of decisions and actions.

One of the biggest contributors to managerial procrastination are emotions. Time spent in worrying about installing
new state-of-the-art computer terminals is time stolen from
getting everything and everyone ready for the installation.
Likewise, the department head should not become so emotional-
ly involved in a personnel problem that he finds himself burn-
ing up the energy needed to remove the problem. Emotions
should be put to work in getting jobs done, not in worry or
in procrastination.

Develop short cuts. Most innovations come from people
who want to do their jobs quicker and easier than before.
The department head, too, can save time by seeking quicker
and better ways to get things done. Almost every cataloging
activity can be performed a little more efficiently and therefore in less time. An especially effective short cut is to do
two or more things at a time. The department head cannot,
of course, hold a departmental meeting at the same time he
writes his annual report. But he can at least jot down a few
notes while he waits for the meeting to start or, better yet,
take notes while he is on a coffee break, riding the bus, or
sitting in the doctor's waiting room. The alert department
head can easily add an hour or more to his working day by
making his leisure, waiting, eating, traveling, and break times
pay double.

Avoid interruptions. By definition interruptions are unexpected, often unavoidable. But interruptions waste time
and the department head should do whatever he can to prevent them. Sometimes the only way to avoid interruptions is
to establish a personal hideaway, either in the library or outside, perhaps a quiet corner in the reference room or a study

carrel in the stacks. Or the department head might have to
stay at his desk after everyone else in the department has
gone home or bring his work home to the kitchen table. One
hour of uninterrupted time can be worth several hours in a
normal interruption-filled workday.

Career Development

A department head who fails to grow in his job is being
unfair to himself and to the library. Growth means to the
career-conscious librarian step-by-step advancements within
the library and perhaps eventually an advancement to a position in another institution. The catch is that in many libraries no one knows for sure what the policies for advancement and promotion are. And where specific policies do exist,
they are not always administered uniformly and they will
usually differ from the policies found in other institutions.
Yet despite inconsistencies and uncertainties, there is a good
deal that the department head can do to advance himself in
his career.

Know the job. The head of a catalog department must
be an expert in bibliographic control as well as possess in-
depth knowledge of librarianship in general. He must keep
abreast of changing technologies, cataloging codes, and managerial philosophies. He should know the administrative policies and practices in his library and understand thoroughly
his specific departmental responsibilities. Of course he must
know his staff, especially how to lead and motivate them. He
must cultivate the habit of positive dissatisfaction and be continually on the alert for ways to improve the department's
operations. He must know what other units in the library are
doing and how his department fits into the total picture.
Finally, he must be aware of how other libraries are solving
their day-to-day bibliographic problems.

Be a professional. Professionalism means more than
memberships in professional organizations. Mainly, professionalism is an attitude. It is personal integrity and having
the respect and confidence of other professionals. Professionalism is being a leader, but a leader willing to listen to
others; it is a mastery of one's performance, and a readiness
to take risks where necessary. Professionalism means active
participation in workshops and conferences, accepting positions

of leadership in professional organizations, and keeping up
with as well as contributing to the literature.

Seek responsibilities. One of the more obvious characteristics of a professional is to seek new challenges and to
follow through on these challenges. The career-minded department head is expected to get things done. He must serve
the library and he must volunteer his services to his profession and community.

Delegate responsibilities. The measure of the department head's success depends as much on the performances of
those he supervises as on his own performance. Invariably,
the department head is held responsible when staff members
succeed in their work. He must, therefore, make maximum
use of the talents of his people. By helping staff grow in
their jobs, he grows in his. Each person in the department
should be groomed to step into the next highest position, including that of the department head.

Work hard. Nothing succeeds like hard work, which often means putting in extra hours on day-to-day departmental
responsibilities. Besides getting the job done, the hard-
working department head is a model for others. Hard work
coupled with smart work equals a successful career.

Plan a career. The same career-building techniques
used by the department head to guide his staff (see Chapter
5, "Career Development") should be applied to the department head's own career development. If he has doubts about
the direction his career is taking, he should talk with his
division head and with other more experienced librarians, perhaps even seek professional career counseling.

To successfully plan his career, the department head
must be aware of his strengths and weaknesses and then build
on his strengths and try to eliminate whatever weaknesses
he might find. He must decide where exactly he wants to go
in his career even though it may be different from what others
might expect from him; he should seek advice but never
should he abdicate career planning to others. He will, of
course, have to make adjustments and compromises along the
way, but if he is willing to take charge of himself, he will
eventually reach his goals. The career-minded department
head must carefully plan his career, never let his career plan
him.

Chapter 3

CURRENT ISSUES

As we learned in the previous chapter, the head of a catalog department is, among other things, a decision maker. In the day-to-day management of a catalog department he is continually faced with and expected to solve many problems. Particularly critical are those issues that focus on how the department is effectively to process materials the library is acquiring. The department head will have to consider such things as which outside processing services to select, whether to catalog certain materials briefly, how to organize various A-V materials, and which card reproduction method to use. In approaching these and similar questions he will have to analyze such factors as patron access, department organization, and available resources. He will, of course, be influenced by the operations of other departments in the library; and certainly he will be limited by parameters established by the central administration. But no matter how complex the problem, the head of the catalog department, as its chief administrative officer, will have the responsibility of gathering, examining, and evaluating all pertinent facts, and, after careful deliberation, passing along concrete, well-defined recommendations to the library administration.

Centralized Processing

To process books efficiently, every library, large and small, must have a good portion of its cataloging performed by an outside source. This source can be the Library of Congress (the biggest of them all), a commercial processing firm, a bibliographic network such as OCLC, or a book jobber that furnishes "cards with books." The processor may do its own cataloging or it may adapt the cataloging of LC and others to the specific needs of its clients. This service may represent individual cards (or the equivalent) from which the library can produce its own card sets, full card sets, complete processing kits, or even shelf-ready books.

By far the largest and most important of the central processing agencies is the Library of Congress. It not only offers a great volume and variety of bibliographic information to libraries of all sizes and types, but, understandably, many commercial processing firms and regional networks base their services on cataloging copy from the Library of Congress. Included in the array of services offered by LC are the National Union Catalog, printed catalog cards, MARC tapes, Cataloging in Publication data, and a microform edition of its authority file.

The National Union Catalog (NUC) contains reproductions of all LC printed cards as well as the cards of contributing North American libraries. Entries are arranged by author or main entry. This is an extremely valuable tool for any library that can afford both the retrospective catalogs and the monthly service--valuable not only for cataloging purposes but for interlibrary loan, acquisition, and general bibliographic work. Besides the National Union Catalog, LC publishes individual catalogs for music and phonorecords, manuscripts, and motion pictures and filmstrips, plus a union catalog arranged by subject headings.

Libraries can use NUC for the verification of authors and titles, and, more importantly, to copy bibliographic information for the production of catalog cards. Since typing individual cards is very time-consuming, most libraries reproduce the entries through photographic means using commercial photocopiers. Special attachments affixed to these copiers enlarge the images to standard catalog card size. After the picture is taken the image can be cut to proper card size and duplicated by Xerox or other means to produce complete card sets.

The Library of Congress also sells printed cards. A library may order one card or complete sets for any title LC has cataloged. Although the tracings, LC call number, and usually a suggested Dewey Decimal Classification appear at the bottom of each card, none of this information is printed at the top of the cards. The headings and call numbers must be typed locally.

Any library requesting cards should order them by the LC card number which appears in the lower right-hand corner of each catalog card and on the verso of the title pages of most American imprint books and in many published indexes and bibliographies. A library can also order cards by author and title, but at increased cost.

To order cards, the library must use the standard machine-readable order forms furnished free of charge by the Library of Congress. Information on the subscription plan is available from the Catalog Distribution Service of the Library of Congress.

On July 1, 1971, the Library of Congress formally established the Cataloging in Publication (CIP) Program. The purpose of CIP is to provide participating American publishers with LC cataloging data for publication in their books, usually on the verso of title pages. LC catalogers construct the CIP data primarily from galleys supplied by the publishers. Although the CIP data do not include such information as subtitle, collation, and citation of pages, enough data are reproduced to allow a clerk to type catalog card masters. The list of participating American publishing houses is impressive and continues to grow, and someday it is to be hoped that most foreign presses will be included.

Besides providing cataloging information on printed cards, in book format through NUC, and on the verso of title pages in the form of CIP data, the Library of Congress will send data in machine-readable form on MARC (Machine-Readable Cataloging) computer tapes. The tapes, sent to subscribers on a regular basis, contain all the bibliographic information needed to produce catalog cards. Needless to say, to benefit from the MARC subscription service a library must have the necessary hardware and software capabilities. Libraries that have their own computers not only can produce card sets from MARC tapes but have the capability of printing accession lists and bibliographies of various kinds. There also exists the potential for a library to integrate its cataloging, serials, acquisitions, and circulation operations and thus eventually develop a completely automated library system.

Other central processing services, especially popular with small and medium-size libraries, are the "processing kits," "cards-with-books," and various pre-processing plans offered

by many processing firms and commercial book vendors. In
a typical cards-with-books plan the vendor will send with
each book ordered by the library a complete card set, often
with call numbers and headings printed on the cards. Usually
in such plans, the library has several options. It can choose
either Dewey or LC numbers, select how it wants the numbers
printed on the cards, and eliminate or add certain bibliographic information. With the processing kits, the library
usually receives shelf-ready books complete with book pockets,
dust jackets, spine labels, plus card sets--again, tailored to
the library's specifications. To be of value, though, such
cataloging services, like all other library services, must satisfy specific library needs. Programs of certain firms are obviously aimed at small libraries, others at larger institutions.
Many companies advertise customized processing, yet nearly
all cater to specific types of libraries and answer specific requirements. In selecting the service best suited to a library's
needs the department head must, therefore, consider carefully
many points, including the following:

1. To whom is the service directed? What size and
type library can best use the service? Catalog cards tailored
to the school library would probably be unacceptable to a
large research library. Conversely, many of the extra services demanded by a larger library would be of little value to
the smaller one.

2. What exactly is provided in the service? Will the
library receive catalog cards with books, complete kits, shelf-
ready books? Will the firm print headings at the top of added
entry cards? Are name and subject cross-references provided?

3. How customized is the service? Will the firm furnish
duplicate sets of cards for branch libraries? Will cards be
formated to local specifications? Will appropriate symbols for
reference books, juvenile books, and fiction appear above the
call numbers?

4. What adjustments will the library and patrons have
to make? If the service is computer-based, will the black subject headings conflict with the red headings now used? Will
the new cards provide the same annotations patrons have been
accustomed to seeing?

5. Will any changes have to be made on the cards?
Often the time spent in changing and adapting a set of cards
to local specifications can be more costly than performing the
entire operation locally.

6. Is the card service linked to a book purchase plan?
If so, how comprehensive is the selection? Will the firm
furnish all the titles needed? Will the cards come with the
books or must you order separately? Must the library buy
books to get cards, and vice versa? If cards are unavailable for a particular title, will the service hold the book for
cataloging or send it uncataloged, forwarding the card set
when available?

7. Does the service follow standard descriptive cataloging rules, classification systems, and subject headings?
If it catalogs as well as using LC copy, are the two compatible with each other and with the catalog department's own
cataloging?

8. What are the costs? Compare the costs with other
services, particularly the costs of the extras and options.
The catalog department may, for instance, find it cheaper to
buy single cards and duplicate the complete sets locally; or
it may want to buy card sets but do its own labeling. In
estimating costs consider personnel, supplies, equipment--
and future costs. Too many libraries have found that after
contracting for a service the price is suddenly doubled to
cover new technology, added services, inflation, or whatever.

9. Can the catalog department perform the service
more efficiently, economically, and effectively than the firm?
After learning of a new cataloging service, many department
heads believe they can, given the proper equipment, do the
job more economically themselves. This is often true, but
not always. Certainly one important consideration is trained
personnel to operate and maintain equipment.

10. Efficient service. Will the firm provide prompt
delivery and service? Will it follow through on its commitments? The best way to discover the reliability of a company
is to query a few of its customers. Does the firm have competent representatives on call who will quickly run down lost
shipments and rectify poor service? In other words, how
much control will the department head really have over the
service being considered?

11. What happens if the service is discontinued or radically changed? If, for whatever reason, the library or the firm discontinues the service, will the library be stuck with expensive materials, equipment, and personnel? Remember also that many companies not only lease equipment, but the data as well. In any case, when starting a new service do not discard the old one, at least not until the catalog department is on firm ground with the new venture.

12. How much of the catalog department's output will the service cover: one-fourth, one-half, three-quarters? To be worthwhile, it should take care of a relatively large portion of the library's present cataloging operation. Too many different services will add confusion rather than efficiency to the department. In retrieving LC copy or other cataloging data from a particular system, the greater the yield on the first search the less handling and sorting of books, further searching, and overall transactions required--therefore, the more efficient the total operation. A search in a microfiche file that yields only 60 percent hits will mean that 40 percent will either have to be researched later, searched in another information base, or given original cataloging.

13. How will the service fit into the department's total operation? Will it be compatible with present job-streams, or will there be costly adjustments that will disrupt department routines?

14. In what format will the information arrive? Although the format most libraries consider ideal is catalog cards, libraries can also receive cataloging copy in book form, computer tapes, or microfiche, to mention only a few current possibilities. If the catalog department is receiving cataloging copy on microfiche it must have the facilities to search and reproduce it economically on catalog card format.

15. How will the new service affect department morale? If it eases much of the department's repetitive and tedious work, this in itself is an important consideration.

16. How does the service compare with others? With the variety of services available, and more coming on the market, it is important to shop around. Look at journal ads, talk to representatives, write for brochures, and examine exhibits at conventions. There is no obligation to buy.

AACR2 and Closing the Card Catalog

The decision by the Library of Congress to freeze its card catalog, as of January 1, 1981, and to start a new automated catalog has stimulated other libraries to consider closing and even freezing their catalogs. The chief reason given for closing has been the publication of the second edition of the Anglo-American Cataloging Rules (AACR2) and the difficulty that many libraries have been having in incorporating the new and previous codes into one catalog. Mentioned also has been the expense of maintaining deteriorating catalogs filled with worn and illegible cards, catalogs that are becoming more and more expensive to file into and to update. Still another reason has been the decision by some libraries to automate with the first step being to close their old card catalogs.

To close a catalog, the library simply decides as of a certain date not to file any new cards into the present card catalog and to start a new one. All materials processed after the cut-off date go into the new catalog and everything that had been cataloged before that date remains in the old card catalog. The new catalog could be a book catalog, a COM catalog, an on-line catalog, or a second card catalog.

The library also has the option of freezing its catalog, as did the Library of Congress. Besides no longer adding new titles, the library makes no changes at all. No new cross-references are put into the old catalog, no changes in location are made, and no indications are given of withdrawals and added copies. All records remain as they were at the time of closing. Freezing can work well in a large closed-stack library such as the Library of Congress, but medium-size and smaller libraries will find out-dated catalogs difficult and confusing for patrons to use.

The first problem the department head must face in closing a catalog is to explain the decision to patrons, especially if the reason for closing is a revised cataloging code. Cataloging rules have been changing for years and will continue to change. Few patrons understand the need for code revisions in the first place, and fewer still would understand the need for maintaining two (or more) catalogs because of a revision, no matter how extensive the revision might be.

It is important, therefore, that a library planning to close its catalog also begin planning immediately for a new automated one and, just as important, that it begin preparing for the eventual integration of the old card catalog into the new automated file. Patrons realize that a library preparing for a computer-based catalog will want to start with a relatively clean file in which all entries are based on the latest cataloging code, and if they are assured that someday they will have a more efficient computer-generated catalog to use, most will accept the temporary confusion of searching two catalogs.

Meanwhile, the catalog department must begin linking the old and the new catalogs in a way that will cause patrons and staff a minimum of confusion. This means asking and answering some important bibliographic questions. What, for example, is the library to do with added copies and new editions? Should older editions be recataloged so they will file in the new catalog next to the earlier editions, or should the various editions be linked by cross-references and information cards, which could mean a substantial number of references?

What about serials? It is confusing enough for patrons to deal with title changes, new issuing bodies, and code revisions when everything is contained in one catalog, but the confusion is compounded when a serial is scattered in two catalogs. The same confusion exists when monographic series are split between an old and a new card catalog.

To integrate a major code revision into the library's existing card catalog is not a simple matter either. First, the department head must estimate what sort of impact the new code will have on the catalog. Most code revisions and changes, including those brought about by AACR2, involve certain types of headings more than others. If, for example, the library has a large proportion of serials where entries have changed from issuing body to title or a large number of law, music, or religious titles which could mean many changes in uniform titles, the effect on the catalog could be substantial. On the other hand, changes could be relatively slight for public and school libraries that house mostly English-language publications, few of which are issued by corporate bodies. Or the library might have a large number of technical reports or other materials that must be weeded continually and therefore require few heading changes since most will be withdrawn eventually.

After studying the impact of the code changes on the card catalog, the department head can then examine the alternatives: change the obsolete headings to conform to the new code; interfile obsolete headings with new ones; or establish split files of old and new headings connected by cross-references and linking notes.

Most libraries, over the years, have used all three methods and no doubt should continue the practice. In other words, where a large number of titles already exist under the old headings, the old and new headings will have to be left, with cross-references made to connect the two (or more) forms. Where only a few headings exist under an old form, they should be changed to conform to the new rules. Finally, where differences in headings will have little if any effect on the filing, the new headings can be interfiled with the old forms. In short, to keep abreast of continuous code changes, including AACR2, most libraries will have to establish and maintain a system of linking and interfiling within their catalogs, recataloging where necessary and as time permits.

Brief Cataloging

One of the most perplexing problems for a department head is his backlog. Catalog departments, large or small, seem to be perpetually faced with backlogs and arrearages of one kind or another. Some departments have accepted them as a way-of-life, others have, at some point or another, decided to do something. Invariably this something has been to hire more staff, automate the library's cataloging operation (for example, join a computer-based network), or, if funds are unavailable for either of these, institute some form of brief cataloging, or what has been variously called fast cataloging, limited cataloging, instant cataloging, and brieflisting.

Specifically, a library will turn to brief cataloging, in whatever form, for one or more of the following reasons:

1. To eliminate a long-standing, stubborn backlog.

2. To compensate for a lack of professional catalogers to fully catalog and classify materials the library is acquiring.

3. To make available to the public, as quickly as possible, recent purchases that are awaiting catalog cards or other cataloging information.

4. To provide at least limited access to certain materials (usually either ephemeral or nonbook) that the library feels need not be fully cataloged and classified.

5. To make available to users a special bulk purchase or gift collection which the catalog department does not have the time or resources to process in the usual manner.

The forms that brief cataloging takes vary from library to library. In some libraries brief cataloging means simply taking a few simple short cuts; in others it will mean no cataloging at all. Some may abbreviate the descriptive cataloging, eliminate the subject headings, and classify by accession number; others will rely completely on published indexes for access to certain items in their collections. The following are the four main techniques used for brief cataloging of books and other materials.

1. Brieflisting: To brieflist the library simply performs a brief or greatly reduced type of cataloging. This is done by reducing the descriptive cataloging (listing only the author, brief title, publisher, and date of publication), omitting all subject headings, and classifying by accession number. The point is to keep the cataloging information simple enough so that a clerk can, with book-in-hand, quickly type a catalog card in a reasonably standard format. The clerk takes the information directly from the title page with little concern for the standard descriptive cataloging rules; nor is any thought given to punctuation, capitalization, and other grammatical decisions. Except in larger libraries, little if any verification is done, although both reader and librarian should be able to identify the book correctly through the main entry. Libraries that do not want to verify even questionable entries can enter the brieflisted books under title. This is especially convenient if acquisition records are entered under title.

Besides the standard bibliographic information of author, brief title, and brief imprint, it is a good idea to stamp or otherwise indicate on the card that the book has received brief cataloging, and to note its location in the library. One way to identify brieflisted items quickly is to use color-coded catalog cards. In addition, the library may want to indicate somewhere on the card the number of copies and volumes in the library, if and when catalog cards were ordered, and whether or not an entry is available in NUC.

Instead of classifying by Dewey or LC, most libraries simply number their brieflisted books consecutively as they arrive. Others use their book order numbers. In either case, staff members are able to remove and catalog items fully in the same order as they arrive in the library.

A library using this brief cataloging technique usually does so for books awaiting catalog cards. For patron convenience, books can be shelved in a special "new books section" located near the circulation desk, where they can be checked out under the book numbers. As a further aid to patron browsing, some catalog departments classify by a broad Dewey or LC class number followed by an accession number. In marking brieflisted books, the department can either apply removable labels or use its regular marking technique and place the permanent Dewey or LC labels over the old book numbers when the books are fully cataloged. Libraries with a relatively small brieflisting program may not want to number the books at all, but merely shelve by author, title, or broad subject.

2. **Order card listing:** An even simpler brief cataloging technique is to place one of the 3 x 5 multiple order slips in the card catalog under either author or title. The slip selected must, of course, be sturdy enough to withstand the abuse it will undoubtedly receive. The duplicate order slip can be placed in the catalog either when the book is ordered or after it has been received. If the library does file slips during the ordering process, it is a good idea to stamp the arrival date on the slip when the book is placed on the new book shelf. When the book is scheduled for full cataloging (perhaps the cards have arrived or the title has been requested by a patron) it is retrieved from the shelf and the order card is pulled from the card catalog. The order card can be used as a work slip when processing the book.

3. **Photolisting:** Another brief cataloging technique is

to reproduce, through a photographic process, title pages on standard catalog cards. Over the years, the reproduction techniques used in libraries have changed with advancing technology until today the most popular method is to microfilm the title page with a microfilm camera, develop the negative microfilm, enlarge it and cut the copy to standard catalog card format.

In order to file the title page reproduction into the card catalog, most libraries reproduce the main entry along the top edge of the card. This is done by either typing the entry on the card after it has been produced, or, perhaps more suitable, inserting an information slip on the side of the title page when it is photographed. The insert should contain the main entry plus the book number and perhaps a statement indicating where the book is shelved in the library.

The main advantage of photolisting is that all the information found on the title page can be quickly and accurately reproduced onto a catalog card, which is, after all, what descriptive cataloging is all about. Understandably, then, photolisting has become popular with libraries wishing to quickly eliminate stubborn backlogs or to catalog materials where accurate transcription of titles is difficult (materials in non-Roman alphabets, for example). Many libraries, particularly in Europe, use title page photography for full, permanent cataloging.

As convenient as it sounds, title page photography is suitable only for larger libraries that have both large backlogs to process and the funds to invest in such a program. Costs of equipment, trained technicians, and supplies are important considerations; and these costs exist whether the library performs all the operations locally or contracts most of the work. In addition, while the technical problems are surmountable, they are nonetheless complex. Simply to reproduce title pages of different sizes and colors clearly and legibly requires a trained operator who can expertly adjust exposures, settings, and reduction ratios.

4. <u>Brief indexing</u>: Many materials, particularly non-books, arrive in the library already numbered and indexed. Most U.S. Government documents, for example, are classified by the Superintendent of Documents numbering system and indexed in the <u>Monthly Catalog</u>; all phonorecords have manu-

facturers' numbers on both the records and jackets, and are indexed in the Schwann Record Catalog; and many microform series come to the library numbered and accompanied by indexes. The point is, these materials have numbers printed on them, and can be reached through one or more published indexes. They are, in effect, self-indexed. To many catalogers, this means that little if any furhter cataloging or classification is necessary. These materials need not even be listed in the public card catalog since published bibliographies and indexes can be used for at least limited access.

A few libraries even use union catalogs, indexes, and bibliographies as access to their book collections. Most popular of all has been the use of Readers' Guide and other published periodical indexes to reach magazines. A library using its periodical indexes exclusively neither catalogs nor classifies its periodicals but simply shelves them alphabetically. The patron consults the standard indexes and goes directly to the shelves to retrieve the title. A library can even use NUC, BIP, and other standard tools as access to its monographs. To locate an item, the patron consults the published index as he would a card catalog, copies the number penciled beside the title, and retrieves the book from the stacks. If no number appears beside an item, he knows that it is not part of the library's holdings.

The chief advantage of brief cataloging is that it speeds the time a book reaches the patron. In many libraries, it is literally the only way a patron can read a best seller before it becomes out-of-date. Granted, brief cataloging is not a panacea. For one thing, brief cataloging nearly always results in increased pressure on reader service personnel. Yet limited access is better than none at all. Also, brief cataloging provides relatively inexpensive access. For any catalog department planning to institute such a program, here are a few points to consider.

1. Consider, first of all, user needs. Is it more important for users to have immediate yet limited access to materials arriving in the library or to have full access as soon as possible, even if it takes several weeks or months (or years) before the books are fully cataloged? Also, consider the importance of a subject approach to the user, an approach which is nearly always neglected in brief cataloging.

2. Is the brief cataloging to be temporary or permanent? The two should not be confused. If the library is implementing a temporary method, it should not become permanent. If the brief cataloging is indeed permanent, both patrons and librarians should have as complete access to the collection as possible through indexes, information cards in the card catalog, well-placed directional signs, and effective reference service.

3. What is the nature of the materials? Popular novels that will soon become out-dated should reach patrons as quickly as possible, yet certain other materials can perhaps await full cataloging. Also, because of their complex entries and the need continually to add single issues and volumes to library records, most brief cataloging techniques are not recommended for serial publications.

4. Consider carefully the problem of entry verification. Usually the author can be taken directly from the title page, in most cases using only last name and initials. In larger libraries, however, if main entries are not accurately verified they may become lost in the public catalog.

5. Can the library effectively coordinate two collections--one briefly cataloged and the other fully processed? There can be both bibliographic and logistical problems. Certainly one problem will be duplications. Not only are the main entries briefly entered but there will be no added entries, title entries, or series entries. The catalog department may, for example, fully catalog a title as a serial and at the same time briefly catalog it as a monograph.

6. How much duplication of work will there be? When the catalog department first briefly catalogs and later fully catalogs a book it is actually processing the item twice. The point is, keep brief cataloging brief.

7. How far is the catalog department willing to go to insure that patrons are inconvenienced as little as possible? To lessen confusion should title entries, cross-references, and added entries for editors and joint authors be included? Remember, though, that the more the catalog department provides for various contingencies, the less the time that is saved.

Cataloging Nonbook Materials

The cataloging and classification of nonbook materials
has become a concern in libraries of all types and sizes.
How should the small public library catalog and classify its
phonorecord collection? How should the art library arrange
its slides? What should the junior college do with its cassettes? Unlike books, for which there exists only one set of
descriptive cataloging rules (AACR), two possible classification systems (LC or Dewey), and two subject heading lists
(LC or Sears), the array of control methods used for nonbooks
is staggering. Every library seems to have developed its
own, many using different techniques for different materials.
There is, unfortunately, no standard--not to mention ideal--
methods of cataloging and classifying any of the nonbook materials flooding our libraries. Nonetheless, until the uni-
versal system does evolve, nonbooks, like books, must be
controlled in some fashion. What, then, are the possibilities?
Although specific techniques differ widely from library to library, all seem to fall into one or more of four basic categories: book system, home-made scheme, alphabetic or serial
arrangement, and publisher's indexing system.

Ideally, nonbooks should be cataloged and classified in
the same manner as books, with all the library's holdings integrated into one general collection. In this way all library materials, regardless of format, would follow AACR2, be classified either in the LC or Dewey systems, and be assigned
either LC or Sears subject headings. The advantages are obvious. Book systems are familiar to patrons and librarians alike,
compatible with existing control and circulation systems, and
maintained and updated by the Library of Congress and other
organizations that furnish subject heading lists, catalog cards,
classification schedules, and descriptive cataloging rules. But
as desirable as this may sound, it is not always practicable.
Although the second edition of AACR does devote several
chapters to the cataloging of nonbooks, the present flood of
materials has made the descriptive cataloging of individual
items extremely time-consuming. Nor is there adequate provision for most nonbooks in either the LC or Dewey schemes.
Libraries using the Dewey Decimal system do have the option
of applying the standard subdivisions .022 (illustrations and
models) and .0208 (audiovisual treatment) to selected nonbook
materials; and the LC system does provide for music scores
in the M schedule and for maps in the G schedule. But to

integrate materials such as sheet maps, phonorecords, slides, and microfiche with books is cumbersome, to say the least. Nor, in fact, do most nonbooks have the same subject relevance as books. Often, too, materials such as microfilms and phonorecords will have more than one title or subject on each physical item, negating the value of traditional subject classification systems and headings.

To meet the special needs of both the materials and patrons, many libraries have constructed their own cataloging and classification schemes for certain nonbooks. The advantage of a tailor-made system is that it can be modeled to local needs. On the other hand, the cost of developing and maintaining locally devised descriptive cataloging rules, subject heading lists, and classification systems is monumental. A library can compromise by using an abbreviated AACR for descriptive cataloging and a Sears or other published listing for subject headings (or eliminate headings altogether), then constructing an elaborate home-made classification system as the prime approach to the collection. Certain materials more than others have traditionally been controlled through home-made schemes. Slide and picture collections, for example, are often arranged by close subject classification schemes, as are large map collections. To avoid the expense of developing and updating tailor-made systems, a library can adopt an already published (or unpublished) system created by another library or individual. It is important, though, when adopting an existing system to select one that is periodically updated and that will fit local requirements.

One of the simplest ways to arrange a collection of nonbooks is to shelve them alphabetically by author, title, subject, or issuing agency. Alphabetic arrangements work particularly well for either open shelf collections (periodicals, for instance), where patrons do not need a subject approach through the card catalog but can go directly to the items from a bibliography or index, or with materials such as vertical files that can be filed and approached directly by broad subject. The chief advantage of the alphabetic subject system is that it is self-indexing. If materials are filed by subject, intermediary finding devices are usually unnecessary. Moreover, an alphabetic system can be easily expanded, and expanded indefinitely. An alphabetic arrangement also allows for direct access browsing. Of course, for multiple access a card catalog or index is still necessary. If, for example, materials are arranged by author or title, a subject approach can be provided through a card catalog or index. When access is through a card catalog the descriptive cataloging can follow AACR, although brief descriptive cataloging will usually suffice for most materials.

Many libraries prefer to arrange their nonbooks by simple accession or serial numbers. Materials such as microforms that do not lend themselves to browsing are often placed in serial order. As with the alphabetic system, the advantage here lies in simplicity; the chief disadvantage is that serial order provides no indication of subject. An index or card catalog is necessary for author, title, or subject access.

Finally, many libraries have begun arranging certain of their nonbooks by the numbering systems developed by the publishers and issuing bodies, with access through published indexes and bibliographies. A good example of this is the control method provided by the Superintendent of Documents for U.S. Government documents. Libraries can shelve items by Superintendent of Documents numbering system, using the Monthly Catalog and other indexes as access. The advantage is savings in time and money. As depository documents arrive in the library, a clerk can look up numbers on the shipping lists, write them on the items, and send them directly to the stacks without complete cataloging and classification. In fact, many government documents already have the numbers printed on them. The library can use the Monthly Catalog for a subject approach to the materials, while anyone wishing to consult the publications of a specific agency can easily do so by browsing in the stacks.

Besides Government documents, many other materials are numbered and indexed by their respective issuing bodies. Phonorecords, for example, arrive in the library with numbers already assigned by the various record companies. These numbers appear on the records, jackets, and LC catalog cards, and are recorded in the Schwann Record Catalog and other listings. Many maps, too, are classified and indexed in one form or another. The U.S. Army Map Service, British Army Geographical Section, and U.S. Coast and Geo-Survey are three services that number their maps. In the last few years, several companies have begun numbering and indexing their microform series. However, to locate individual titles in indexed series, patrons must know that indexes do indeed exist;

and they must know the locations of these indexes in the library.

Thus libraries have developed various ways of handling nonbooks. Actually, they have developed too many ways. The result is a complete lack of standardization. Which system or combination of systems is best for a particular medium in a specific library is not as yet evident, at least not to most librarians. Nonetheless, until we do have some standardization, each library must select the system appropriate to the material at hand, even if this means only a temporary solution. Although circumstances will vary, some general principles exist to help the librarian select or construct the system best suited to the material under consideration and to the library concerned.

The first principle is that librarians must reject the concept that all materials, nonbook as well as book, can and should be cataloged and classified under one standard system. Sheet maps, cassettes, microforms, phonorecords, and the like are not books, and they need not be cataloged and classified as books. This means that the public card catalog will not necessarily reflect all the library's holdings. Users may have to consult other tools and search other locations if they expect to find certain materials.

A second and important principle is: when in doubt as to how to organize a particular nonbook collection, follow the archival principle of "provenance," which states that the library must maintain the materials in the organic units in which they were accumulated or created by the agency, publisher, or issuing body. Thus microfilms, archival materials, government documents, and phonorecords that are indexed and numbered in some fashion should remain intact and not be integrated with other collections. Again, this implies that in many cases little or no access will be provided through the public card catalog, except perhaps for information cards indicating that certain materials can be located through appropriate indexes and bibliographies. Exceptions should certainly be made for individual microfilms and certain other nonbooks that are reproductions of books and for which patrons, not realizing that the titles they are seeking are in nonbook form, would automatically consult the card catalog. Also, heavily used materials which are classified in series, such as certain Government documents, may have to be removed from their locations and individually cataloged and listed in the public catalog.

Whenever possible the principle of provenance should apply to non-indexed materials, as well. A group or collection of materials which is neither numbered nor indexed should be kept in the same organizational framework as when first produced. The catalog department should not, for example, try to regroup, chronologically, geographically, topically, or in any other predetermined way, a manuscript, archival, or document collection. The records of each group and subgroup and of each series should be kept intact and not merged with those of other groups, divisions, or series.

If a group of nonbooks does not possess an inherent system of arrangement, it must then be arranged, classified, and/or cataloged in the simplest and most practical way possible for effective servicing. Again, this means the nature of the materials must dictate their organization. A large quantity of miscellaneous sheet maps, for example, should be cataloged and classified not in the traditional author-title arrangement, but organized in drawers by country and sub-arranged by locale, type of map, date, and so on.

Another important principle: whatever the control system, it must be both simple and flexible. Too often the tendency has been to start with a relatively simple scheme and evolve into a complex one. The system should start simple and remain so. At any rate, the system must be flexible enough to allow for expansion, alteration, and even complete change.

The principle that nonbooks need not be treated as books implies that for efficient servicing they must be housed separately. More and more, libraries are segregating materials by type, less and less by subject. Periodical rooms, A-V centers, microform areas are not uncommon in libraries today. Although it is practical for a library to catalog and classify fully a few U.S. Government publications and integrate them into the general collection, when the library becomes a depository receiving thousands of books and pamphlets each year, it must re-assess its control methods--specifically, classify by Superintendent of Documents system and house the collection separately. Similarly, a few microfilms will be no problem if fully cataloged and classified and placed behind the

reference desk, or even sent to the stacks. But if the number of reels becomes large enough to be considered "a separate collection" they should be recognized as such and an entirely different control method devised, with the collection
then housed in its own media center along with appropriate
viewing devices and supervisory personnel.

Another important point is that the less emphasis the
library places on the public card catalog and traditional (book)
descriptive cataloging rules and classification methods, the
more patrons must rely on reference and other library personnel for assistance. In other words, to give users the best
possible access to the materials the cataloging, classification,
indexing, equipment, staffing, and storage facilities must
complement each other.

Following is an alphabetical listing of some of the materials libraries are now organizing into special collections,
and the methods most often used to control them.

Archives. Most libraries follow the principle of provenance, organizing their archive and manuscript materials
within the groups in which they were originally conceived.
Out of these original groupings the cataloger develops a broad
classification scheme, usually with a mixed notation, with individual items receiving at most accession numbers. A typical
archival number might look like this: AMA 2-B6. The letters AMA stand for the American Mineral Association; the
number 2 indicates a particular committee; the B designates
a group of correspondence; and the number 6 is a specific
series of letters. Patrons can approach the materials directly
on the shelves or through the calendars, inventories, or other listings maintained by most archivists.

Cassettes. Cassettes, like phonorecords, can be arranged by manufacturer's numbering system, serial system,
or, in a small collection, alphabetically by title. While other
possibilities do exist, it is preferable to keep the arrangement
simple. If possible, cassettes should be cataloged according
to AACR. As with most A-V materials, however, the descriptive cataloging can be simplified, with brief title entries placed
in the public card.catalog.

Government documents. In smaller libraries, U.S. Government documents should be cataloged and classified like books,

with ephemeral items placed alphabetically in vertical files by either issuing agency or subject. Libraries with large depository collections should, however, classify by the Superintendent of Documents system, using the Monthly Catalog as access.

Microforms. Because microfilms, microfiche, microprints, and other microforms do not lend themselves to patron browsing most libraries arrange them by simple accession systems with sets and serials subdivided decimally. Frequently, the library will assign a broad Dewey or LC class number followed by an accession·number. If possible, titles should be fully cataloged according to AACR with cards filed into the public card catalog. In the case of large microform series the library may have to fully catalog only the series and approach the individual titles through the indexes and bibliographies provided by the issuing agencies.

Music scores. Nearly all libraries catalog and classify music scores in the same manner as books. Most, however, find it convenient to segregate music from books on the shelves, which for a library using the Dewey system means adding "M," "MS," or some other symbol above the class numbers on scores.

Phonorecords. For browsing purposes small public libraries often shelve their phonorecords in open shelves by broad subject categories (symphonies, sonatas, operas, and so on) or alphabetically by composer. Larger libraries that maintain closed stack collections will usually arrange records by either manufacturers' numbers or accession systems. If a professional music cataloger is available, records should be fully cataloged by AACR; otherwise a brief author-title listing will have to suffice.

Picture collections. Picture and photo collections lend themselves best to subject arrangement in file cabinets. An important exception would be art pictures, where medium and artist are more important.

Sheet maps. While atlases can and should be integrated into the general reference collection, sheet maps, because of format, should be arranged geographically in special map cabinets. For a large collection, a simple home-made classification system may be useful. A typical map system will have a number for location, a letter for type of map (nautical, transportation, geological, agricultural, etc.), a Cutter number for the author, and perhaps a date. Whenever possible, however, the library should use the indexing system established by the publisher.

Slide collections. Slide collections, like picture collections, can be arranged alphabetically. Art slides, for example, should be arranged by artist, and architectural slides by place. Large collections, however, are often arranged by home-made classification schemes, and approached either directly or through an index, card catalog, or other auxiliary finding aid. Indexing should be as brief as possible, especially if a rather detailed subject classification scheme has been developed. Generally, the arrangement of art slides is by form, century, country, and finally by artist and individual slide numbers. A typical number might look like this: P20/ES/P4/46. P is for paintings; 20 for the twentieth century; E for Europe and S for Spanish artists; P4 Cuttered for Picasso; and slide number 46.

Vertical files. In most libraries vertical file materials are arranged in folders by broad subjects with, if necessary, an author-title index. To be consistent with their book collections, a few libraries arrange vertical files by Dewey or LC.

Card Reproduction Methods

As with any service or piece of equipment, the selection of a card reproduction method must be based on local needs. No single system is suitable for all libraries or for all library needs. Some libraries in fact use two or more methods. By far the simplest method of duplicating catalog cards is to type each card in the set individually. This is also the least efficient method. An exception might be the small public library that has its cards produced at a central processing center and which might occasionally retype a worn card or reproduce an extra card for local needs. A school library that has sufficient student help might feel it can economically type full sets of cards, particularly if the cataloging copy is brief. It is, however, not only time-consuming to type cards individually, but each card must be proofread and necessary corrections made. Whether typewriters are used for card reproduction or only for typing masters and adding subject headings, the department head must choose each machine carefully. All department typewriters, preferably electric, should have standard library keyboards including square brackets, foreign diacritical markings, and the script ℓ.

One of the more typical reproduction methods has been stencil duplication. Stencil duplicators, available today in a wide variety of sizes, models, and prices, are all based on the same principle: a master copy is typed on a stencil which is affixed to the duplicator; pressure is applied by either rotating a drum or through direct contact; ink is forced through the perforated stencil to produce an image on the blank catalog card.

The smaller hand-operated stencil duplicators designed specifically for duplicating catalog cards are ideal for smaller libraries with limited production; and the larger and more sophisticated electric duplicators will provide fast and efficient service for medium-sized and even larger libraries. Stencil is an inexpensive process and maintenance and operation are simple. However, quality is not as good as with the more sophisticated duplicating machines, production is relatively slow, and, depending on the type of machine and the ink used, the process can be slow-drying, messy, and require at least some cleaning time. Although it is possible to use the more advanced machines for other library duplication needs, for best results the department should use stencil duplicators exclusively for card production.

In the last few years, the electrostatic copiers, especially the Xerox models, have become a popular method of card duplication with all but the smaller libraries. Xerox copiers are most suitable for larger operations, but if the machines are used for other duplicating jobs in the library they can be economical for smaller departments as well. The machines must be adjusted and the stock changed every time a library switches from card production to paper copying, but this is a relatively simple operation.

Another important feature of the Xerox copier is that it can reproduce typed cards, printed cards, photocopy from NUC, and various other masters. Depending on the model, it can duplicate four, six, or even eight masters at a time. The equipment is rented, with the fees based on production; thus there need not be a large initial outlay for equipment. And though more complex than most stencil duplicators, the

Xerox and other electrostatic copiers can be operated by a clerk or student assistant. Most communities have competent company representatives to service machines.

Offset printing is a method popular with libraries that require a large volume of card production. The quality of image is good and production is relatively fast. However, it is definitely a duplication method suitable only for a larger catalog department, unless, of course, the library contracts the work to a commercial processor. The equipment is expensive and requires a skilled operator and a trained service person. To help defray expenses, most libraries that have purchased their own presses use them for other in-house duplication needs. The offset master is produced either by typing directly on the master or by photographing the copy. Although the optical method requires an extra step and is therefore more complex and slightly more expensive than the direct method, it does allow the library to photograph printed cards and other copy.

Libraries that have automated their cataloging operations will have their cards produced in-house by printers attached to the terminals. Besides a computer printer, most automated libraries must also maintain an electrostatic copy machine or other more traditional method of card production to reproduce extra cards and cards in non-Roman alphabets not printable by printers.

In addition to the techniques mentioned above, many other possibilities and combinations exist, including various photographic processes and transfer techniques. There will continue to be refinements of traditional methods and developments of new techniques, which means that deciding which of the many reproduction methods is best for a particular library will not be easy. Many factors must be considered, including the following:

1. Quality of reproduction: The variety of reproduction methods available today also present a wide range in the quality of reproduction. Important considerations include clarity of image, sturdiness and size of stock, and permanence of the ink.

2. Quantity of cards and card sets required: Generally speaking, the more volume required the more sophisticated

the reproduction method needed. For a library belonging to a network and receiving cards from a central computer center or buying card sets from a central processing service and only duplicating a few hundred titles a year for local needs, a small hand-operated stencil machine would be the most economical solution; a library processing under 10,000 titles a year will generally find the standard-size stencil best; and the library cataloging over 10,000 titles would probably need a Xerox machine or offset press.

3. Turnaround time: Whether reproducing cards locally or having them duplicated by an outside service, an important consideration will be how long the library (and the public) must wait for the cards.

4. Headings: Does the reproduction method provide for subject headings and added entries printed at the top of the cards? If so, are they reproduced in the desired format? If headings are printed in black capitals and patrons are accustomed to red headings, what adjustments must be made?

5. Proofreading: The time necessary to check for errors can be costly. If each individual card in a set must be proofread or if there are a good many errors, the library had better consider another method.

6. Wastage: Although the costs of wastage, through either human or mechanical error, may be negligible in a small library, in larger operations this expense can be a major consideration.

7. Other possible uses: Efficient use of a duplication machine can often be increased if it is used to reproduce correspondence, memos, and other library communications.

8. Type of master: Will the method reproduce all types of copy required--printed cards, typed masters, and photocopies?

9. Total costs: As with any cataloging operation, all costs must be considered: equipment, time, materials, supplies, personnel. Is the library renting, leasing, or buying equipment and services?

10. Trained personnel: Many of the newer and more

complex reproduction methods require skilled and highly trained operators. This bears both on production costs and the catalog department's ability to produce quality cards.

11. Service representative: A method of reproduction should not be considered unless the catalog department is either assured of a local representative who will service and maintain equipment and provide sound advice, or has a staff member who can properly maintain the equipment.

12. Inconvenience of equipment: Is the equipment noisy or dirty? Will it soon become outdated and have to be replaced?

13. Down time: The more sophisticated the process, the more likelihood of breakdowns. Whether a postcard-sized stencil machine or a computer printer is used, the possibility of time lost in repairs and straightening out problems must be considered.

14. Supplies: Are the card stock and other supplies top quality, readily available, and moderately priced? Many reproduction methods will accept only certain card stock. Also check to see that the catalog department has access to spare parts.

15. Present library equipment: What equipment does the library already own? Is the library leasing a Xerox machine or is there a stencil duplicator in the supply room that can be used for reproducing cards?

16. Nature of catalog copy: It may, for example, be economically feasible to type sets of cards individually with brief descriptive cataloging in the English language; yet it might be difficult, even impossible, in non-Romance languages.

Dividing the Catalog

Many people, including both librarians and patrons, feel that the traditional dictionary card catalog is not the "key to the collection" it is heralded to be. Most dictionary catalogs are cumbersome to use, difficult to understand, and costly to maintain. In desperation some libraries have either returned to the book catalog or advanced to the COM catalog, and many institutions that have automated their catalogs have indeed switched to these forms; others have experimented with various substitutes including indexes and published bibliographies; still others have divided their catalogs into what they consider more palatable segments. According to most who have tried this latter method the results have been, if not spectacular, at least an improvement over the traditional dictionary concept.

Generally the division has been a two-way split into an author-title catalog and a subject catalog. A few libraries have gone further and made three-way divisions into author, title, and subject catalogs.

Why have libraries divided their catalogs? Briefly there are six major factors that have influenced the decision to divide, and any department head contemplating a switch should give them serious consideration.

1. Catalog use: Will patrons and librarians make more and better use of a card catalog in a divided form than in a dictionary arrangement? Most libraries that have segregated subject cards from non-subjects did so because they believed patrons would find a divided catalog more convenient to use. Many patrons do, indeed, have problems distinguishing between subject and non-subject entries. By dividing the catalog, this distinction is clarified, and the number of cards a patron must search for a known item is significantly reduced. Acquisition and other library personnel have also found it easier to verify authors and titles in a divided catalog. In a divided catalog, however, double searches are often necessary for complete coverage. There will be times, too, when it is more convenient to browse through all possible entries at one location than to go back and forth between catalogs.

2. Reader assistance: Closely related to reader use is the improved assistance many librarians believe they can provide patrons through a divided catalog. Certainly, it enables users to better visualize the subject approach to the collection. The fact is, many librarians are themselves confused by filing rules and thus feel more at ease when assisting others in using a catalog in a divided form. Dividing the catalog should also help reference personnel study patron use and aid librarians in identifying problems associated with the card catalog.

3. Catalog maintenance: It is generally agreed that segregating subjects from non-subjects in the catalog simplifies its maintenance, particularly the filing of cards. It is easier for a supervisor to teach filing rules and less confusing for clerks who must learn them. The result is faster and more accurate filing. The larger the catalog the more complex the filing, and the more benefits will result from a division of the catalog. The catalog department will, however, have to duplicate many guide cards and cross-references and place more emphasis on title cards; it may also want to make subject cards for autobiographical works.

4. Physical arrangement: A library dividing its catalog must consider available floor space and the arrangement of the catalog. Even though the size of each catalog is reduced by division, the total floor space needed actually increases. Instead of space to house one large card catalog the library must provide an even larger area with a clear geographical separation for two (or three) smaller catalogs. Physical arrangement is therefore an important consideration. Dividing the catalog nearly always means layout changes.

5. Congestion: The separation of one large catalog into two or more smaller ones should help relieve overall congestion, although in larger libraries the result may be the opposite in certain areas, particularly in the author-title section. The enlarged floor space, in itself, should relieve congestion and improve the flow of users. Also, since patrons can presumably locate specific items more easily when subjects are segregated from non-subjects, catalog searches should take less time.

6. Future applications: Future plans for the use and structure of the catalog will often influence a decision to divide. For example, a library planning a computer-produced book catalog which includes separate subject and author sections might, as a first step, divide its card catalog. Or a library purchasing computer-produced catalog cards with black subject headings may consider dividing its catalog to lessen the confusion between the older red and newer computer-produced black headings. The fact that a library is planning to contribute to a union catalog may also influence the decision to divide, as may the form of existing catalogs which readers must use in other libraries in the area.

Put in its most obvious terms, the decision to divide the card catalog or not should depend on user needs and, to a lesser extent, on staff needs. Determining these needs will be difficult, more difficult than the actual dividing; for even in the largest library the physical division is a relatively simple operation. It does take manpower, of course, and beyond this, planning; but if the department head has experienced clerical help and is willing to work out details in advance, the changeover can be accomplished smoothly and effectively.

The best way to divide the catalog--that is, with the least amount of confusion and inconvenience to both patrons and librarians--is to do it in three distinct stages. The first stage is to divide the subject cards from the others within each drawer, placing all subject cards behind subject dividers in the drawers; or, in a three-way division, divide each drawer into author, title, and subject sections. Another equally effective technique is to make a division within each section by placing all author-title cards in the top rows and all corresponding subject cards in the bottom rows of each section. In either case, signs should be placed on the catalog cases informing users that during the changeover they will find subjects segregated within each drawer or section. If the segregation is within each section, it is also a good idea to use colored labels for the subject drawers.

In step two the subject cards are removed from each drawer and placed in separate drawers in empty cabinets. If there are not enough extra empty cabinets, drawers can be stacked on tables until enough space is available from the old dictionary catalog to begin the new subject section. As the subject cards are removed, the author-title drawers should be condensed, and temporary labels made for both sections. Since this second phase can be quite hectic, it is best to do it after closing time, using as few people as possible.

The third phase, which begins immediately after the catalog has been physically divided and the sections relocated, is to make permanent labels. This final phase need not be rushed and should include readjusting the number of cards in each drawer and making and filing extra guide cards.

Department Facilities

Department facilities and how they are used will have
much to do with the way the department is managed and organized. Conversely, how the department is organized will
affect, at least to some extent, the physical layout. But while
the department head may have a good deal to say about the
organization and administration of the department there may
be little he can do about net assignable square feet, electrical
outlets, washroom facilities, furnishings, and the many other
things that make the department both comfortable and functional. More likely, he will have to simply "make do" with
inadequate surroundings. Staff will be expected to work in
a cramped, poorly lighted, non-ventilated, illogically planned
corner of an inadequate structure built to house a department
half the size.

The department head who becomes involved in planning
a new building (or renovating an old one) must plan intelligently. He must look ahead to the time when his department
is fully automated, his library is acquiring twice as many materials as it now does, his staff has doubled, and the department is processing as many nonbooks as books. He must not
scrimp on equipment or furnishings, either. If the lowest
bid must be accepted, he will insist that specifications be
tight enough to ensure that materials and services will still
be of top quality. Certainly he will seek input from his staff—
they are the ones who must live with the results. Just as important, he will make sure the library administration knows
exactly what is expected in the new department. He will accept nothing less. Finally, the department head will consider
the following points to make sure nothing has been overlooked.

1. Arrange the layout on a functional basis. Books
    and other materials must flow naturally and logical-
    ly through the department.
2. Provide direct access (either vertically or hori-
    zontally) to the card catalog and reference areas.
    Also important is easy access to the other technical
    service departments, and to the stacks.
3. Insist on maximum flexibility. Use the landscape
    planning concept to separate units with shelving,
    furniture, and movable partitions. Avoid fixed in-
    terior walls.
4. Make sure the department is well lighted, either

with artificial or natural shadow-free lighting.
Maintain at least 75 candle-power at desk height
throughout the department; 100 candle-power is
best.

5. See that the department has enough electrical out-
    lets. Maximum flexibility must be provided for lo-
    cating electric typewriters as well as for audio-
    visual, data processing, duplication, labeling, and
    other equipment. Also provide ducts for data pro-
    cessing cables, even though the department is not
    as yet automated.

6. Keep in mind the comfort of the staff. This means
    automatic air-conditioning and heating, of course.
    Avoid objectionable noise distractions from either
    people or equipment. Create a fresh, clean appear-
    ance. Provide adequate restrooms and water foun-
    tains.

7. Make sure there is enough space for all work areas.
    Staff work stations should be at least 120 square
    feet per person. Binding and marking areas will
    need twice that much.

8. Insist that the department head's office be located
    in the catalog department, not in an administrative
    suite two floors above. It should be a private
    office that is indeed private. A glassed-in office
    is best; and it must be soundproof.

9. Plan for all department space needs. There must
    be enough room for shelving, book trucks, A-V
    equipment needed to catalog nonbooks, reference
    tools and table space to use them, card catalogs,
    terminals, and supply cabinets.

Streamlining Department Operations

Despite stagnant or declining budgets there will continue to be increased service demands on libraries. Every
catalog department will be expected to maintain and, if possible, increase production. It behooves the department head,
therefore, to think not only of efficient solutions to department problems but, where necessary, of short-cuts and stop-
gap remedies. We have looked at a few of these, including
various brief cataloging techniques, and in subsequent chapters we will examine others. For the present, and by way of
review, here are a few of the techniques a department head

can use to increase production while maintaining reasonable control over library holdings.

1. Allow outside processing services to do as much cataloging as possible. Centralized cataloging is usually more economical than local custom processing.

2. Standardization is vital. It is all right--and in many cases necessary--to take short cuts in the cataloging and classification of certain types of materials, particularly nonbooks and ephemeral materials; but it can be disastrous to make frequent and elaborate exceptions to established practices. For efficient processing, the library must accept and adapt to the standards of outside processing firms, networks, and co-ops.

3. In organizing nonbooks try to maintain the materials in the same organizational units in which they are received in the library. Whenever possible use the published indexes and numbering schemes provided by the issuing agencies. If the library must develop its own cataloging and/or classification schemes, they should be kept simple and flexible.

4. To get books to users as quickly as possible, give serious thought to some form of brief cataloging. But the cataloging must indeed be brief or the purpose of the program will be defeated.

5. The most important product of the catalog department's activities is the public card catalog. It is also a costly product to construct and maintain. A short-cut which many libraries have initiated is to underline added entries at the bottom of the cards instead of typing headings, and to file the cards behind headers in the card catalog. The same technique can be used with call numbers; i.e., not typing them in the upper left-hand corners but simply leaving the numbers as they appear at the bottom of the LC cards.

6. Cut revision to a minimum. After a cataloger has proven he can do a professional job, the only revision should be for clerical errors. The same principle should apply to all cataloging operations. If the number of mistakes found in revising a certain activity does not justify the time spent in revision, then the revision step should be eliminated. At any rate, never revise the same work more than once.

7. Never duplicate information in card catalogs, files, or indexes. For example, an authority file that duplicates information found in the public catalog, NUC, or other working tool is redundant. Also, be careful not to duplicate information found on various serial records including card catalogs, check-in files, computer printouts, and order files.

8. To speed the searching procedure, most catalog departments follow a "no conflict" policy. That is, as long as the entry does not conflict with entries in the card catalog it should be taken as it appears on the title page. The same principle can apply to subject headings. Headings should be accepted as they appear on purchased catalog cards, unless and until a conflict is discovered at the point of filing.

9. Call numbers appearing on the bottom of the cards purchased from LC or other central processor or appearing on records in the data base of a computer-based network should also be accepted. To avoid call number conflicts with the library's local cataloging some libraries add a symbol (a lowercase "x," for example) to the Cutter number on all original cataloging. Still other libraries omit Cutter numbers altogether--a workable solution for many smaller libraries but a questionable and confusing practice for medium sized and larger institutions.

10. To make maximum use of pre-processing services many smaller libraries not only accept the processing service's subject headings, call numbers, and descriptive cataloging without editing, but disregard edition, collation, and imprint conflicts. Although again, this is perhaps an expedient approach for the small or understaffed public library, it will eventually cause confusion in larger institutions, at least if carried to extremes. Generally, the time required to revise and modify copy is short enough to make it a worthwhile practice for most libraries.

11. Catalog departments are turning more and more to support staff (paraprofessionals, clerks, and even student assistants) for much of the processing work once considered strictly professional. With the continuing emphasis on central processing services, the use of nonprofessionals is becoming both feasible and economical.

12. Finally, question each step in every department

routine. In most catalog departments there are many time-honored practices that can and should be altered or even eliminated. Does the library really need to accession books? Today, most librarians think not. Do you need temporary slips to reserve call numbers in the shelflist? Because of the time necessary to type the temporary slips and the low percentage of duplicate numbers, many catalog departments have eliminated temps altogether. Rule of thumb: Never continue a routine simply out of habit.

Chapter 4

EFFECTIVE STAFFING

Personnel is the backbone of the catalog department. The physical layout, equipment, working tools, and outside services are of no value without catalogers, clerks, and student assistants. Even if the library buys catalog cards from the Library of Congress or elsewhere, or has a totally automated catalog department, it will still need people to run the machines, catalog and classify materials for which cards are unavailable, type and input information, file cards and maintain catalogs, edit and revise work, and perform a hundred other tasks that neither outside services nor sophisticated machines can accomplish. The fact is, the more efficient the staff the more useful are the tools, services, and machines.

But if the department head wants an efficient staff he must recruit one. He must carefully select the people he thinks best qualified, orient and train them, and, finally, evaluate their performances. The selection, training, and evaluation is a continuing process, and one that takes a good deal of time. Much can be delegated and much will be the responsibility of the personnel officer and division head, but the ultimate responsibility lies with the head of the department.

Staff Recruitment

Although most of the routine paper work is a function of the library personnel office, the actual selection is, or at least should be, the job of the department head. Before recruiting, however, there are a few preliminary decisions to make. First, what are the possible recruiting sources? Some libraries concentrate on one or two sources; others tap as many as possible. If experience has shown that certain ones are more productive than others, no doubt these will be emphasized. In any case, one of the first areas to which the department head will turn for help will be the library itself. The library not only represents a good reservoir of experienced manpower, but the very fact that the administration considers promoting and transferring its own people before going outside shows an interest in their future. While the library will be the first place to which the department head will turn, in actual practice he will get most of his help, particularly for the beginning position, from outside. Even if it were possible to fill most department vacancies internally, the need to continually inject fresh blood into the department means looking elsewhere for talent. Particularly for professionals, the department head will want people with different backgrounds and varied viewpoints. For this reason, he should recruit different kinds of individuals from different sources. Here, then, are some of the possibilities.

1. Recent high school and college graduates--one of the best sources, especially for beginning clerical and cataloging positions.
2. Unemployed--another possible source for professional librarians.
3. Employed but dissatisfied--many experienced catalogers are continually on the lookout for better positions.
4. Retired--a resource overlooked by too many libraries.
5. Minority groups--an area that, more and more, libraries are successfully tapping.
6. Handicapped--because of past discrimination this source has too often been a last resort.
7. New entrants--in many communities married women entering (or returning to) the labor force have become an excellent source.
8. Overseas--many larger libraries look to foreign countries for area and language specialists.

In selecting the sources and methods of recruiting staff, the department head must consider such things as civil service regulations and union contracts, and he must read carefully the guidelines set up by the library administration. It may be, for example, that department heads are expected to give preference to present employees by filling certain vacancies through promotions. Or perhaps certain recruiting sources must be used, such as ads in specific professional journals or in local newspapers. And certainly the department head will be expected to fill all his vacancies without discrimination as to race, sex, age, or any other factor.

Recruiting Methods

Once the department head has determined the caliber of applicant required, has perused the hiring parameters established by the library, and has considered the available sources the next step is to examine possible recruiting methods. Which he should use will depend on many factors including type of library, position being filled, previous experiences in filling similar positions, money available for recruiting, and the specific qualities required in an applicant.

Employment agencies. Many catalog departments rely heavily on public and private agencies for their clerical help. Except for a few special libraries that can use specialized agencies, they are, however, of little value for recruiting professional catalogers. If an agency is used, the department head must see that it thoroughly interviews, tests, and screens each applicant. If an agency sends people who do not match position specifications, it is not doing a proper job. Also, the agency must provide each applicant with appropriate forms listing test scores, references, education, and employment history.

Advertisements. One of the most economical and most effective (thus one of the most used) recruiting methods is newspaper and journal advertising. More than likely, the library will place ads in local newspapers for clerical help and in professional library journals for catalogers. The main drawback is that newspaper advertising lacks the built-in screening process that presumably is available from an employment agency. So, to screen out as many unqualified readers as possible, ads must be written carefully. The wording should make the reader feel that the catalog department of the library is a desirable place to work, while making it clear that there is no point in applying without the specified qualifications. A problem with professional library journals is the time lag between submission of the copy and the appearance of the ad in the journal.

Library school recruiting. Many of the larger libraries send representatives to various library schools to interview prospective graduates. There are two distinct advantages in library school recruiting. First, the representative can paint an attractive, personalized picture of the library and the catalog department; secondly, he will provide advanced screening of candidates.

Nearly all library schools have placement offices that offer facilities for traveling recruiters. If the library cannot afford to support a representative, the department head or personnel officer can send the catalog department's job requirements to the library school placement office; résumés of qualified applicants are usually sent by return mail. Also, many library schools have monthly listings of job openings with which the department can post its vacancies. These listings are sent to interested graduates.

Convention recruiting. Libraries often send representatives to library conventions to interview candidates. The American Library Association as well as most regional associations provide special recruiting services at their annual and semi-annual meetings where interested recruiters and recruitees can get together. Convention recruiting is particularly convenient since presumably at least one person from the library will be going to each national and state convention. If properly coached beforehand, whoever attends can act as a part-time recruiter.

Unsolicited applicants. Every library receives occasional unsolicited letters from librarians seeking possible openings, not to mention scores of inquiries about part-time jobs from students and housewives. Few of these queries will meet department needs; but some may. The better the reputation of the library the more unsolicited letters and the more walk-ins it will receive. And if the library happens to be the only one in the area, it will find that it is standard procedure for newcomers interested in library work to apply. For future reference, either the department head or personnel office should keep a file of better-qualified unsolicited applicants.

Word-of-mouth. Word-of-mouth recruiting can be a profitable searching technique, especially for experienced catalogers. By word-of-mouth, we mean such sources as referrals by present staff members, recommendations from neighboring librarians, rumbles from the grapevine, calls from former professors, and even recommendations from friends of friends. Generally, when a present employee recommends a new cataloger or even a student assistant a certain amount of screening does take place. Often, too, when considering a recommendation the department head can get some idea of the candidate by looking at the sponsor. Word-of-mouth recruiting can, however, lead to cronyism and nepotism.

Recruiting methods will differ from library to library, department to department, and job to job. If the clerks are unionized the department head may want to turn to the union for help; if the position is under civil service the opening can be posted with the civil service; and if the department needs a month or two of typing help for a special reclassification project the library can lease personnel from a "temporary help service." Other possibilities include: an internship program through a local library school, spot announcements on the radio, a booth at the local high school career day, a "help wanted" sign on the reference desk. The method selected will depend a good deal on whether the department is seeking a professional, paraprofessional, or nonprofessional. For clerks the library will concentrate on the local labor market; for catalogers it should cover the country. What is important is to use the method appropriate to the position and the caliber of person the department wants to attract. Beyond this, at least some preliminary screening should be provided. Nothing is more frustrating than for the department head to have to read through stacks of résumés and interview dozens of persons who are neither interested in nor qualified for the job.

Periodically, therefore, the recruitment program should be evaluated in terms of its success in obtaining competent personnel. If the department is not getting the applicants expected, alternatives should be considered. Maybe the library is not using the most effective methods. Perhaps the administration is reluctant to spend money on recruiting. Are the advertisements being placed in the right journals? Do the ads say what they are supposed to say? Is the personnel agency sending qualified people? Are certain library schools giving better service than others?

Selection Process

The process of selecting qualified personnel for a cata-

log department is, in many ways, a process of elimination.
Each stage passed is another step in the elimination of certain applicants and the retention of others. The initial screening, the résumé review, the reference check, and the interview are steps through which all applicants--catalogers, support staff, and student assistants--must progress if they hope
to reach the final selection decision. Although the steps need
not be followed as presented here, each is important if the
department head expects to find competent, qualified people.

Step 1: Job analysis. In analyzing a particular job,
the department head must determine what qualifications he is
seeking in his applicants. For a general cataloging position
an applicant should have the MLS degree plus a general subject background. In addition, catalogers who are expected to
work in specific subject or language areas must have formal
training in these areas, preferably graduate degrees. If,
for example, the position is that of a music cataloger, applicants should have appropriate music training. Despite the
obvious need for specialists, however, the first concern
should be for professionals with broad library and educational backgrounds. Catalogers must have the subject and language competencies required to catalog and classify the materials assigned them, and certainly they should have demonstrated, either in library school or on the job, an understanding of bibliographic organization, but the truly successful
cataloger will be a professional librarian first, a cataloger
second.

The department head should seek librarians with prior
relevant cataloging experience, of course. Failing this, he
should insist on sound library school training in cataloging
and classification. On the other hand, an applicant should
not be expected to be thoroughly conversant with the specific
variations to AACR applied in the department. Anyone with
a good general background and an overall understanding of
the principles of bibliographic organization and control will
be able to adapt to local procedures.

An important prerequisite is that the applicant have a
sincere interest in bibliographic organization. This interest,
difficult but not impossible to determine, is best identified
through reference checks with former professors and supervisors. The department head must be careful, though.
Someone who has demonstrated an interest in the theory of

cataloging may not care at all for day-to-day practice. In the last few years, it has been particularly difficult to equate classroom performance with on-the-job success, primarily because the trend in graduate library schools has been away from the actual cataloging and classification of materials and toward the study of the theory and administration of bibliographic organization. The department head must make sure that the applicant wants to catalog books and not just theorize.

This is not to say that librarians with little or no administrative potential are to be accepted. Both the ability to work as part of a team and leadership potential are essential for just about every professional cataloging position. With the increased need for nonprofessionals, catalogers are being called upon to train, revise, and supervise clerks and paraprofessionals in various processing activities. The catalog department is no longer a haven for the extreme introvert, if indeed it ever was.

Besides the subject and language background necessary to catalog and classify books assigned to him, the cataloger must have an understanding of nonbook materials. He must be willing and able to adapt what he has learned in library school to the organization of specialized and unique materials. In addition, no matter what position the graduate (or the experienced cataloger) fills in the department, he must be familiar with--and be willing to master--a great variety of both traditional and innovative tools. Automation will sooner or later, directly or indirectly, touch every catalog department. The cataloger must be willing to adapt to microfiche printouts and computer terminals in the same way as he is expected to use NUC and the electric typewriter.

Certainly the applicant must have the time-honored appreciation for accuracy, and a feeling for details, but he should not be so obsessed with minutiae that he will overlook the broad bibliographic picture. When necessary he must be willing to take calculated risks and do what is expedient to get materials moving through the department. He must have a respect for tradition and the "Rules," yet be willing to adapt to the changing needs of materials, and, most important, be capable of relating what he has learned in library school or in his last position to the local setting. He must, in other words, think and react as a professional, not as an undergraduate.

Many of the same qualifications sought in the professional cataloger will be applicable for most support staff positions. The clerk must, for example, be both a team worker and a potential leader; be attentive to detail yet have the ability to see the total picture; possess specialized typing, filing, and other skills, but also have a broad educational background; know and use the traditional clerical tools, and, just as important, be willing to master new ones. There are, of course, certain qualifications essential for the professional that are not generally required in the nonprofessional. For one thing, the department head, although seeking career-minded people, is not looking for "a professional." Little if any emphasis need be placed on such considerations as graduate degrees, certification, outside professional activities, or research and creative potential. Also, since certain basic skills (typing speed, for example) are essential for just about every clerical position, test scores become a much more important consideration. Generally the employment agency, or perhaps the library itself, will provide clerical aptitude and performance tests. Such tests, including those designed for general business positions, can fairly accurately predict library job success. Skills such as typing, filing, and record keeping acquired in general business courses are applicable to most library work. The department head must, therefore, know the type of tests given to applicants and be able to relate raw scores to ability. He must know which test scores are relevant to his job needs and which are not, and be able to identify above and below average scores.

For paraprofessional positions the department head will of course set paraprofessional qualifications. Undoubtedly the paraprofessional will have at least some supervisory responsibilities, and should therefore possess leadership qualities similar to those required of any supervisor. Recently, most libraries have insisted that their paraprofessionals have both classroom and practical library exposure. This means, in most cases, at least two years of college (or even an undergraduate degree) with ten to fifteen hours of library science, plus related library experience. There will also be quite specific qualifications for machine operators and other technical positions.

Clearly the skill requirements will differ from position to position, yet the same general qualifications will apply to all potential staff members, whether student assistant, card typist, marking supervisor, or serials cataloger. What is sought in all applicants is not just someone who will adequately perform the technical duties listed on the job description (although these must be clearly outlined and understood by both the department head and the applicant) but a team member who is sympathetic with the goals and objectives of the library and who will contribute to making the department a smooth and efficiently run organization.

Step 2: Preliminary screening. Since qualifications of the position have already been established in the job analysis, the department head has, in a very real sense, screened out certain candidates. Beyond this, some preliminary screening must be done by the employment agency, the library secretary, or the personnel manager. The purpose of this preliminary screening is to insure that the department head spends time only on well-qualified applicants. Whatever the job, professional or clerical, there will be certain minimum qualifications (MLS degree, two years experience, 60 wpm, and so on) that the library secretary, library school placement officer, or someone else can use as the basis for a decision on whether to offer the application blank or politely say, "Sorry, not qualified." To eliminate possible misunderstandings, the minimum standards should be made as clear and precise as possible, and in writing if necessary.

Step 3: Application form and résumé. The application and biographical data forms are traditional requirements of all persons applying for library positions. A typical form, usually furnished by the library personnel officer, will provide such information as education, background, work experience, references, and relevant personal data. Because of the different job requirements, the department head should insist on separate forms for professional and support staff positions. The completed forms should be read carefully before meeting the applicants. Actually, many department heads consider the application a sort of test. By weighting and scoring various questions statistically according to predetermined values (ten to twenty points for relevant experience, five to ten points for high grades, and so on), a potential supervisor can get a fairly accurate rating on each of the applicants. But no matter how an application is analyzed, there is a lot to be gleaned from it.

Besides the basic information regarding background

and education, the department head should be able to tell the applicant's ability to organize his thoughts and present facts clearly and precisely, an important consideration for any cataloging position. He should also look closely at the education and work record to see if the applicant has consistently progressed to better jobs, and see how education relates to work experience. These and other factors such as prior income and professional affiliations may help predict future success. Careful reading of the application will also provide a departure point in the interview; and the references listed on the application point out areas for further inquiry.

Step 4: Reference check. Most references listed by an applicant will fall into one of three categories: character references, school references, or work references. Exactly how much checking of the applicant's references is necessary will depend on possible doubts about him and the position for which he is applying. Usually, the higher the position the more necessary is a reference check.

For most applicants a check of character is of little value since the applicant usually supplies his own character references. Any inquiries will result in favorable comments. And school references are only important in recruiting people directly out of library school. The most valid references, particularly for catalogers, are those from former employers. Whatever the reference being checked, an important rule-of-thumb is: be as close to the referee as possible. This means that in questioning a former employer, a face-to-face conversation is best; next, a telephone call; and least reliable is a letter. Referees will nearly always speak more freely and candidly than they will write.

Also, when checking a reference it is important to speak directly to the applicant's former supervisor (the department head, chief typist, or cataloging revisor) rather than calling the personnel department or library director, neither of whom is likely to be able to give the kind of information needed. Likewise, the department head should do the telephoning himself and not relegate it to the personnel department, particularly when considering a cataloger or other higher-level position.

The specific queries will depend on any doubts that may have risen from the review of the application and, of course, on the circumstances that attracted the candidate in the first place. Typical questions would be: Why did he leave your employ? Would you re-employ him? Was he cooperative? Did he get along with others? The department head should concentrate on those questions for which answers are obtainable from no other source.

Step 5: The interview. The interview is the most widely used and, in most cases, the most important of the selection tools. The interview, although by no means a foolproof method of assuring top-quality people, can, if used properly, serve a number of purposes. For one thing, it provides an opportunity to learn as much as possible about the candidate. Not only will the department head reinforce what he has already gleaned from the application and reference check, but he should learn things unavailable from any other source. It is, therefore, as much a search for negative as for positive evidence.

Also through the interview, the applicant has an opportunity to learn something about the library, the department, and the position he is considering. It is a selling job on the interviewer's part and a learning situation on the applicant's. Whether the candidate becomes a member of the catalog department or not, the department head is, in a manner of speaking, doing public relations work. Perhaps most important, the interview, no matter what else it accomplishes, interjects much needed personal warmth into what can otherwise be a sterile process.

Most employment interviews fall into one of three categories: the patterned interview, the stress interview, and the nondirective interview. Exactly how the department head defines his own technique will depend on how the interview is structured and the way in which he communicates with the applicant. The same basic principles apply whether conducting the interview alone or as a member of a selection committee.

By far the most often used technique is the patterned or standard interview. As the name implies, the patterned interview is relatively structured. In its extreme form the interviewer follows a detailed checklist of prepared questions with little or no deviation. After the session, the interviewer carefully analyzes the answers and rates the applicant in terms of his responses. In the less extreme and more popular form the interviewer, while covering selected aspects of the applicant's background, does deviate when necessary and often follows through on specific points of information. The interviewer thus follows a predetermined plan, but not slavishly.

While the patterned interview, no matter how loosely structured, relies on covering specific topics and asking certain questions, the nondirective interview is completely unplanned. The department head may introduce a topic to get the session moving, but during the rest of the period the candidate is allowed to talk on any subject and say anything he wishes. The interviewer remains silent, offering neither advice nor comments. At most, he simply repeats some of the candidate's phrases to encourage him to continue his monolog. Theoretically, a trained nondirective interviewer can induce a person to reveal more of himself than is possible through any other technique, but the nondirective interview is not as simple as it appears. First developed by the psychologist Carl Rogers as a counseling technique, it requires a good deal of skill on the part of the interviewer if he is to achieve sound interview objectives. It is also very time-consuming.

In the stress interview the interviewer deliberately tries to antagonize, embarrass, or frustrate the candidate. The object is to force him to lose control of his emotions and thus test his reactions under stress. The opposite of the nondirective interview where the interviewer plays a passive role, in the stress interview the "interrogator" continually criticizes and interrupts the applicant. Again, as in the nondirective technique, the interviewer must be well trained. Neither the nondirective nor the stress techniques are recommended for most library situations, yet elements of both methods can be incorporated into the more traditional patterned interview.

Assuming that the department head is planning to develop a more or less patterned interview, his first step would be to prepare for the candidate. The interviewer should study the application blank, biographical summary, college transcripts, test scores, and the information gained from the reference checks. Then he should jot down any questions that stand out from the review--not that he should read from a prepared script, only that he may need a few notes to jog his memory.

The interview should be held in private, comfortable surroundings--and sufficient time allotted. This may be anywhere from five minutes for a student assistant to a day or two for a prospective cataloger. The department head should determine if there is anyone else in the department the candidate should meet. If there is a selection committee involved they certainly must be included.

The interview should begin with questions that deal with the applicant's work history and education, questions which he expects to be asked. If there is enough time, the applicant should be invited simply to tell his life story. At any rate, the opening conversation should deal with items free of emotional overtones. The department head should try to create a friendly, relaxed, informal atmosphere conducive to the free flow of information, and to encourage the applicant to talk freely. Questions that can be answered with a simple "yes" or "no" will reveal little. The interviewer should avoid leading questions that give him a ready-made answer. If the applicant is asked, "Did you get along well with your former department head?" he will not only be put on the defensive but need only answer with a simple "yes," saying nothing about the circumstances.

In order to get the applicant to do most of the talking the interviewer must be a good, attentive listener. He should not criticize or show disapproval. Displaying negative feelings about anything the applicant says will discourage him from talking freely. The interview situation in which one person automatically assumes the dominant role is not conducive to friendly give and take. Unless the interviewer is deliberately conducting a stress interview, he should not aggravate the confrontation by constantly criticizing.

Nor should he be afraid to ask subjective questions. He is interviewing the whole person, not just one segment. Although the department head has no right to interfere with a cataloger's personal life, he still has an obligation to know how such things as health and domestic situation may affect the applicant's professional career. If questions are asked naturally and directly in a matter-of-fact tone, and not at all in a discriminating way, the applicant will respond in kind.

While the candidate is supposed to talk freely, the department head will be expected to do some talking, too. Cer-

tainly he will want to explain carefully the duties, responsibilities, and future of the position offered. And he should
be candid in his explanations, emphasizing both desirable and
undesirable features. Tasks such as filing, typing catalog
cards, and marking books are boring to many people. If
certain aspects of the work are unattractive to the applicant
he should politely withdraw from consideration.

The applicant should be taken on a tour of the department and introduced to various staff members. If the position is a professional one, other librarians should talk with
him. Later, the interviewer will want to contact staff members to get their impressions of the candidate. Incidentally,
the department tour provides a good opportunity to feed in
questions about the applicant's previous jobs.

To avoid confusion and embarrassment, the interviewer
should give some overt sign when he wants to close. He
should let the candidate know when a decision will be made,
and how and when he will be notified. Then, after the candidate has left, the department head should immediately record
his impressions on paper. If several people are being inter-
viewed for a job, much of what was said will be forgotten if
each person is not evaluated while the details are fresh in
mind.

As a quick review of the preparation, handling, and
evaluation of the interview, here are a dozen do's and don'ts
to remember:

1. Do prepare for the interview. The department
    head should show the applicant that he cares enough
    about the interview to plan ahead.
2. Don't take copious notes during the interview.
    Nothing is so annoying as having someone take
    down everything you say as you are talking.
3. Do keep control of the interview. The philosophy
    of the patterned interview is that the interviewer
    structures, conducts, and controls the session to
    gain specific objectives.
4. Don't bother to interview obviously overqualified
    people. If someone is hired whose education and
    background far surpass the job requirements, he
    will become bored and soon quit.
5. Do ask open-ended questions. The applicant should

be encouraged to answer questions in-depth and in
detail.

6. Don't misrepresent or exaggerate working conditions
in the department. Just as the department head
wants honesty from the applicant, the applicant expects honesty from him.
7. Do keep the interview natural and informal. One
way to do this is to get out from behind the desk.
8. Don't be inflexible. Although the department head
may be using a patterned interview, he should go
into it willing to pursue certain topics and skip
others, depending on immediate needs.
9. Do ask the same key questions of all applicants.
Flexibility is important for an informal atmosphere,
but if certain job-related questions are asked of
one applicant but not of others, the department
head could be guilty of discrimination.
10. Don't become personal. It is important to create
a friendly atmosphere, but the department head
must be careful never to cross the line that divides the applicant's personal and professional life.
11. Do make sure the applicant meets everyone with
whom he will be working. This is important both
for the candidate and for the staff.
12. Don't play the "big shot." The interview is not
the place to try to impress the applicant with the
department head's cataloging expertise.

Step 6: Selection decision. After all the information
about each applicant has been gathered, rechecked, evaluated,
and digested, and after each candidate has been discussed
with others in the library, the department head makes his
decision. Ideally, all decisions on the selection of catalog
department personnel are the department head's. The personnel department should screen applicants, supply information, administer tests, and do the paper work. Others in
the library can help with the interviewing and give advice,
and the final decision must be discussed with the division
head and the library director, as well as with those with whom
the newcomer will work. Most importantly, the final decision
must be based on recommendations from the candidate's immediate supervisor, whether the chief typist or head of the marking section. But while the responsibility for the decision may
be the library director's, and the immediate supervisor may
be allotted the major portion of the input, the final decision
is the department head's.

What, then are some of the points that should have been noticed in the interview, phone check, and application review? If the candidate is a recent library school graduate, his transcripts will have been studied for language and cataloging courses. If he has had previous cataloging experience his work record will have been investigated. His reasons for leaving his last position have been checked. If he is being offered less than what he was making before, the department head will want to know why he wants the job. Does he really want to be a cataloger, or does he want the job only until something opens up in the reference department? How well did he get along with his co-workers and with his former department head? In the final analysis, the decision may be obvious or it may be difficult, but if the above steps have been followed and the decision has been given careful consideration, the odds are it will be the right one.

Departmental Assignments

After the staff has been selected the department head will need to make necessary assignments, perhaps even some re-assignments. As new members are added the department head, in consultation with others in and outside the department, may have to make certain adjustments and changes in the structure and organization of the department. If the department is a large one he will probably want to divide the professionals into senior and junior catalogers. In a public library whose catalogers are on a civil service scale or in an academic library whose professionals have faculty status, this division will be a natural byproduct of the overall institutional system. The senior members, called revisors in many libraries, should be responsible for training new catalogers and, most especially, for revising their work. In addition, they should share some of the department head's administrative responsibilities. He may even want to form an advisory council made up of senior catalogers.

The department will also need one and probably more paraprofessionals, called in many libraries subprofessionals, library technical assistants, or library technicians. They should be experienced, on-the-job trained clerks with at least two years of college, including some library science courses. Their primary responsibility will be to supervise the various clerical functions. As libraries transfer duties from the professional sphere, paraprofessionals are becoming more and more important to department operations.

It is the clerks, along with the other support staff, who will form the backbone of the department, and will represent the larger portion of the work force. Although in past years most departments have considered a ratio of two nonprofessionals to every professional about right, today a four-to-one ratio is considered more realistic. With the growing emphasis on centralized cataloging and with more and more libraries joining computer-based networks, a six- or eight-to-one ratio will soon be standard. The clerks will type and file cards, label and mark books, catalog books with LC copy, input and search on terminals, and perform all the other operations basic to an efficiently run department. The department will no doubt also have several student assistants, particularly if the library is on a college campus or is part of a school system. Students will assist clerks in such tasks as filing cards, retrieving materials from the stacks, and marking books.

The size of the staff will, of course, depend on the amount of cataloging and related activities the department is expected to perform. Obviously, there should be sufficient staff to do the job.

Professional versus nonprofessional. An important consideration in staffing a catalog department is, therefore, the library's definition of professional and nonprofessional functions. The trend has been, and will continue to be, toward nonprofessionals assuming more and more cataloging responsibilities, particularly in those areas requiring a minimum of bibliographic interpretation and judgment-making. Below are a few examples.

1. Searching. Much of the department's pre-catalog searching can be assigned to nonprofessionals. Actually, if the technical services division is properly organized, a good deal of searching will have been performed before the materials reach the catalog department. But no matter where the responsibility is placed, establishing the authority of authors, titles, and perhaps even subject headings should be done by nonprofessionals. Clerks can easily match work slips against established bibliographies, authority files, standard subject heading lists, NUC and LC copy, network data base, and the library's own card catalog.

2. <u>Reclassification</u>. If the library is reclassifying from
Dewey to LC, all but the supervisory work should be assigned
to nonprofessionals. A properly trained paraprofessional is
quite capable of changing numbers on books and cards, ordering or replacing catalog cards, and even assigning call numbers by checking the library's titles against LC copy. A
cataloger must, of course, classify those books where neither
the titles themselves nor other editions are available in LC.

3. <u>Assigning Cutter numbers</u>. If the department is a
large one where specialization is considered the most economical way to divide cataloging duties, support staff can be
assigned the shelf-listing. Shelf-listing consists of simply
checking a book against the shelflist and fitting the author
number into its logical place in the number sequence.

4. <u>Processing added copies and new editions</u>. The entire operation of adding copies, volumes, and even new editions should be delegated to nonprofessionals. If the department is large enough, a separate section should be established.

5. <u>Original cataloging</u>. In at least a few libraries nonprofessionals are being assigned certain original cataloging
operations. To be sure, these nonprofessionals must be experienced, and the cataloging limited to specific categories.
Nonprofessional cataloging of fiction books has proven especially successful. All that is required is the transcription of
the title page and the relatively automatic assigning of a call
number checked against the shelflist. Usually no subject
headings are required for novels. In some libraries clerks
do the descriptive cataloging for all books, regardless of subject, with professionals responsible for assigning subject
headings and classification numbers.

6. <u>Descriptive cataloging of special materials</u>. If the
department head is fortunate he may find a nonprofessional
with specialized knowledge that can be put to good use.
Many academic and special libraries, for instance, have clerks
and even student assistants with foreign language abilities
who can transcribe title pages and even assign subject headings to books in non-romance languages.

7. <u>Computer inputting</u>. Inputting cataloging copy from
formatted workforms should be performed by the clerical staff

under the supervision of a paraprofessional. Besides supervision, revision, and training of terminal operators, well-trained paraprofessionals can also be responsible for bibliographic searching on terminals, formatting of workforms, checking on-line authority files, and even for the more complex decision-making responsibilities such as determining whether or not to accept the records of contributing libraries, modifying records to fit local standards, and completion of cataloging copy.

8. _Filing_. Filing of catalog cards, including the training and revision responsibilities, is clearly a nonprofessional function. If a department head has a core of well-trained clericals and a competent paraprofessional supervising, it is not impossible to divorce the entire filing operation from professional responsibility.

9. _Maintenance of authority files_. The maintenance of subject and name authority files should be assigned to support staff. And certainly the maintenance of subject headings and cross-references in the public catalog is clerical in nature. Generally, though, the overall supervision should be professional.

10. _Revision_. Although revision is usually considered a professional responsibility, if it is limited to checking for typing errors and minor discrepancies in call numbers, it should be delegated to nonprofessionals. Whenever clerks revise professional work, however, they should not make corrections themselves. Rather, they should refer their findings back to a cataloger for changes. In this way the cataloger is kept aware of his mistakes and the clerk is assured that an error is indeed an error.

11. _Cataloging from LC copy_. In most catalog departments the entire cataloging operation using computer printouts, catalog cards, CIP data, NUC, and other records based on LC copy has become a nonprofessional operation. Properly trained paraprofessionals can even make minor changes where the library's edition does not match LC copy.

12. _Supervision_. Support staff can also assume many of the supervisory and training responsibilities. Besides the filing operations mentioned above, the typing, bindery, and marking units can be successfully supervised by nonprofessionals.

The main reason for relieving professionals of clerical duties is, of course, an economic one. If a clerk is assigned duties formerly performed by a professional, the cataloger is not only released to do more professional work, but the library saves money. Even though the shortage of competent professional librarians is not as acute as it once was, libraries are not averse to processing their materials as economically as possible.

As more and more libraries join bibliographic networks there will be a continuing decrease in the need for in-house professionals to do original cataloging. This is especially true for those institutions willing to accept member-library cataloging with a minimum of revision and adaptions. There will always be a need for professional catalogers in supervisory positions, and catalogers must catalog those materials not handled by networks and processing centers. The future will also find catalogers more engaged in research and in preparing bibliographies and indexes for materials not appearing in the public catalog.

In addition to the obvious advantages in delegating more responsibilities to support staff there are also problems. Nonprofessionals are not motivated in the same was as professionals, they lack the broad bibliographic background of professionals, and they are not as flexible as professionally trained persons. The library must, therefore, provide extensive on-the-job training. Also, in most libraries the turnover among clerks is much greater than among professionals. Nor is it always easy to recruit nonprofessionals with the necessary bibliographic and language backgrounds, or with the supervisory and decision-making abilities needed for most paraprofessional positions. Fortunately, this situation is changing. Junior colleges and even a few universities are now offering library technician courses. Libraries, too, are establishing extensive apprenticeship and in-service programs designed specifically for support staff. And, as salary scales are adjusted to accommodate the paraprofessional, the quality of staff will surely improve, and the turnover rate decrease.

Specialization. Directly related to the continuing need to define and identify professional and nonprofessional functions is the growing emphasis on staff specialization. In the past specialization has been primarily a professional consideration, but the introduction of new manual and automated techniques is making it a nonprofessional concern as well.

Libraries will soon have to look outside the library profession for professional help and many are already doing so. Systems analysts, programmers, and machine operators are, today, a necessity in many libraries. These needs will continue, and others will emerge. For some specialist positions the catalog department may require a thorough knowledge of librarianship, for others a specialty competence will suffice. For some positions special in-service training programs will be necessary; for others the library can rely on library and technical schools for qualified personnel. But however or wherever specialists are acquired, the department must consider carefully each applicant's bibliographic and specialized knowledge, and then use it effectively.

The dual assignment. Another organizational concept that could someday affect the way catalog departments are organized is the dual assignment. In the dual assignment, an example of the division by staff specialty, librarians are assigned both to the catalog department and to one of the public service units. In the past, most such assignments have been given to reference librarians, departmental librarians, and bibliographers willing to spend some time, usually half a day, in the catalog department processing books in their subject or language fields. Usually they were either recent library school graduates who wished to broaden their professional exposure or senior librarians with a subject or language specialty valuable both to public services and the catalog department.

The most frequent argument in favor of the dual assignment has been that the dual assignee, through a close acquaintance with both public services and technical processing, becomes a better all-'round librarian. His cataloging experience, for example, helps him to use the card catalog more effectively and thus better equips him to assist patrons. Through his cataloging duties he becomes acquainted with materials in his field as they pass over his desk, and, again, is better equipped to aid others in interpreting the collection. Theoretically at least, his subject or language specialty also helps in processing materials; being closely attuned to patron needs, he can judge which books he should give priority and which should be analyzed or otherwise given special consideration. He better understands how and by whom the materials will be used, and can adjust his cataloging activities accordingly.

As with every organizational concept, there are both advantages and disadvantages to the dual assignment. It is questionable, for example, whether it is worthwhile to spend the time and money necessary to train a librarian to do two distinct jobs. Can, in fact, a professional librarian do two half-time jobs as effectively as one full-time job? Cataloging, in particular, involves many detailed and complex procedures. It is difficult for most department heads to maintain uniformly high standards with full-time professionals, let alone with part-time help. And how many librarians have the desire, experience, and personality to do both public service and cataloging work? Also, while it is assumed that a librarian will acquire a broader professional knowledge through a dual assignment, his divided (some would say conflicting) loyalties could cause problems.

Thus, so far at least, most dual assignments have been initiated out of necessity, not because the idea was considered basically sound. It has simply been the only way out of an awkward situation. Slowly, however, a few libraries are beginning to consider this a fundamentally sound approach. In the opinion of many administrators it would eliminate much duplication. Could not bibliographers who must search, verify, and analyze materials during the selection procedures, and whose expertise is similar to that of catalogers, also do the cataloging and classification? Bibliographers using LC copy in their selection process could quite easily adapt it for local cataloging purposes or simply pass the information along to their clerical staff for complete cataloging and classification. Again, however, how well the dual assignment concept will work in a particular library will depend on the quality of the staff and on local circumstances.

Chapter 5

ORIENTATION, TRAINING,
AND EVALUATION

Although every new staff member should receive a formal orientation before arriving in the catalog department, it is also
important that a more personal welcome be provided at the
department level. Too often, the initial introduction to the
library is cool, formal, and unnecessarily structured. In contrast, the department orientation should be relaxed, informal,
and personalized. Exactly how detailed a presentation is provided will depend on the new employee's background and on
the position. A transfer from the acquisition department will
not receive the same introduction as someone from out-of-
town; and the professional cataloger will get a somewhat different orientation than a typist. The orientation should come,
however, either from the head of the department, the newcomer's immediate supervisor, or a senior member of the department. A beginning typist, for example, can be turned
over to the chief typist, and a new cataloger to an experienced professional. Whoever conducts the orientation should
understand its purpose and accept the responsibility for making the newcomer feel at home. Orientation should not be
done haphazardly.

The first step for the department head or other person
assigned to welcome the newcomer is to prepare himself. This
means a review of the résumé, application, and any other information that would help relate the newcomer's background
to the new job. In addition, someone should see that the
staff member's desk has the proper supplies and the necessary reference tools. When the newcomer arrives he should
be given a warm, friendly welcome. Throughout the orientation it is important that the department head's manner be relaxed and poised. The employee's first impression will re-

main with him for a long time, and for this reason it should
be positive and friendly.

The department head might begin with a brief discussion of the cataloging functions and an explanation of the department in relation to other units in the library. The new
employee's position in the department should be reviewed,
and he should understand to whom he reports and is directly
responsible. Also important is a review of the policy manual
furnished by the personnel office, including working hours,
lunch periods, coffee breaks, pay periods, merit ratings, and
so on. If there are any rules or regulations that the department head wants stressed, such as punctuality or promotion
policies, this is the time to present them. For catalogers,
professional aspects of the position should be emphasized.
Any professional activities that the cataloger personally or
the catalog department in general might be expected to engage
in should be mentioned.

In the initial discussion the department head should go
over the newcomer's background and interests. Perhaps the
library can help him get settled in the community. Possibly
he will need information about housing, transportation,
churches, or public schools. Next, the new employee should
be taken on a tour. If the library has a formal orientation
given by the personnel officer which includes a detailed library tour, the department tour can be limited to the immediate work area with a quick review of washrooms, lockers,
employee's entrance, elevators, smoking areas, lunch room,
and other facilities he will be using the first day or two.
The department tour should be systematic, starting at the
point where the materials enter the department and carrying
through to where they leave, with a careful explanation of
the flow-patterns.

The newcomer should be shown his desk and work area,
of course, and be introduced to fellow workers who sit near
him and do the same work, even if he has met them before.
It is important that he be given a brief explanation of the
duties of everyone to whom he is introduced. He will not
only get a better picture of what the department is all about,
but will realize that the administration has a sincere respect
for the skills and knowledge of all staff members. This is
also a good time to emphasize such things as length of service
and promotion policy, facts that will both reassure the new-

comer and pat the veteran on the back. If the new employee is a professional it is important to point out the reference room and card catalog plus any other tools with which he will be working. These will be thoroughly explained during the in-service training period, but it is still a good idea to emphasize their locations in relation to his work area.

Points to remember in the orientation include the following:

1. Be friendly. If the department head is dejected and sullen or tries to put the newcomer in his place, he may not return the next day.

2. Organize the presentation. If necessary, write out a checklist. If the presentation is disorganized it will be evident in the orientation and will probably show up later in the newcomer's work.

3. Explain all possible assignments. The orientation is the ideal time to let the cataloger know that although he is assigned to catalog serials, he is also expected to process other materials when necessary.

4. Listen as well as talk. Most people like to talk more than they listen. If the orientation is successful, the department head will learn as much about the new staff member as the newcomer will about the department.

5. Emphasize the positive. When walking through the library the department head should not stress backlogs or the volume of work. It is easy for a new cataloger to imagine himself buried under an avalanche of books.

6. Do not oversell. When describing the filing and typing routines to a new clerk the department head should be honest. If part of the job is boring, it will become evident later anyway.

7. The orientation is for the benefit of the staff, too. The department head not only hopes to educate and impress the newcomer with the cataloging operation, but he should try to give the staff a favorable impression of their new colleague.

8. Do not expect the newcomer to remember every-thing he is told the first day. The department head should plan to go over important points more than once. He should not become impatient if he has to repeat himself.

9. Encourage questions. All important points will not be adequately covered unless the department head re-ceives feedback.

10. Vary the presentation with each new employee. The orientation should be tailored specifically to the position and the individual.

If more than one employee is scheduled to start work on a particular day, the department head can conduct a group orientation. If the group includes both professionals and non-professionals, however, it may be necessary either to stagger portions or to delegate part of the orientation to another mem-ber of the department. There will be aspects that apply to professionals but not to clericals, and vice versa.

After the initial session the department head must not lose contact. He should drop by the newcomer's desk at least once a day for a few days to find out how things are going. Then, in about a week or two, he can have a brief, casual talk to review the progress to date and check for pos-sible problem areas. The department head should discuss any difficulties the newcomer is having adjusting to the rou-tines, ask if there is any information he still needs, try to discover his attitude toward the department, and encourage suggestions to improve the work. Finally, if the library has a formal probationary period (and it certainly should), the department head will call in the new employee at the comple-tion of this period to congratulate and welcome him as a permanent member of the department.

In-Service Training

The specific training programs established by the de-partment head will vary from job to job. It should be stressed, though, that the department head does not have a choice of whether or not to train the new cataloger--his only choice is _how_ to train him. If formal training is not provided, the newcomer will train himself, by trial and error or with the help of a co-worker. It is important, therefore, to make sure that training is formalized, not haphazard. No matter how much time and effort are involved in training new staff, it will be time and effort well spent, especially considering what will be gained by eliminating the acquisition of poor work habits which the newcomer may otherwise continue throughout his employment.

To train a person on a new job the supervisor (department head, chief typist, catalog revisor) must know the job himself, and know it well enough to subdivide it into logical parts and to teach each activity without losing sight of the whole. Before beginning the training, then, the supervisor should go over in his mind, step by step, the entire procedure, and determine exactly how each routine is to be presented. Will the trainee be taken out to the card catalog at this point? Will the supervisor type an example? Will he review the entire marking process?

Generally, the first step is to explain the sequence of the entire operation. Then, with the department manual in hand, the supervisor goes through the procedure, explaining each step and pointing out key points in the manual. If the manual has been written properly (manual writing is described in Chapter 11), the trainee should be able step by step to follow the entire sequence. After the routine has been explained, the trainee should read through the manual by himself; then, after digesting the material, go through the operation, actually searching the data base, cataloging the book, or assigning the call number, under the watchful eye of the supervisor, of course.

The first few days, the department head should insist that the trainee stick strictly to the procedure as outlined in the manual, so that nothing is omitted. After the newcomer has all the steps clearly in mind and realizes how each relates to the entire operation, he should be allowed to adjust the sequence to fit his own style, particularly if he is a professional. In fact, if either a cataloger or clerk deviates from a routine and can demonstrate that the deviation is indeed an improvement over the original procedure, it should be incorporated into the manual. The best procedure for one person, however, may not suit another. Some catalogers, for example, can batch twenty or more titles when checking against the card catalog or NUC, others can handle only five or ten successfully.

The newcomer's work should be closely checked during the first few weeks, and periodically checked for several weeks thereafter. The cataloger should be under a revisor, either the department head or a senior cataloger, who will review all the newcomer's work for at least two or three months. Even an experienced cataloger will need close revision until he can adapt to department routines. Just as important, every new employee should have one person to whom he can turn for help. At least for the first few weeks, the new cataloger should save all his questions for his revisor. If he is free to ask questions of anyone in the department, it is inevitable that he will receive conflicting answers. Also, the closer contact the revisor has with the cataloger the better he will understand the newcomer's strengths and weaknesses, and thus the better equipped he will be to gear the training program to specific needs. The traditional revising method is for the cataloger to send his completed copy, along with the book, to his revisor, who blue-pencils corrections. The revisor returns the copy and book to the cataloger with, if necessary, verbal or written comments. The cataloger then makes necessary changes and sends the copy on for processing. In noting corrections, it is important that the revisor accompany all corrections and comments with specific references to AACR, the department manual, or other working tool. The cataloger can then compare the problems at hand with the official rule or routine.

The same basic principles that apply to any learning situation are applicable to catalog department training programs. Below are listed the most important.

1. Make the training period a friendly, relaxed experience. If the supervisor begins to feel frustrated or senses that tensions are building, he should stop and switch to an alternative approach. In outlining the training schedule, it is a good idea to determine the concentration time of each operation, and proceed accordingly.

2. Establish goals in the training program. Each day the trainee should be told he will learn specific operations: classify books, type headings, or search the card catalog. The supervisor thus provides a challenge as well as a method of judging progress. At the end of each session, both the trainer and trainee can look back with satisfaction on their accomplishments.

3.   Compliment and encourage at each key step.   In order to be able to compliment the newcomer on his progress, progress must be insured.   If more is attempted than can be grasped at one time, the newcomer will become discouraged.

4.   Always provide opportunities to practice each routine immediately after it is explained.   No one can learn how to type a catalog card or input a record on a terminal by simply reading about it in a manual.   Practice is essential.

5.   Each routine should be presented in various ways. The new cataloger should read the routine in the manual, have it explained to him, explain it to the revisor, and finally perform it.

6.   Present all routines in their logical sequence.   The new typist must see the relationships of each step of the operation.   Just as important, what has already been learned must be related with what is presently being learned.

7.   Proceed from the whole to the parts.   In every procedure the entire operation should be explained first, then broken into learnable segments.   One part must be learned at a time, going on to the next step only after the first is digested, always keeping in mind the place of the part within the entire operation.

8.   Start with the known before attempting the unknown. The trainee will learn most easily by beginning with something already known, then moving on to the unfamiliar.   With a recent library school graduate, for example, the revisor should begin with what has been learned in library school, then build on that until specific routines have been mastered.

9.   Likewise, start with the elementary before attempting the complex.   Catalog typing routines can be complicated. Therefore the chief typist must begin the in-service training as simply as possible.

10.   Encourage questions.   If the newcomer is not asking questions, he should be asked questions to make sure that he understands thoroughly.

11.   Emphasize the key points.   This is done through verbal repetition and through using marginal notes and underlining in the manual.

12. Be positive in the training. Encourage rather than discourage; praise rather than reprimand; reward rather than punish; exclaim rather than complain. Be enthusiastic, not apathetic.

13. Remember also that no two persons learn at the same pace. Whether professional or support staff, each comes to the department from a different background, and is motivated differently. Each will react to the training program in a different way.

14. End each training session on a note of progress and encouragement. The marking supervisor should not, for instance, abruptly stop after several typing mistakes have been pointed out to the student assistant. Quitting at this point will not only over-emphasize these mistakes but will discourage further progress.

Training Programs

The education of catalog department staff members does not end with the initial in-service training period. At this point, education has really only just begun. Training is a continuing operation that takes many forms, requires various approaches, and fulfills different objectives. Briefly, most catalog department training programs are aimed at one, and usually more, of the following.

1. To impart information: Clearly this is the basic purpose of all departmental education programs. It is especially important for the professional cataloger who must keep abreast of changes in cataloging codes, one or more subject fields, two or more languages, terminal coding procedures, and a growing profession.

2. To increase productivity: Programs that will increase the quantity and quality of output (cards filed, microfilms cataloged, books marked, and so on) are vital to the catalog department. Most programs will have this as either a primary or secondary objective.

3. To develop supervisory skills: The objective of many programs established in recent years has been to develop leadership skills in supervisory personnel, including department heads.

4. <u>To reduce supervision</u>: A properly trained cataloger will supervise himself. The better trained he is the more he can work on his own and the less time a revisor must spend supervising him.

5. <u>To increase morale</u>: Every program should contribute toward department morale. A terminal operator who is properly trained, who is confident of her abilities and skills, and who takes pride in her work, will have good morale.

6. <u>To change attitudes</u>: Closely related to increased morale are changes in work attitudes. A cataloger who is performing poorly has a poor attitude toward his work and his profession.

7. <u>To reduce mistakes</u>: The reduction of mistakes, probably more than any other single factor, has motivated department heads to re-examine their training programs. When a rash of filing errors appears in the card catalog or when misspelled words are spotted in the subject headings, the department head should instinctively look to the training program, or lack of program. Training reassessment, in any event, should be a continuing process.

8. <u>To increase department efficiency</u>: The need to maintain department efficiency is particularly evident when a crisis occurs, such as a sudden influx of gifts or the resignation of a particularly valuable cataloger. If personnel are unable to adapt to changing circumstances, something is lacking in the training program.

Effective training programs do not emerge overnight. There is much to consider before embarking on even a relatively straightforward plan. First, does the program have the support of the library administration? While most library directors now realize that in-service training is essential for an efficiently run catalog department, the support is seldom unqualified. The library director may agree that it is necessary to have well-trained catalogers, but when it is necessary to commit resources to a specific project, the catalog department may find that it receives more excuses than support. Moreover, support must be moral as well as financial. If catalogers get a signal that the library administration understands and supports a particular program, the program will succeed; if the signal is negative, it will not.

Another important point, and an area in which many programs fail, is the establishment of a precise set of objectives. If, for example, the department head wants to improve the quality and quantity of filing, then that is the objective. But the objective must be specific. Improve by exactly how many cards filed per hour? With what percentage of accuracy?

Still another consideration is financing. While the objectives will determine the program, so can the budget, at least to some extent. Lack of funds need not, however, be a major deterrent. The creative department head will find the necessary equipment, facilities, and personnel within the library. Perhaps he can convince the administration to buy equipment which will not be used just in the catalog department but in other library units as well, or for several different programs. If training involves expensive hardware, perhaps it can be rented at a reasonable fee. But whether notepads or computers, all supplies and equipment must be ready to go before the sessions begin.

As for facilities, usually all that is needed is a comfortable, soundproof room with the capacity to seat the number of trainees involved. Finding competent training personnel should be no problem, even on a limited budget. Training leaders need not, and in some cases should not, be professional teachers. The department head or one of his catalogers will know more about local needs than an outsider. The experience and background of the trainer are important considerations, but it is not difficult to develop teachers from within the department.

For a program to succeed, participants must be motivated to learn. Unless a person is willing to learn a skill and wants to submit to a specific program, it is a waste of his time and the library's money to force him. The best instructor and the most elaborate program cannot train someone who does not want to learn. To allow a cataloger time off to attend a language class, no matter how important it is to his cataloging responsibilities, is simply a waste unless he really intends to learn the language. Another important consideration is that theory and practice must go hand in hand. Studying the Russian language does not make a Russian language cataloger; that is, unless he actually has a chance to catalog in the language. Although any information a staff member gains will presumably be of some future use, training time is too precious to use it indiscriminately. A staff member who is trained for a specific skill which he has no hope of using will, sooner or later, become frustrated and discouraged, and eventually reject all training no matter how practical.

How many persons will be included in the program? This will certainly affect training plans. If it is a one-time need, or if only one or two persons are to be trained each year, it may be more economical to have an outside organization do the training. Tuition, travel, and living expenses could be less than the costs of setting up a program within the library for just one or two staff members. Or perhaps a network, book vendor, or other outside group will provide personnel to do the training in the library. How long will the program last? The time factor is important in considering the type of program developed, and whether, in fact, a staff member can be spared. It may be more economical to hire better qualified people than to train staff within the department for specific jobs.

Certain programs may suit one job requirement better than another; other programs may be adaptable to just about any need. It is important, therefore, to understand the possibilities, and know how each can be used to best advantage. Following is a brief review of the training techniques in use today, and how each can fit the needs of the catalog department.

On-the-job training. No matter how much practical experience and formal education a cataloger has had when he arrives in the department, at least some on-the-job training is necessary. This training--the show-and-tell method discussed earlier--should be provided by the immediate supervisor during the first few weeks (or, in some cases, months) of the newcomer's employment. Usually the supervisor demonstrates the job, stressing the key points; the employee then performs the job, and the supervisor provides feedback.

On-the-job training can take various forms. Apprenticeship training, in existence ever since the beginning of skilled trades, is still used today in many catalog departments. A few library schools, for example, have developed internship programs in which, in lieu of writing a thesis, the student is sent to a library to "learn the trade." Another approach is the "assistant to" position often used in libraries as a means of learning supervisory positions. Certainly the head of the catalog department should have an assistant who can step in and take over when necessary. His exact title is unimportant, but a clear understanding of his duties is imperative. Another quite successful on-the-job program is the "rotation position" where a staff member is systematically moved from position to position to provide experience in several areas of the library. Although most rotation positions are reserved for recent library school graduates, more experienced professionals can also benefit from such a program.

Lecture. The lecture method is particularly useful for presenting factual information to a large number of people. For instance, a lecture presentation would be a particularly good way to acquaint staff with a new retirement or insurance plan. The effectiveness of the lecture method depends a good deal on the interest of the material presented and on the ability of the lecturer.

Conference. Because the conference provides more opportunity for trainee participation, it is generally considered more effective than the lecture, especially where the objective is to change attitudes and behaviors. The conference technique might be used to acquaint department personnel with a controversial plan to automate the catalog department; or, the library might hold a management conference for all department heads and supervisors.

To insure group involvement, essential for any conference, participation should be limited to about 25 people; at the lower end of the scale, less than ten does not generate much cross-discussion. The conference leader, to be effective, must be familiar with the topic and have an understanding of conference techniques. While it is important to give the group a good deal of freedom it is also necessary to have the objectives in mind and to work always within a general framework.

To provide more realistic approaches to library problems and to encourage a greater degree of trainee participation, educators have, in recent years, developed several new conference tools and techniques, one of the most popular being the case study. This method, like other simulation methods, is normally used to help participants analyze and solve management problems. The procedure is to present a management situation for analysis by the participants, who, after studying the situation, provide some tentative answers. From these discussions, individuals draw basic management principles which they can transfer to their own departmental situations.

In the role-playing training method, a simulation technique designed to analyze interpersonal relations, conference participants play the parts of certain characters and act out events in typical library situations. Those trainees not involved in the role-playing take notes and later discuss their reactions to what they saw, the objective being to discover the most effective means of handling similar situations.

The in-basket simulation method is still another technique popular today with conference groups. The in-basket technique, designed to sharpen participants' decision-making abilities, involves allowing participants separately to examine a dozen or so items, including memos, letters, and notes on various cataloging problems, that might typically be found in the "in-basket" on a department head's desk. Usually, participants are told that the situation calls for a quick decision because the department head must leave town that day. He is forced, therefore, to pass on certain problems quickly to the division head, turn over others to a cataloger, write memos to the library director, and leave instructions with the chief typist. The obvious disadvantage of the in-basket and similar simulation techniques is that they do not necessarily relate to actual practice.

Conventions and meetings. All professionals (and, where appropriate, nonprofessionals) should attend state, regional and national conventions. It is not so much the knowledge gained from listening to speeches and viewing exhibits that is important to professional growth, but the opportunity to meet other professionals and talk over mutual problems. Committee work, in particular, exposes catalogers, too often sheltered from active professional work, to learning experiences available from no other source.

Short courses and institutes. Throughout the year, many universities and professional organizations hold special courses for librarians. A library school might conduct a two-week summer course on automated cataloging, or the American

Library Association may sponsor a two-day institute on re-classification to precede its summer convention. Because such courses often relate to specific, practical, and immediate cata-loging needs and are usually conducted by knowledgeable people in the field, short courses and institutes have become a valuable training vehicle. An important concern, though, is that courses relate to the specific needs of catalogers. The exact content of a particular course is not always apparent from the title or even from the published brochure. As part of his professional responsibilities, the department head should keep abreast of local and national institutes and insist that the library administration give financial and moral support to department members who can benefit from participation.

Vestibule training. Vestibule training, the opposite of on-the-job training, is training away from the actual work area, usually outside the library itself. Department terminal operators will probably receive training at network head-quarters or at a special workshop set up at a nearby library. Although the training conditions are often quite different from the actual working environment, vestibule training does offer better controlled supervision and an opportunity for concen-trated instruction, conditions particularly conducive to learn-ing machine operations.

In-house media. Probably the least used, most misused, and least understood of the many training vehicles are library media, including such devices as newsletters, bulletin boards, memos, and reports. Properly used, in-house media can furnish staff with up-to-date, authoritative information not only from the department and library but from the library world in general. Unfortunately, few departments use their local communications to full advantage. Chapters 9 and 10 describe some of the in-house communication techniques found in the catalog department.

Special assignment. Committee work, report writing, and other special assignments (also discussed in Chapters 9 and 10) are learning techniques too little used in libraries. Yet, if they are properly organized, a cataloger can learn more from committee or other special assignments than from just about any other learning situation. Just as important, he can contribute to the development of the library.

Formal course work. Both professionals and nonprofessionals should be encouraged to take formal classes. Catalogers can benefit from language, computer science, and other job-related courses, and clerks should find any library science course valuable. Staff can take these courses either through correspondence or in the evenings at a local college. The library should grant compensatory time to anyone willing to enroll in a work-related course. It is important, however, for a course to fit the job requirements as well as possible. The traditional academic assumption that the university professor knows what is relevant to the student's needs at a specific point in time, is able to present information in a relevant manner, and, finally, can accurately measure and evaluate student learning through contrived tests is not always valid when applied to catalog department training needs.

Audio-visual presentations. A-V materials can be useful in conjunction with just about any training program, or they can be used by themselves. Films, filmstrips, and slides have been particularly valuable in orientation programs. The library should establish an A-V orientation program not just for patrons, but as an introduction for new employees.

Laboratory groups. The most controversial of the recent training ideas has been the laboratory techniques variously called sensitivity training groups, T-groups, and encounter groups. Sessions usually last anywhere from one day to two weeks, and are presented in relatively unrestricted situations. The technique goes something like this: after a brief explanation by the group leader, participants break up into groups of ten to twelve to discuss openly themselves, each other, and anything else that comes to mind. With the leader acting as a catalyst, participants air their personal feelings and attitudes, not to mention hostilities. Through this strong emotional experience, it is hoped that each will derive a better understanding of the others, and a good deal of self-knowledge as well.

Many different opinions exist as to the value and place of sensitivity training in library development programs. Some critics claim great benefits, others believe it a waste of time, still others maintain that because of the strong emotional experience involved a good deal of harm is possible. But if participants are properly selected and the leader professionally trained, sensitivity training can bring about at least short-term improvements in interpersonal relationships.

Whatever training techniques are used, it is important to remember that individuals are not just being trained to perform certain specific duties but, at least in the case of catalogers, to be professionals. Theoretically, a cataloger becomes a professional when he receives the MLS degree; actually, he can have two, three, or more graduate degrees plus many years of cataloging experience and still not be a professional in the true sense. It is the responsibility of the head of the department, therefore, to see that each of his catalogers becomes a professional, and, just as important, that each continues to grow in professional competency.

Workshops

More and more bibliographic training is being carried out through a vestibule training technique known as the workshop. An afternoon workshop for catalogers on the latest changes in <u>AACR2</u> might be held in the library conference room as a part of the catalog department's in-service training program; or a two-day workshop sponsored by a computer-based network might be presented at network headquarters for terminal operators from various libraries in the region. Because of the growing popularity of workshops, chances are that sooner or later the department head will be called upon to conduct one or more sessions, maybe even asked to organize an entire program. Chances are also that workshop participants will come not only from the department head's own library, but from various other institutions as well.

The first consideration in planning a workshop is, therefore, who and how many will be attending. If attendance is voluntary, limits may have to be put on the number of participants. If trainees are to be chosen by their supervisors, those doing the selecting should have an understanding of the objectives of the workshop and the qualifications necessary for attendance. In selecting a location for the workshop, the department head will want to consider, among other things, facility and equipment needs. If, for example, a workshop on computer inputting is held away from the workplace, the site should include terminals and be as similar to the work situation as possible. Other equipment and facility considerations might be a lectern, chairs, and tables; audio-visual materials and equipment; duplication facilities; and a reception area and special meeting rooms. Lighting, acoustics, and the general comfort of participants, including accommodations for the handicapped, are still other concerns. The department head will certainly have to consider such supplies as tablets and pencils, handouts, workforms, and perhaps even things like application forms, name plates, identification badges, and certificates of workshop completion. Some materials can be supplied by the participants; others, introductory films and videotapes, for example, can often be obtained from a professional organization, book jobber, or bibliographic utility. Still other materials will have to be purchased from a library supply house or perhaps made up by the department head and duplicated for use by the trainees. The department head will also need to identify which materials to send to participants before the workshop begins. He may also be expected to arrange for transportation, lodgings, and food service, including refreshments for the morning and afternoon breaks and possibly banquet facilities. He will need to test all equipment to be used at the workshop and see to it that everything is in good working condition. Above all, he will need to arrange for qualified trainers and perhaps seek volunteers to help with registration and other related activities.

The department head should learn something of the background of the trainees and try to gear his presentation accordingly, breaking down the information into realistic bits and logical steps, always proceeding from general principles to specific examples and from familiar to more challenging activities. He should decide if the objective of the workshop is to apply previously learned skills to new problems or if the material will be completely new to everyone. He should use a variety of teaching methods and gear the workshop to practical applications, providing as much hands-on experience and individual practice time as possible. If the trainees are a relatively homogeneous group with a common set of needs and experiences, the workshop can be more structured than if participants come from different backgrounds. If they do represent varied backgrounds, he may have to offer the sessions on different levels. In any case, at least some adjustments will no doubt have to be made once the workshop starts.

Each session should start the moment the participants enter the room. First impressions are important, especially when dealing with people from different backgrounds. The department head should try to greet personally each trainee as he or she enters. A little small talk enhances self-confidence and helps ease the uncertainties that seem to arise when strangers come together. Participants should be allowed to seat themselves where they choose. Before the first session begins, the department head should distribute name badges and ask participants to write their names on cards to be placed in front of them. He should begin by reviewing the objectives of the workshop and explaining how these objectives will be achieved, including what equipment, handouts, and manuals are to be used. This assures everyone that learning is about to take place. The department head wants also to give participants confidence in his ability as a teacher and, just as important, confidence in their ability to learn from the workshop.

Evaluations

Even if a new cataloger is not exposed to a formal training program, he will in some manner train himself. The same principle applies to job evaluations. The department head will evaluate his people whether or not he has developed a formal, systematic program. The question is, should evaluations be formal or informal? The answer is both.

Informal evaluations. Even in a relatively formal evaluation situation, most of the information will be gathered informally. The department head will gather data not only to evaluate specific members of his staff but to see that materials are flowing through the department, books are properly labeled, and cards are being filed into the card catalog. If a problem is spotted, the department head will intervene with an interview, memo, shift in assignments, disciplinary action, or whatever he thinks necessary to rectify the situation.

The information gathering can be done in many ways. One method is through direct contacts with the staff, including formal interviews and informal observations. Some of these checks will be on a regular basis, others will be done randomly or whenever the occasion arises. The number and frequency will depend on how well or how poorly things seem to be going. Staff members will also initiate contacts, which again may be on a regular basis or spontaneous. The library director might meet with his department heads every Monday morning at nine o'clock to discuss department activities.

while the chief typist may appear at the department head's desk only when a problem arises. Unfortunately, too many department heads take staff-initiated contacts less seriously than those they themselves initiate or that are originated by the division head or library director. Both are important. Exactly how often the department head is approached by staff will depend a good deal on his attitude. If he disregards or ignores contacts, staff will eventually stop supplying information.

Even a walk through the department, watching catalogers search NUC, students label books, and clerks type cards, can reveal much about how individuals are progressing. Granted, much of the information gathered in this way is intuitive, but by constantly observing staff in action the department head will soon learn what to look for and the implications of what he observes. He must not, of course, march through the department every hour on the hour peering over the shoulders of his terminal operators. Yet he should make a point of consciously contacting or observing each member of the department every day.

Statistical checks are another common method. Certainly they represent the most objective evaluation technique. How many books did Jane Smith catalog last month? How many errors did she make? How many days was she late for work? But simply to collect information is not enough; the information must be interpreted and something done with it. The point is not simply to accumulate an assortment of unrelated statistics, but to collect information that will help interpret just what and how individuals are doing. The department head must be particularly aware of trends and patterns. Is the serials cataloger processing fewer and fewer titles each month? Why? Should a change in assignments be made? Should the department head have a talk with him? Through constant monitoring, the department head not only evaluates the performances of individual staff members but can determine the overall progress of the department, uncover bottlenecks, and keep abreast of department morale.

What should the department head look for when evaluating his staff? In his professional catalogers he wants to know exactly how professional they are. Is the cataloger performing professional work, making professional decisions, and both following and leading as a professional should?

Certainly the department head is concerned with quality and quantity of work, how many titles each cataloger is processing and with what degree of accuracy. Although quality may be difficult to assess objectively, quantity can be gleaned from monthly statistics. The department head must, however, be careful of statistics. They can be misleading. Catalogers and catalog departments are too often judged merely on titles and volumes processed, and important factors such as quality of bibliographic control are often disregarded in assessing cataloging production. The reference librarian, who keeps an equally detailed count of the types and quantity of reference questions answered, is seldom evaluated on these statistics. Neither should the cataloger be. Where quantity is considered it must be weighed in light of the parameters within which each professional--whether a cataloger, bibliographer, or reference librarian--is forced to work.

Also important is the cataloger's ability to work as a member of the team and to get along with others. This is not to say that the cataloger must be a conformist or that he cannot be an individual. He should indeed be an individual who, in his own way, contributes to the department, the library, and the profession; and he must--again, in his own way--do his part to see that the department attains its goals and objectives.

Certainly, the department head will expect the cataloger to be reasonably punctual and to be dependable. If he cannot be depended upon for the cataloging of books as well as everything else expected of him, he is not living up to his professional responsibilities.

The cataloger must know the bibliographic tools, too, and know how to use them. He must be thoroughly familiar with the cataloging codes, classification systems, and subject heading lists used by the library. He must be comfortable working within the subject fields and languages assigned him. Equally important are the less tangible qualities expected of all staff members: judgment, adaptability, attitude, initiative, and so on.

Although support staff are not expected to possess the same professional qualities as the cataloger, much the same personal traits are desirable. Like the professional, the clerk must have the traditional qualities of dependability, judgment, initiative, and adaptability. The department head will also want to know that the clerk possesses the skills needed to perform the job, and that both the quality and quantity of work is satisfactory. The nonprofessional must work as a member of the team, too, and if he or she is in a supervisory position, leadership qualities must also be assessed.

Formal Rating Systems

Over the years, libraries have developed a wide range of formal evaluation systems. Unfortunately, most have been established by administrators who have had neither enough knowledge of the specific jobs involved nor an understanding of the principles of job evaluation. If the head of the catalog department is confronted with a form that has little relation to his department's operations or objectives, there is really little he can do with it. But if he should have a voice in developing either a departmental or library-wide system he must make sure the final plan meets department needs. If an evaluation program is not initiated by the library administration, the department head should develop his own. To ensure orderly growth of an organization, members of the department, including the department head, must keep abreast of progress. This necessitates periodic evaluations. By way of review, here are some of the basic evaluation techniques used in libraries today.

Rating scale. One of the oldest, simplest to administer, and most widely used evaluation methods is the rating procedure. Although conceived in many different forms, it is basically a listing of qualities (attitude, initiative, dependability, cooperativeness, and so on) against which the department head rates his people. To rate someone, job performance is compared with each quality listed, and the degree of performance marked on a rating scale ranging from, say, "poor" to "superior."

The rating scale is easy to administer, simple to tabulate, and facilitates comparisons among employees. However, the validity of these comparisons is questionable. A cataloger's rating of, for example, fifteen "goods" and five "very goods," too often has little meaning when compared with a similar score of another cataloger. Even more confusion exists when comparing the scores of a cataloger with those of a reference librarian.

Checklist. To overcome some of the problems of the rating scale, a few libraries have turned to the checklist method. This consists of a list of words or phrases which can be compared with an employee's job performance. Each statement in the checklist has certain value or weight. (Thus the system is often called the "weighted checklist.") After marking those statements that most closely describe the individual the rating sheet is tabulated and numerical score achieved.

In a slightly different checklist method, called the forced-choice technique, the listing is divided into groups of four statements, two considered favorable and two unfavorable. The department head selects the single phrase most descriptive of the employee's performance; and, again, the results are tabulated and a score produced. If the checklist is to be effective, whoever constructs it must be familiar with each job; even more important, he must be qualified in constructing evaluations.

Essay. The essay evaluation has proven one of the more successful of the library rating systems. The essay evaluation, usually by the department head, can be completely unstructured or may follow a predetermined format, perhaps grouping comments under broad headings. The prime drawbacks of the essay evaluation are that it takes a good deal of time and ability to write informative and readable essays.

Field review. In the field review method a library administrator (the division head, library director, or personnel officer) discusses the progress of each library employee with each department head. The interviewer usually has several factors which he compares with the job requirements and performance of the job holders. After the interview, he writes his reports and, with an overview of the library's operation, makes recommendations on salary increases and suggests how various employees could and should improve.

Critical incident method. The so-called critical incident method has been most successful in academic libraries where tenure and promotion decisions involving professional librarians are based on an accumulation of facts. Other libraries use this method to reinforce other approaches. In this method, the department head records significant (or "critical") incidents, favorable and unfavorable, in a notebook or in personnel folders. At evaluation time these notes are reviewed. In using this sytem, the department head must be careful not to give the impression that he is continually spying on his staff. It is too easy for staff members to get the feeling that the department head is constantly looking for something to record in his "little black book."

Group evaluation. In the group evaluation method department and division heads meet to review the performance of the entire library staff. Because of the nature of library duties, department heads often have contact with staff members outside their own units; thus, through group sessions they can bring a wider perspective to the evaluation program than is possible with an individual department head evaluation. In academic libraries professionals are often evaluated by their peers, particularly when tenure and academic promotions are involved. The performance of catalogers who do committee work, engage in research, and are active in professional organizations is often best determined by a number of raters.

Ranking method. In the ranking method the department head simply ranks his people from high to low, usually in three separate categories: professionals, paraprofessionals, and nonprofessionals. After rank orders have been established, individuals are then divided into above average, average, and below average categories, or some other grouping dictated by the purpose of the ranking. This method is often used in libraries to determine salary distributions. The result is not unlike the A, B, C, D grading system used in the classroom.

Regardless of the method used, an evaluation is only as good as the evaluator and the purpose to which the system is put. A poorly done evaluation put to a questionable use is worse than no evaluation at all. Human weakness and error have invalidated too many well-conceived programs. The evaluator must be particularly alert to personal bias and prejudice. Unaware of his real feelings, the department head may, for example, react unconsciously to the dress, lifestyle, or personality of a cataloger. Also, there is the tendency to rate a person either too low or too high because of feelings about a single trait: this, what writers on personnel call the "halo effect," is perhaps the most prevalent form of bias in evaluation. It is not uncommon, for example, for the chief typist to rate a clerk low on all traits simply because

she is habitually late for work or because of some other particularly annoying habit.

The evaluator should be careful never to let a single
incident color the evaluation. A rash of filing errors or a
disagreement over a cataloging procedure just before the rating period may prejudice the assessment of a clerk's entire
year's work. A lack of knowledge of a person may also result
in an incomplete or even unfair evaluation. If the head of the
department has not had an opportunity to observe a new cataloger he should be careful not to give a cursory rating. It
is better to give an incomplete rating, or no rating at all,
than an uninformed one. Confusing quantity with quality is
still another problem. Simply because a cataloger processes
an above-average number of books or a clerk can type headings faster than anyone else in the department does not mean
they are productive. The time necessary to correct errors
may negate above-average production.

Although the evaluation program should have a specific
purpose, the purpose should not bias the evaluator's judgment.
If, for instance, the department head knows that the ratings
he is giving will affect the pay increases of his catalogers,
he must not unconsciously (or consciously) rate them higher
than they deserve just to insure that they will receive their
raises. Likewise, if the evaluation is designed to improve
the work of the catalogers (which all evaluations should do),
the department head must be careful not to over-emphasize
weak points (and de-emphasize strengths) simply to show
where improvement is needed.

Another tendency found in too many evaluators is to
give people consistently low, high, or middle ratings. Uniformly low ratings are usually given by the department head
who secretly believes his people are inferior to him or who
has an inferiority complex which can be assuaged only by
putting everyone else in his place. Another department head
will give high ratings to show how much his clerks have improved since the last rating period, or to gain easy popularity. Still another evaluator will rate his staff in the middle
range to play it safe, wanting neither to praise not to con-
demn.

Performance standards. Performance standards are
usually defined as the output during a specific period of time

for a staff member, the department, or a unit within the department. Quantity and time are the most common performance criteria, but performance can also be measured in terms of quality, costs, or a combination of factors. Quantity would be the standard when a staff member's performance is measured by the number of titles cataloged (cards filed, records inputted, volumes labeled, etc.) each day, week, or month. Quality would be the measurement when judging the acceptability of output as determined by error reports, rejection rates, or other established set of quality standards. The usual way to tabulate output is for members of the department to record on standardized statistic sheets the number of items they process. One of the benefits of computer-based cataloging is that production can often be recorded automatically.

One problem in initiating a monitoring program is that staff members tend to resist efforts to measure their production. They seem to feel that the department head is implying that they are not working hard enough; and they think of production in terms of stopwatches, time and motion studies, job transfers and terminations. Frequently the reason staff members do not see cataloging production the same way the department head does is that no one has taken the time to explain what the term "performance standards" really means. The department head must, therefore, explain to his staff that monitoring programs benefit both the library and individual staff members. Employees must understand that the chief reason for monitoring their production is to give them a basis for self improvement, not to provide supervisors with a way to look over the shoulders of their people. And, of course, data gathered from a monitoring program is necessary in preparing the library's annual and other reports.

The department head should begin his monitoring program by focusing on exactly what it is he wants to measure and why; then he must set specific production goals. A goal might be a 10 percent increase in titles inputted by the department or 50 more titles cataloged each month, but never simply "more production." He should, of course, invite suggestions from everyone in the department. A good way to generate ideas is to form a committee to help set up the program.

To be effective, the monitoring method must show both short- and long-term progress, and the procedure must be understood by everyone. Forms for gathering data should be clearly headed with adequate space to tick off numbers (see "Forms Management," Chapter 9). Finally, the department head must make it clear who will be involved; normally this would include everyone engaged in a certain activity.

The procedure for gathering data should be made as straightforward as possible. A frequent complaint of catalog department employees is that monitoring systems interfere with the actual work. Only relevant data should be recorded and only actual performances monitored. Data should be recorded by each staff member promptly after performing the activity, submitted to the department head on a regular basis (usually on the last day of each month), and immediately calculated.

A critical point comes in collating the data, which includes checking for accuracy and completeness and analyzing and comparing performances. Comparisons should be made internally to see how production levels have changed over a period of time and how individuals are performing in relation to department norms. Performances can also be compared with external sources, either by using data collected from other libraries or by measuring department production levels against national standards as published in the literature.

To encourage self-appraisal, data should be made available first to the staff member whose performance it mirrors rather than to the immediate supervisor. The significance of the data should be periodically reviewed by the department head and staff member, usually at evaluation time, so that each person performing an activity gains an understanding of his or her progress in relation to past performance and department goals. It is essential that the department head make continual use of the results. Measurement for the sake of measurement is a waste of time and resources. Besides self-appraisal, performance data should be used for the reappraisal of department operations, for the refinement of production goals, and for making adjustments in the data-gathering process itself, including the reformatting of reporting forms.

The department head should consider the following factors when comparing and evaluating individual performances:

1. Type of activity. Certain activities are easier to

perform than others. All things being equal, a cataloger processing English-language novels will be able to put through more titles than another cataloger who is working with scientific foreign-language treatises.

2. Facilities and equipment. State-of-the-art computer terminals can make a measurable difference in production. So can a spacious well-lighted, properly ventilated work area.

3. Processing methods. A logical unimpeded work-flow is essential for high production. Duplication of effort by staff members in the searching of incoming materials can generate impressive statistics when counting the number of searches performed each day, but in no way would this data reflect the efficiency of department operations.

4. Conditions and status of materials and equipment. Excessive downtime on the computer or even an outdated work form can hinder efficiency and impede productivity.

5. Human factors. Experience and formal education are important considerations. Morale and job satisfaction also play an important part. An effective training program, positive personnel policies, and appropriate job assignments are essential for high production. So are supervisors who can lead, motivate, and communicate effectively with staff. Often low production can be traced directly to the department head. It may be, for example, that productivity has slipped because the department head has neglected production. Perhaps his attention has been focused on solving the problems associated with joining a bibliographic network and he has assumed that production will take care of itself once the department goes online. In many libraries no one, not even the head of the department, is "in charge" of production. Although every manager endorses high productivity, not every one is willing or able to explain what it means, let alone develop an effective monitoring program.

Evaluation Procedure

The first step in evaluating the overall performances of staff members is to analyze the job duties and responsibilities, and establish job standards and good job descriptions. It is important that the department head discuss these standards with his staff so that each knows what is expected of him or her. Each must understand what the evaluation means in terms of salary, promotion, and goal fulfillment. Then a timetable for evaluation and interview sessions should be set.

Ordinarily, the evaluation is made by the individual's immediate supervisor and reviewed by the next upward in line. The chief typist would evaluate the members of the typing pool and these evaluations would be reviewed by the department head. In departments where assignments are varied it is perhaps best for the head of the department to do all the evaluating, with, of course, advice from others. In a department where a clerk types cards under the supervision of the chief typist, files cards under the supervision of the catalog maintenance chief, and withdraws books under the direction of still another supervisor, it is difficult to define the chain of command, at least for evaluation purposes.

At the designated time the evaluations should be filled out by the department head, reviewed by the division head, and finally, interviews should be held with each staff member. During the rating conference--the most important part of the evaluation procedure--the department head discusses the ratings with each staff member. Also at this point, the department head and staff member should discuss future development, review duties and responsibilities, examine ways of improving performance, set new objectives, and discuss career goals. Finally, special projects should be assigned. The evaluation conference is the time for frank give and take in which all problems and misunderstandings are aired and resolved. It is also imperative to explore ways of keeping open the lines of communication.

In summary, to have an effective evaluation program the department head must do the following:

1. Make sure his staff, both professionals and support staff, are fully aware of the evaluation plan used in the department, including the specific dates on which the evaluations and interviews are to take place.

2. Make sure the evaluation program is an on-going process with formal interviews held at regular intervals.

3. Do not wait for scheduled evaluation periods to

counsel members of the department; evaluation should be a continuing, everyday process.

4. Keep in mind the effect of the evaluation on the staff member's future performance.

5. Emphasize a supportive role in the evaluation; de-emphasize the punitive role.

6. Not only point out areas of weakness in a staff member's performance but, even more important, show him how to improve.

7. Establish objectives and standards of accomplishment for the coming year.

8. Document joint decisions made regarding future objectives, and discuss them periodically.

9. Be tactful, but do not sugarcoat; convey, as truthfully as possible, exactly how the person is performing.

10. Find out how each staff member feels about his performance; ask him what can be done to help him improve.

11. When in doubt on a specific point, ask the person how he thinks he should be evaluated--and take him seriously. He knows more about how he is performing than anyone else.

12. If the evaluation shows obvious inconsistencies, look to outside factors which may be affecting performance.

Perhaps the most important point to remember in any evaluation program is exactly how much responsibility the department head must assume for the performance of his staff. Has he given them all the help and support he can? Has he made sure that there are no policies, procedures, or people blocking their performances? Does he keep them informed on progress? Has he placed each member of the department in a job for which his or her talents and experience fit? If the answer to these questions is yes, both the department head and his staff will receive "superior" ratings.

Career Development

In the past, department heads have done little or nothing to help employees plan their careers. What career planning did exist was based almost entirely on the needs of the library, seldom on employee needs. This attitude is changing. When making promotion and transfer decisions, department heads are beginning more and more to take seriously the aspirations of their staff members. Many department heads are even helping their career-minded employees advance to positions in other institutions.

If the personnel office does not provide a formal career development policy for the library, the department head should establish an informal program of his own. Among other things, career development makes maximum use of staff. The more accurately the department head can match people with jobs that fit their skills and ambitions, the better performances he receives from them. A career development program avoids obsolescence, decreases turnover, and reduces on-the-job frustrations. Career planning establishes the staff member's identity and status, satisfies his need for personal fulfillment and self-determination, and helps him gain better control over his life. When employees find little or no growth opportunities within an institution, their attitudes weaken and job performances are affected. Also, an active career development program enables the department head to recruit better qualified staff, since career-minded people usually give preference to libraries that support their career aspirations. Finally, career development at the department level contributes to the institution's affirmative action program. By identifying career paths, the department head helps upgrade the working lives of his staff, especially minorities.

Of course the department head cannot ignore institutional needs in order to satisfy individual aspirations. Compromises have to be made, both by the employees and by the library administration. The point is that when making staffing decisions, the department head should consider seriously the goals and skills of employees, not simply department needs. Career development is a responsibility that should be shared by everyone in the library: staff members, department heads, library personnel office, and central administration.

The department head can either consider career planning

a separate activity or he can incorporate career development into his yearly evaluation program; preferably both. In any case, a systematic approach seems to work best. One such approach is to break career planning into the following basic steps:

1. Self-appraisal. With the help of the department head, the staff member questions his career interests and assesses his potential. What skills do I possess? What interests do I have? What would I really like to be doing? The department head should encourage the staff member to ask himself just how important are things like financial rewards, job security, career challenges, supervisory responsibilities, and interactions with co-workers and library users. The staff member should realistically assess his background and education and try to identify his strengths and weaknesses in bibliographic, supervisory, technical, and interpersonal skills. Of course, aspirations are likely to change over the years and a reappraisal of career goals will have to be made at each stage in life, but the department head should at least provide the opportunity for each member of his staff to start his or her own appraisal process.

2. Review career opportunities. For career planning to succeed the staff member's skills and interests must relate to present and future employment opportunities. Here again the department head can help by reviewing job descriptions with the staff member and by discussing qualifications for present and future openings. The department head will want to outline promotion and transfer possibilities within the library and also discuss the nationwide job situation. Finally, he should recommend publications that contain occupational information.

3. Set career goals. After the staff member, under the guidance of the department head, has analyzed his occupational strengths and weaknesses, identified his interests, and reviewed possible job opportunities, he is ready to develop his career goals. The department head should encourage the staff member to make his goals as compatible as possible with his abilities, desires, education, experience, and psychological needs; above all, career goals must be realistic. Both self-awareness and an understanding of job opportunities are essential.

4. <u>Prepare career strategies</u>. Here, too, the department head can help by assisting the staff member in outlining
the steps he should take to achieve his goals and possibly
help him identify alternative strategies. The staff member's
career plans must take into account his needs and skills and
include future education and job experiences. Besides receiving help from the department head, the staff member may
want to talk with others in the library, perhaps even consult
a professional career counselor.

5. <u>Implement strategies</u>. Although implementation is
up to the staff member, the department head can help by
carving out career paths within the department and by making
these paths available to qualified staff. Each position in the
department should contain at least two steps, each related to
the other and each requiring more responsibility and at least
one new skill. Besides the library's formal job-posting system, the department head will want to announce job openings
on the bulletin board and circulate notices through department memos. To help prepare members of his department for
advancement both within and outside the institution, the department head should make available special projects and committee assignments, provide access to workshops and in-
service training classes, and encourage staff to enroll in continuing education courses. He should also develop special
work experiences within the department, including job rota-
tions, dual positions, and acting supervisory assignments.

Chapter 6

STAFF RELATIONSHIPS

The management of a catalog department is the management
of people. By its very nature, people management is a close,
personal relationship, difficult to identify, impossible to measure accurately. Yet this relationship, intangible as it may
seem, forms the basis of the department head's responsibility
both to his staff and to the library administration. Traditional concerns, for example, volumes cataloged and hours
worked, take second place to staff relations. If the department head has a good working relationship with others in and
outside the department he will also find an increase in the
books cataloged, cards filed, records inputted, and hours
worked--and he will discover fewer mistakes, shorter coffee
breaks, and less absenteeism.

How the department head relates to his staff is a critical question which he must answer--and continue to answer--
as best he can, if he expects his department to fulfill its
goals and objectives. To find out just how effective is the
staff-relations-quotient of a department head (or other administrator, manager, or supervisor), the following questions
should be answered, honestly and objectively:

1.   How often does the department head contact his
staff? It is not enough to announce that he has an open door
policy; the department head must have an open mind policy
as well. If staff members do not come to him, he must go
to them.

2.   Does he know the members of his department? If
the department head expects to maintain a good working relationship with his people, if he expects to anticipate reactions,
understand attitudes, and evaluate morale, he must know the

members of his department not just as names and faces but as individuals, each with his or her own personality.

3. What are the attitudes, positive and negative, of the staff? If a terminal operator has a negative attitude, it is up to the department head to recognize it, discover the underlying causes, and do something about it. Granted, a department head should not meddle in the employee's personal problems, but he should at least recognize a problem when it exists and understand how it is affecting the person's work habits.

4. Does the department head have a positive attitude toward his staff? If so, the staff will react in kind. The department head's attitude toward any aspect of the department's operation will affect the attitudes of others. Whether training, advising, or disciplining, he must be positive. If he expects high standards from his staff, he is likely to achieve high standards. If he expects low standards, he will get them, too.

5. Is the department head considerate of others? Does he take into account the feelings of his staff and does he try to anticipate the effects his decisions and actions will have on others?

6. Does he at any time or for any reason belittle his staff? Whether demonstrating a new routine or pointing out an error, sarcasm will only cause problems, not solve them. Even an indirect or unconscious remark can create a barrier between the department head and a staff member.

7. How effective are the work assignments? Chances are the department includes a good deal of talent among its professionals, paraprofessionals, clerks, and student assistants. If so, it is the responsibility of the head of the department to make sure that these talents are used effectively. Whether assigning books for cataloging, cards for typing, or librarians to special projects, it must be done wisely. If assignments are ineffective, it will be evident to everyone.

8. How do staff members feel about their working conditions? Too often, the department head is unaware of things like supply shortages, dirty typewriters, poorly lit video display screens, and inadequate air conditioning. A clerk will

complain once about a faulty typewriter; then, when no action is taken, she will keep future complaints to herself. The
result will be a disgruntled typing pool complaining among
themselves about poor working conditions, both real and
imagined. In a smooth-running department, the department
head will show a genuine interest in the conditions under
which the staff must work.

9. Do staff members know their roles in the library?
Everyone should understand his or her purpose in the department. No one, professional or nonprofessional, should
have to ask "why?" For a typist to know only that she is
typing something called subject headings at the top of 3 x 5
cards is not enough; she must understand the purpose of it
all and know how her work affects the total library operation.

10. Is each staff member growing in his or her position? No one in the department should feel unchallenged.
If necessary, the department head should provide extra assignments and projects. Professionals, in particular, must
know that the department head is interested not only in the
future of the department but in their futures.

11. Are opportunities provided for advancement within the department? A marker who does not have a chance to
advance to a typing position (that is, of course, if she is
qualified and, indeed, wants to advance) will become stifled,
and the department will suffer. A person who is bored, feels
trapped, or is not realizing his or her potential will become
unhappy and frustrated. Each member of the department
should be able to take over a position one step higher than
his or her own, even if the next step is the head of the department. If it is necessary to transfer a staff member to
another department to insure advancement, this should be done.

12. Are all members of the department interested in
self-improvement? No matter what the job, everyone in the
department can and should improve. Both on-the-job and off-
the-job education must be encouraged. Every member of the
department (including the department head) is capable of improvement.

13. Are staff members willing to help out when the
need arises? If a cataloger is ill or if a backlog mushrooms
in the marking section, are others in the department, including

the department head, willing to step in to clear the bottle-neck? Whenever possible, back-up should be provided; more importantly, a spirit of togetherness should prevail that auto-matically assumes that professionals and nonprofessionals will cover for each other when necessary.

14. Are professionals contributing to the profession? If catalogers engage in research, read professional journals, attend professional meetings, and are continually thinking of ways to improve the department's operation, the department is truly professional.

15. Are staff members deluging the department head with suggestions and new ideas? They should be. If they are not continually suggesting new ways of doing things, ob-viously a block exists, perhaps a block set by the depart-ment head.

16. Does the department head ask questions? Not only must everyone in the department feel free to ask questions of the department head; he must feel free to ask questions of them. He should not be embarrassed to ask a cataloger how to establish a corporate entry or how to apply a filing rule. Staff members already know the boss does not have all the answers, and he should know it too.

17. How successful is the department's in-service training program? Is it a continuing program? In-service training is not merely the welcome the newcomer receives when he or she first arrives in the department; it is an on-going, flexible, in-depth program tailored to the needs of each individual in the department, a program that takes into consideration each person's capabilities, aptitudes, and ambi-tions. In-service training is both an educational experience for the staff and a way to learn how the department is func-tioning. An on-going training program also tells members of the staff that they are valuable enough to deserve specialized education.

18. Does the department head set a good example? He cannot expect others in the department to maintain high standards if he does not set the same standards for himself.

19. Does the department head give credit where credit is due? If not, he is discouraging, if not blocking, progress.

Neglecting to compliment a cataloger for above-average production or, even worse, taking credit for someone else's idea, is poor management. No matter who receives credit for a specific idea, the head of the department will be credited with good management.

20. Does the department head admit his mistakes? No one can manage a catalog department and not make mistakes. If he is not making mistakes, he is not trying. Admitting errors is not only the honest thing to do, it is the way to gain the respect and confidence of the staff.

21. Is he impartial? The department head who plays favorites or shows prejudice will automatically alienate everyone, even those he favors. He must also recognize when someone in the department is trying to manipulate him.

22. Is the department head consistent? Or is he subject to changes in mood and manner? Unpredictable behavior is unlikely to win the confidence and cooperation of others.

23. Do staff members take pride in their work? If they are enthusiastic about their assignments and are willing to put extra effort into getting the work done, a healthy department relationship exists. But if the department consists of clock watchers who consider their work a drudgery, problems exist that need attention.

24. What is the reputation of the catalog department among other units in the library? A healthy rapport among individuals and departments is essential for an efficiently run organization. If others in the library look upon the catalog department with pride, staff will, in turn, take pride in their department.

25. How is department morale? If the department head does not know, he should find out. He should look for such signs as interdepartmental feuds, excessive rumors, sloppy work, waste, and absenteeism. Morale will, of course, change from month to month, week to week, even day to day. Good overall morale is, nonetheless, vital to a smooth-running department, and must be constantly evaluated.

26. Does the department head allow staff members to solve their own problems, or does he feel that no one but

himself has the authority or the brains for problem-solving?
It is often more difficult for a supervisor to stand aside and
allow others sufficient time to work out solutions than to step
in and solve the problems himself. Whether he knows--or
thinks he knows--more about problem-solving than others in
the department is not the point. The confidence he shows
in his people and the experience they will gain in the process
is what really counts.

27. Does the department head include everyone in the
department in the decision-making process? If staff feel that
they have had a say in a decision they will be much more
likely to help implement it than if they have had no input in
the matter. And if a decision has to be the department head's
alone, he should be prepared to explain the why of it.

28. Does the department head delegate responsibility?
Does he look for staff members who are ready to take over
decision-making and other responsibilities? If opportunities
do not arise, the department head should make them arise.
Delegation not only relieves supervisors of unnecessary details, but provides others in the department with opportunities to prove themselves. This is basic to a growing department.

29. Does the department head emphasize results rather
than rules? "Going by the book" can stifle creativity. Un-
orthodox solutions sometimes work the best.

30. Is each staff member kept informed of his or her
progress? Everyone wants to know how he or she is doing.
Keeping department members informed, both through formal
evaluations and informal comments, helps boost morale, improve performances, and promote initiative.

31. Is the department head open with his staff? Is
he, for example, frank when discussing annual evaluations
and does he offer his staff clear and honest explanations of
what he considers their relative strengths and weaknesses?
If, at any time, the department head senses misunderstandings
on any subject, he must be willing to step in and clear them
up.

32. Is the staff kept up-to-date on changes in the department and in the library? The department head is in an

ideal position to pass along information. If he fails to keep his staff informed on what is new in the catalog department and in other departments, they will be working in the dark. Staff must not be forced to rely on rumors for information.

Departmental Relations

Just as important as healthy relations between the department head and his staff are good working relations among staff members themselves. Departments blessed with good inter- and intra-departmental relations function relatively smoothly, while those experiencing continual conflicts falter. Unfortunately, many catalog departments seem to fall into the latter category, and this is not too surprising. For one thing, cataloging remains a mystery to most non-catalogers, a situation perpetuated, at least in some cases, by the catalogers themselves. Too many catalogers assume the role (if not always the status) of experts who consider the opinions of others, including those who use and are dependent upon their services, perhaps well-intentioned but uninformed. In turn, many public service librarians consider catalogers rigid and inflexible, unwilling to accept reasonable suggestions, unable to see the practical side of librarianship, and too ivory tower in their thinking. Probably the most common criticism is that catalogers have made the card catalog an end in itself; that is to say, catalogers are cataloging for catalogers. According to many librarians, catalogers may know their tiny corner of the library world but seldom see the whole picture. They make decisions only in terms of their own special interests, forgetting that they exist to serve others.

A lack of understanding of what is involved in the cataloging process has perpetuated many such criticisms. The circulation librarian, for instance, may think nothing of sending a truck full of books into the catalog department for reclassification without realizing that it can take just as long to reclassify the books as it did to catalog and classify them in the first place. As a consequence, catalogers, faced with what they see as a lack of understanding of processing procedures, often feel that their efforts are unappreciated. Many are convinced that they are not receiving the credit or the status of other librarians, that their opinions are ignored, and that they are often purposefully kept uninformed on important policy matters. They feel isolated, particularly from the central administration.

But while catalogers may feel slighted by the administration, library directors have their complaints, too. Because of what they consider the secretive atmosphere pervading their catalog departments, many feel forced to allocate too much authority to their department heads. Also, according to many library administrators, catalogers have absolutely no concept of the value of their services in relation to costs. How much value, for example, should be placed on the perfect catalog card, whatever that is? Even more perplexing is that catalog department cost figures seldom reflect the department's work, and never seem to go up or down in relation to volumes and titles cataloged. Department heads, on the other hand, feel that they are not given enough authority, that they are not allowed to make important decisions, and, even worse, that the decisions made for them by the central administration are uninformed, ill-advised, or just plain stupid.

A good many of these misunderstandings stem from conflicts of interest: conflicts between individuals, between groups, and between departments. The interests of the reference librarian who hates to say "no" to a patron will conflict with those of the cataloger whose primary concern is monthly production and a regulated flow of materials. Conflicts exist within departments, too. The department head's interest in getting catalog cards filed on Friday afternoon will conflict with the interests of a filer who has just received a frantic phone call from her baby sitter. In addition, conflicts can arise where individuals or units compete for service. Branch librarians, for instance, will compete to have the catalog department process their books first. Such conflicts are further compounded by communication failures, personnel changes, poor organization, inadequate chain of command, or lack of coordination of demands.

The basic differences in the structure and purpose of various library units will also cause misunderstandings. The catalog department, involved primarily with the flow of materials, is particularly vulnerable to criticism. Delays and backlogs affect not only catalogers but all others who use or work in the library. Public service personnel, dependent as they are on the catalog department, are naturally quick to criticize. Even patron attitudes can contribute to department tensions. In an academic or special library where patrons place excessive demands on the catalog department, processing personnel often, in turn, react aggressively.

Differences in working conditions also tend to polarize people and departments. Even the fragmented hours of reference librarians in contrast to the eight to five, Monday through Friday work week of catalogers act as a natural barrier, as can the physical separation of the two departments. Moreover, these fundamental differences in functions, working hours, and objectives of various departments tend to attract people with different interests and personalities which, in turn, can further separate individuals and groups.

Conflicts occur where different job levels are defined more in terms of ascribed than achieved status. The typical library situation where clerks cannot possibly achieve the status (and salary) of professional catalogers can easily cause internal strains. This is particularly evident in democratically oriented organizations where equality of opportunity is stressed.

Conflicts also occur because of misunderstandings in role relationships. The new cataloger, for instance, may feel forced to choose between the goals set when he was in library school and those imposed by his new department head. The senior cataloger, too, may find himself playing multiple and conflicting roles. He may have to choose among the expectations of him in his roles as a professional librarian, as a member of the catalog department, as chairman of the library social committee, and as representative of the state library association. He may conform to some roles, resist others, and partially comply with yet others. The department head must, therefore, be aware of such conflicts and see that all members of the department understand clearly their role relationships in and outside the department.

Conflicts (inter-departmental ones in particular) are normal, often unavoidable, and sometimes desirable. Actually, purposeful inter-departmental rivalry (as well as such devices as establishing deadlines, setting quotas, and creating emergencies) is a legitimate way to challenge staff. Although perhaps a bit devious, if handled properly, controlled conflict can inspire better performance by adding spirited rivalry to the department; it can even inject a unifying effect. Conflicts

also stretch aspirations, help prevent stagnation, and stimulate interest and curiosity. Conflict is a medium through
which problems can be aired and solutions evolved. It is the
root of change. And in fact, variant goals, new challenges,
status struggles, risk taking, personality clashes, and ri-
valries make conflicts inevitable.

Reducing Tensions

It is not, therefore, always necessary, or even desirable, to reduce tensions. But when it is, there are several
techniques the department head can use to blunt or rechannel
a conflict. One method is to find a common enemy. If, for
example, catalogers start feuding among themselves, the department head can call them together not just to iron out differences, but to re-direct hostilities into more productive channels. Perhaps he can throw out a few statistics from Capitol
City Library or State University, letting his people shoot at
cataloging production instead of each other. Or, even better,
he can make a graph of department statistics to see if he can
challenge his people to improve their past records.

Another approach is to have an arbitrator--the department head, technical services librarian, or library director--
listen to all sides of a problem and then pass down a binding
decision. The mediator should be mutually respected and, if
possible, a mutual boss. Granted, this is a dictatorial approach, but it often works. In many cases, the antagonists
simply need an authority figure (a diplomatic one, to be sure)
to pass judgment and see that they shake hands and make up.
A departmental or inter-departmental feud is often based on
misunderstandings and hurt pride, the solution to which may
be a good cry followed by a pep talk.

Or perhaps the underlying problem is inadequate communications. All that is needed is to re-open or re-affirm
the lines of communication. Generally, the more interaction
between groups and individuals the more understanding and
appreciation of each other's problems. For instance, a disagreement between the catalog and reference departments
over information provided on the catalog cards might be eased
if both realize that they have mutual interests and problems.
Both departments are understaffed and overworked; and both
are dependent on the card catalog. Since one of the responsi-

bilities of the reference department is to interpret the catalog, information not included on the cards must be supplied by them. If the reference people realize how much time and effort are required for catalog maintenance, and the catalogers understand how much reliance the reference department places on this tool, both are more likely to appreciate each other's problems and needs.

The seminar approach can also be used to solve conflicts. This technique has been successful in tackling conflicts between two or more departments, between the clerical and professional staff, and between the library administration and staff. A professor from a nearby library school might be asked to conduct a one-day seminar on a broad subject such as library administration, emphasizing, of course, specific areas where local differences seem to exist.

Finally, there is the option of doing nothing. The department head does not have to "do something" every time a conflict arises. It may be that meddling will cause more harm than good, especially if the facts are blurred. If it seems that action may actually compound the problem the best approach may be to ignore it. If the conflict does not go away, then, of course, action must be taken. If a persistent conflict is not uncovered, underground networks usually exaggerate and distort the truth, often multiplying the tensions and hostilities.

When action is indeed required, the first step is to analyze the conflict carefully, and recognize it for what it is. To understand the extent and depth of the problem, the department head should look for warning signs: absenteeism, ill temper, withdrawal, polarization, communications block. He should be particularly alert to changes in normal behavior. He should then analyze the facts as he sees them. Who is involved? What are the issues? Which are real issues, which are imagined? Then dig for underlying causes. Discover, if possible, the seriousness of the problem. Also important is the urgency. Does the conflict need immediate attention? Can it wait? If not, what can be done about it?

Solutions will, of course, differ according to the nature of the problem. But whatever the ultimate approach, the department head must remember to do the following:

1. Keep the conflict problem-centered rather than personality-centered.
2. Avoid an outcome that labels one side the winner and the other the loser.
3. Make the solution a permanent one, not just temporary.
4. Except as a last resort, avoid a compromise solution; that is usually no solution at all.
5. Be concerned with staff growth, not just with who is right.
6. Recognize that open discussion can be healthy, especially if it brings to the surface problems that need surfacing.
7. At the same time, make sure that no one loses his or her dignity in an attempt to "battle it out."
8. After a solution has been reached keep communications open.

Mutual Problem Solving

An important responsibility of the department head is to resolve the various day-to-day conflicts that arise among members of the department, especially between staff members and their supervisors. The department head can clear up most disagreements by explaining a point of library policy to both parties and then handing down a decision based on policy. Although such solutions might not always satisfy both sides, decisions that are supported by library policy are usually, at the very least, acceptable to everyone. Other conflicts, however, are more complex and therefore more difficult to resolve, especially when there are no policies or precedents to fall back on. The best approach here is for the department head to act as an arbitrator, and try to help both sides examine the conflict in a reasonable and logical way. One such problem-solving technique calls for a step-by-step approach based on an understanding by each person of the other person's needs.

1. Identify needs. If the department head is to help the antagonists arrive at a mutually acceptable solution, he must first make sure that each side understands the other's position, especially the other person's needs. If, for example, a terminal operator wants to take her vacation (release time, lunch period, afternoon break) at a certain time but her

supervisor insists that some other time would better satisfy the needs of the department, there is a conflict. The department head, after outlining the problem, should find out from the terminal operator if another time would not work just as well and then ask the supervisor why she needs the operator to be at the terminals at that particular time. The two parties should not, however, try to justify their needs, but merely bring them out into the open. To help establish a cooperative atmosphere, the department head should point out any needs that both sides might have in common.

2. <u>Look for possible solutions</u>. After both sides have stated their needs, they can begin looking for a solution. Everyone including the department head should pose possible resolutions without stopping to discuss the relative merits of each. As in any brainstorming session, no serious suggestion should be ignored. No matter how impractical an idea might seem at first, it may eventually lead to a workable solution.

3. <u>Evaluate the solutions</u>. After a list of possible solutions has been generated, each should be carefully evaluated. Some will be obviously unworkable and can be rejected at once; and if either party has a strong objection to an idea it, too, should be discarded. The point is to try to uncover at least one solution that will satisfy everyone's needs. If none of the solutions seem satisfactory, the department head should begin the process again by briefly restating each person's needs and once more brainstorming for solutions.

4. <u>Agree on a solution</u>. If the department head feels that they have found a solution that both parties can agree upon, he should restate it in simple terms. Each person should then comment again on the idea, discussing its merits and clearing up areas of confusion. If the solution meets the needs of both parties, it should be restated by the department head and agreed upon by both parties.

5. <u>Implement the solution</u>. To avoid misunderstandings, the solution and a plan of action should be made as detailed as possible, perhaps even written in the form of a step-by-step outline with copies for everyone, including the department head. It is important that both sides have the same clear understanding of the solution and that both know exactly how it is to be executed. The department head may also want

to propose possible variations or suggest one or more alternative solutions so that if the agreed-upon plan is blocked for some reason a substitute can be put immediately in place.

Complaints and How to Deal with Them

One barometer of good or poor inter- and intra-department relations is the number of gripes heard in the department. It has been said that good catalog department relations can be equated with the department head's ability to handle legitimate complaints, and his interest in dealing with these complaints. Unfortunately, though, staff gripes are one of the least understood and most neglected aspects of cataloging management. Department heads, it seems, are too busy attending meetings and writing reports to bother with staff complaints, at least until they evolve into crises. This is indeed unfortunate, for if a cataloger cannot get satisfaction from his department head where can he go? If he confines his complaining to his co-workers, his morale and the morale of others will drop even lower; and he remains unsatisfied. If he brings his grievances to the division head or library director he is guilty of bypassing his immediate supervisor. Even when a cataloger does bring his gripes to the head of the department, they are sometimes brushed aside. The department head may listen to the problem then break off in the middle to rush to a meeting; or he may smile politely and insist that it will all work out in the end--when he knows it will not. Perhaps he will tell the complainant that someone will look into the problem, but that it will take time to fill out forms and get through the administrative tangle.

Obviously, these and similar evasions are unacceptable in a well-managed department. No matter how seemingly trivial the complaint, the department head must give his full, undivided attention, which includes taking the following simple but important steps:

1. Give the complaint a sympathetic hearing.
2. Take the complaint seriously.
3. Display concern.
4. Let the person completely talk out his gripe.
5. Repeat the complaint in the complainant's own words.
6. Agree with the complainant on exactly what is involved.

7. Immediately follow through by gathering necessary
   information.
8. Do everything possible to resolve the problem.

The diagnosis and solution of the grievance may be
quite obvious, or it may be hidden. It may be a simple misunderstanding, lack of information, personality clash, or poor
communications. If an immediate solution is not apparent, an
answer must be found as soon as possible, and the person
told exactly how and when this will be done. Then in the
shortest possible time, the department head must return with
the information and, if at all possible, a solution.

Whatever solution is eventually reached, it must be an
honest one. If it is temporary, if it is a compromise, even
if it is not the answer the complainant is obviously seeking,
he must be told exactly why it must be so. As long as it is
a considered and a fair solution, it will be accepted in the
spirit in which it is given.

If there is one group of individuals from whom the department head will receive a disproportionately large number
of complaints and problems (or so it may seem), it will be
the senior members of the department. The typist who has
been in the department "since the building was built" and the
cataloger who was cataloging books "before the boss was
born" are inevitably the ones who cause the department head
(and others in the department) the most concern. Too often
they will be suspicious of the department head; even worse,
the department head will be suspicious of them. These sus-
picions will surface in many ways. The department head may
accuse older staff members of using their seniority to gain
special privileges, of not giving their best to the department,
of constantly blocking progress, and of taking up too much
of his time in satisfying their whims. They, in turn, will accuse the department head of not knowing his job--and they
may be right.

Inevitably, such problems, both the real and the imagined ones, are at least partially the fault of the department
head. Is he unconsciously (or consciously) neglecting the
abilities of the senior staff? Is he taking their talents for
granted? If good staff relationships are to be maintained, the
library administration must give the senior members their fair
share of attention, and then some. No doubt many have been

around for a long time, and will probably be around long after their supervisors have moved on. More to the point, they have learned a good deal about department operations which they can and should share with others. To have an efficient department the worth of each member, old timers as well as young turks, must be recognized and utilized. The department head must insure that the experienced cataloger's abilities are put to maximum use; and also see that his sense of importance is not undermined.

To get the most out of his senior staff, the department head must therefore consider these points:

1. Remember that senior staff have information about the department and library not possessed by others. This information must be put to good use.

2. Think of the experienced staff as forming the backbone of the department. They can provide a continuity that every department needs to function smoothly.

3. Actively seek the advice of senior staff. Although the department head should not ask questions that obligate him to follow their advice, he can still do it in a way that shows he respects their opinions.

4. Form an "advisory council" made up of senior catalogers. While individually each may have certain shortcomings (as everyone does), collectively they represent many years of valuable experience and know-how.

5. Place each new cataloger under the wing of an experienced revisor. Even though the newcomer has had previous experience and the older employee is perhaps not as quick or up-to-date as might be desired, there is still a lot the experienced cataloger can pass on to the newcomer, including friendship.

6. Do not ignore complaints by older staff about their physical (or mental) discomforts. These are real discomforts, and the department head must consider them as such.

7. Do not neglect the senior members of the department in in-service training programs. Although some of the old-timers may claim that they know it all, they will still

appreciate being included in the latest automation seminar, since they like to be considered just as progressive as the younger members of the department.

Correcting Department Errors

No matter how well members of the department work as a team, they are still people, and people are imperfect. They make mistakes. This imperfection in cataloging staff (including the department head) is compounded by the very nature of the cataloging and classification operations. Not only do errors occur, but they are painfully obvious to everyone in the department, as well as to patrons, other departments, and the library director. Errors cannot be completely eliminated, but they can be sharply curtailed, and one of the chief responsibilities of the department head is to keep them at a minimum and prevent their recurrence once they are discovered. It may seem, in fact, that most of his time, and the time of other senior members of the department, will be spent in revising and correcting the work of others. But the question remains: when a goof is found, what should be done about it? If the department head expects to run a near error-free department he must not only sharply curtail errors, but must do it in a way that will improve future performance and encourage those responsible to work even harder. Too often, the department head feels awkward and unsure in his criticisms. Even more unfortunate, those criticized feel antagonistic and defensive when errors are brought to their attention, and consequently will not give of their best in the future. Criticizing a member of the department in a way that will both improve his performance and let him walk away satisfied is a difficult, but not impossible, task. Here, then, are a few basic rules to help the department head in his role as department critic:

1. Get all the facts before criticizing. If a reference librarian points out a drawer of filing errors in the public card catalog, the department head should not race off immediately to confront the new filer with the cards. He must discover the facts first. Have the cards been recently filed? Could the errors be the responsibility of more than one filer? What does the revisor have to say about them? What are the possible reasons for the misfiled cards? Was there a misunderstanding of the filing rules? Improper training? Carelessness

or just plain boredom? Lack of information nearly always results in over-reaction.

2. Criticize positively. The department head should
not simply drop the misfiled cards on the filer's desk with a
sarcastic note; he should point out the specific rules involved,
and show how the cards should be filed. With the rule book
in hand, he should explain exactly how the rules apply not
only to this situation but to others, and then suggest how the
filer might go about digesting the rules of the handbook. If
the supervisor always suggests concrete ways to avoid repeating mistakes, the person will make an honest effort to
improve.

3. Do not assume a superior attitude when criticizing
others. The department head need not remind a typist that
he knows a little more about cataloging rules than she does.
No matter what the situation, if the supervisor "talks down"
to a staff member, a barrier will develop.

4. Admit errors. This does not mean that the department head must automatically take the blame for every mistake that happens in the department. But if, for instance,
a filing error was at least partly the result of a poor inser-
vice training program, the department head should shoulder
at least some of the criticism. More importantly, he should
do something about it.

5. Remain calm. It may be difficult for the department head to keep his temper when confronted with a serious
cataloging error; but not only does losing control not correct
errors, it creates hostilities and thus defeats the main goal
of improving performance. Moreover, the person who cannot
control his temper has no business supervising a catalog department, or anything else for that matter. If necessary,
he should cool off before discussing the problem. If he assumes a reasonable attitude, so will the offender.

6. Always criticize in private. When a revisor catches
a cataloging error, it will only cause resentment to rush over
to the cataloger's desk loudly berating him for the goof.
Public ridicule may, in a few cases, prevent further mistakes
of the same type, but it also causes antagonisms that will
bring repercussions much worse than the original mistake. A
rule of thumb: praise in public, but criticize in private.

7. With every criticism include at least one sincere compliment. It is just as important to get a cataloger in a corrective frame-of-mind as it is to point out a specific mistake. Although he will probably sense he is being softened for a blow, he will still react better than if he is abruptly accused of a mistake. If comments are begun with a sincere compliment such as "You're doing real well in assigning call numbers, but ..." the department head is assuring the individual that the general quality of his work is satisfactory but a few lapses need to be watched and corrected.

8. In writing criticisms, follow-up with a verbal explanation. Naturally, if the revisor is checking the work of a new cataloger he cannot discuss each misplaced bracket blue-penciled on the catalog cards. But even here, the revisor should go over as many of the corrections as possible with the cataloger personally. Not only are misunderstandings cleared up more readily in a person-to-person contact, but the revisor can judge reactions and, more importantly, provide a friendly, understanding atmosphere not possible via comments scribbled on a catalog card.

The Credibility Gap

When actions do not accord with motives, there is a credibility gap. Gaps in credibility exist in politics, news media, and just about everywhere else, including catalog departments. The patron is confused about what he reads (or does not read) on the catalog card, the reference librarian is skeptical of the efforts of the cataloger, and the cataloger is often suspicious of the department head.

Department credibility involves, therefore, staff confidence in and trust of the department head. When there is a gap in credibility, the department head has lost contact with his staff. Members of the department are no longer functioning as a team but as a group of suspicious people, separated from each other and from their supervisor. Credibility is in doubt when the staff is suspicious of the department head's actions, skeptical of his motives, and mistrusts his words. When he shows either uncertainty or overconfidence in the face of a crisis, when the staff finds obvious discrepancies between his words and deeds, or when he relies on authority instead of example to achieve results, a credibility gap will arise.

One reason for a credibility gap is the department head's promising what he cannot or will not fulfill. Whether he deliberately uses words to conceal motives or is simply procrastinating, the results are the same: doubt and disbelief. Similarly, the "do as I say, not as I do" attitude will cause staff to doubt motives. If the department head insists on punctuality but habitually arrives late himself, he will have a credibility gap. If he enforces a rigid no-talking rule in the department but is himself a gossip, a credibility gap will result.

There are many less obvious circumstances that can lead to a loss of credibility. A discrepancy between the goals of certain staff members and those of the supervisor can cause frustrations and misunderstandings, and thus doubts in the minds of staff. While the department head's goals may center on cataloging one hundred titles this month, theirs may be fixed on the up-coming pay raises. Failure to recognize and reconcile conflicting goals will naturally cause gaps.

Both physical and psychological gaps can cause a loss in credibility. If the department head physically (or mentally) separates himself from his staff, he will soon find he has less contact, observation, and understanding of what is going on in the department. The more the contacts with staff the less the danger of misunderstandings.

The department head's preoccupation with his own problems, then, can separate him from his real responsibility-- the staff. Too many department heads bury themselves in paper work and meetings, thus losing contact with their departments. Emotions, too, can separate someone from reality. The anxious, fearful supervisor is too preoccupied with protecting himself to consider what is going on around him. The uncertain and frustrated person is too busy either fighting with or withdrawing from supposed antagonists to keep up with reality. The manipulator, too, will lose the respect of his staff.

Granted, credibility is often difficult to achieve. The very nature of the supervisor-supervised relationship will, from time to time, cause division, and thus a loss of credibility. Gaps are reduced not by following a magic formula but by simply using common sense. First of all, no matter what his style of leadership, the department head must be predictable and consistent, particularly in times of change and stress. Whether his approach to cataloging management is democratic or not, he must be honest, keep his commitments, never promise more than he can deliver, and not confuse action with accomplishment. He may think he is giving the impression of a dedicated, hard-working executive by sitting at his desk reading and re-reading junk mail, or by remaining after five o'clock to shuffle catalog cards--but he is not. Finally, to gain the trust and respect of others, the department head must give trust and respect. It the atmosphere in the department is one of mutual understanding, the department head will have a smoothly operating organizdtion where credibility is taken for granted.

Motivating Staff

The motivational theories of leading authorities in the behavioral sciences are complex and varied. Abraham H. Maslow, for example, rates human needs, considered by him and others as the basis for human motivation, hierarchically. He begins with physical needs and progresses to security needs, love needs, ego needs, and, finally, self-fulfillment needs. His theory states that the higher needs are difficult if not impossible to satisfy until the lower needs are satisfied. Thus when a lower need is satisfied, the next higher need emerges, and so on.

Frederick Herzberg divides motivation into two sets of factors: motivation factors and hygiene factors. The first group he considers high-level factors such as achievement, recognition, responsibility, and professional advancement, all of which concern work itself. The second group, which he calls dissatisfiers, includes job security, salary, company policy, working conditions and status. According to Herzberg, motivation factors, the most important of the two, must be present for job satisfaction, but the hygiene factors, though not directly motivating the employee, must also be present to prevent job dissatisfaction.

Chris Argyris sees the problem of motivation as the opposition between individual and organizational needs. The greater the discrepancy between these two needs, the more dissatisfied is the employee. He defines motivation, then, in terms of the way an individual reacts to this discrepancy.

Douglas McGregor, one of the most popular of the behavioral scientists, has evolved what he calls the Theory X and Theory Y concepts of motivation. He conceives the Theory X concept as the traditional managerial practice based on the premise that the employee inherently dislikes work, and will avoid it if he can. The employee must, therefore, be forced to work. McGregor's Theory Y concept, the progressive managerial theory, states that people do not inherently dislike work, and under proper conditions want to work. Thus under Theory Y, management must promote an environment (primarily through democratic leadership) that encourages the employee to achieve his own individual goals, which then will result in an achievement of the organization's goals.

Rensis Likert, an exponent of participative management, believes that motivation is based on the supervisor's ability to support his employees. To succeed, the supervisor must keep lines of communication open, take a genuine interest in his people, and at all times have complete confidence and trust in them.

Clearly, what these and other behavioral scientists are saying is that the traditional methods of motivating employees (most especially "fear") are no longer valid, if indeed they ever were. All writers in the field seem to agree that to motivate successfully, the employee's need for self-fulfillment must be satisfied, a truly difficult task. The head of a catalog department has only limited powers in determining such factors as library policy, working conditions, and salaries; but whatever powers he does have must be used to the fullest.

Job Satisfaction

Staff fulfillment and motivation depend a great deal on job satisfaction. Yet it is often difficult to determine just how satisfied a cataloger or other staff member really is. The problem of matching needs with satisfiers is complicated simply because we are dealing with such intangibles as feelings and emotions, and when these intangibles are hidden from the department head, as they usually are, it is doubly difficult. Even when the department head has the confidence of his staff, he can never be sure just how "satisfied" they really are.

Because job satisfaction is so subjective a matter, studies yield conflicting results. Perhaps the only valid generalization researchers agree upon is that people with similar backgrounds, education, and interests tend to seek the same benefits from their work. In other words, job satisfaction, morale, and motivation for the professional cataloger would, theoretically at least, be about the same as for other catalogers, yet quite different from those of a typist.

To keep attuned to job satisfaction, then, we must look to the individual, whatever his or her position. We must look behind the facade, look for signs and clues. More than likely these signs will center on one of four general areas: the department head, the work, the work group, and the conditions of employment.

The department head. A good relationship between the department head and his staff is vital to job satisfaction. If the typist feels that the supervisor is interested in her welfare and that he is truly someone to whom she can turn for help, she will be much more satisfied than if she feels alienation. That is to say, the department head must be employee-centered, not job-centered; he must manipulate situations, not people.

The work group. Relationships with co-workers are also important to job satisfaction. Generally speaking, the more status and recognition a cataloger or other staff member gains from his group the more secure and the more satisfied he will feel. Everyone needs to feel a part of his working group. A cataloger not accepted by his peers (either in or outside the department) will, in turn, not accept or identify with them.

The job. Certainly the nature of the work will determine, to a very great extent, job satisfaction. Although it is unrealistic to assume that everyone must feel (or needs to feel) that his work is interesting and a challenge, the department head must at least work toward this goal. He does this by varying work assignments, properly using the individual's abilities, delegating authority, and avoiding, as much as possible, monotonous and tedious assignments. Two additional points: everyone needs to feel he has at least some control over his work; secondly, everyone wants to feel successful in his work, whether he classifies maps, files catalog cards, or inputs records on a terminal.

Working conditions. Related to the work itself are the working environment and the conditions of work. The department setting, salary, hours of work, and job security are very real factors that will either detract from or contribute to job satisfaction. No matter how satisfied a cataloger may be in his work assignment, a feeling of insecurity, justified or not, will color his outlook. Unfortunately, many conditions related to the work are completely out of the hands of the department head and his staff. A clerk may try to do something about a broken typewriter, but if funds are unavailable for repairs, she will not get far. Or, the department head may try his best to make the filing routines more interesting and challenging, but filing is just not that appealing to most people. The point is that everyone in the department must at least try to improve working conditions, and if they are trying, conditions will indeed improve--at least a little.

Chapter 7

RESEARCH AND DEVELOPMENT

The cataloging and classification of library materials is essentially the organization of knowledge, a process basic to all
disciplines. The results of this organization--catalogs, indexes, bibliographies, and similar tools--are the key to research in all fields. The cataloger is, in fact, responsible
for the most complex tool of all--the card catalog. To prepare this and other tools adequately, those responsible must
be expert in the principles of both bibliographic organization
and subject analysis. Catalogers know, perhaps better than
anyone else, the access routes to specific areas of knowledge.
Why, then, should not the cataloger, the one person who understands the practical and theoretical organization of our
heritage, participate actively in the quest for and the recording of this heritage?

Like the college professor whose teaching grows out of
his research and whose research grows out of his teaching,
the cataloger's library duties and research activities can and
should complement each other. Rare books, microfilms, periodicals, pamphlets, and special materials of all sorts pass
through his hands. He examines, studies, and literally lives
with resources that others locate through painstaking searches.
From his position in the library, he can spot a problem that
requires study, a new subject relationship, a need for a new
bibliographic tool, or an application of a new manual or automated technique to the problem of bibliographic control.

The practicing cataloger is, more than anyone else,
aware of the bibliographic problems that confront him. Library school faculty, library administrators, and Ph.D.'s in
other disciplines who now perform much of the bibliographic
research are too far removed from the realities of working

librarianship to appreciate the problems and needs, and this is evident in the research they produce. No matter how much formal education or how much research experience a person has, unless he has actually worked in a field, all he can really understand are the broad philosophical and historical implications, not the day-to-day practical problems that so desperately need study. Also, the cataloger's subject knowledge is usually broader than that of the university professor, and he can thus introduce a new dimension to what have too often been specialized and too minute emphases in past bibliographic studies. Research, and institutional research in particular, must become the domain of the practitioner as well as the theorist. Any cataloger who cares to accept the challenge will find unlimited possibilities.

The cataloger may be eager to produce research and the library administrator willing to encourage staff research, but there are problems to be overcome. Where does the over-worked cataloger find the necessary time? Administrators, no matter how commendable their intentions, are reluctant to allow compensatory time; and catalogers are reluctant to do research (library-related or otherwise) after hours. Even academic librarians, who are expected to emulate their teaching colleagues in research and publication, complain of lack of time. Even more unfortunate, few catalogers are either research-oriented or research-trained. In library school little if any class time is allotted to training in research techniques. Although the term paper and graduate thesis may provide the prospective cataloger with a brief introduction to the mechanics of research, more often than not it also instills a life-long student syndrome. In most graduate schools, students are not only assigned their topics, but the methods of operation and desired formats must be rigidly adhered to. Understandably, the results of post-graduate research are not dissimilar to the typical graduate paper.

Another problem found in many libraries is that research on specific library problems too often prolongs rather than accelerates decisions. The process of information gathering, examination of alternatives, and evolution of a decision takes much more time than the usual quick and easy, off-the-top-of-the-head decision. The need for quick decisions on complex cataloging problems has often forced librarians to settle for short-term decisions at the expense of long-term planning.

Perhaps an even more basic problem is that findings and decisions of research studies are only temporary. This is a fact which most librarians find difficult to accept. It is, indeed, frustrating for the cataloger who has thoroughly researched a subject and subsequently evolved a workable solution to find, a year or so later, that the entire question must be re-studied.

Still another problem is standardization. In undertaking research projects, particularly those involving inter-institutional cooperation, librarians invariably face the question of establishing a set of workable definitions. This is most evident in problems dealing with the accumulation and interpretation of library statistics. A simple request from a government agency for the number of volumes cataloged throws many libraries into confusion. In the volume count, how are pamphlets and other unbound items, government documents, music scores, or volume-equivalencies reported?

Individual Research

Institutional research--sometimes defined as defensive research done when one is attacked by a problem--is unquestionably vital to any growing catalog department. But just as vital to the individual, to the profession, and even to the department is the personal research conducted by catalogers who search out projects on their own. This research can be applied, as is most institutional research, or it can be theoretical. In either case, the cataloger will find an unlimited number of topics. He can investigate the historical, theoretical, or practical approaches to the organization of knowledge; he can perform research in his subject field; or he can carry out research that supports other disciplines. This latter category, which we normally associate with librarianship, would include compiling bibliographies, indexing journals, constructing thesauri, and developing research tools.

Specifically, here are a few research ideas available to catalogers. Some are suitable for institutional projects, others for personal research, most for both.

1. Study the use of the card catalog or other library tool. How do patrons approach the card catalog? What can be done to improve its use?

2. Investigate card reproduction methods. What are the unit costs for each type of card reproduction equipment? Which is best for the library?

3. Index a local newspaper or periodical. Are there serials, reports, or other publications to which the library presently has no access? Would an index be of use to the library? To other libraries?

4. Research the pros and cons of centralized processing. Should the library establish a centralized processing service for libraries in the area? Would it benefit by joining an already established center or network?

5. Study the need for a union catalog. Should the city or region set up a union catalog--book or card? Would it be better to send catalog cards to an already existing union catalog or bibliographic center?

6. Investigate the unit costs of processing different types of materials: books (with and without LC copy), serials, documents, phonorecords, and so on. How much money will the library save by classifying U.S. Government documents by Superintendent of Documents numbering system instead of cataloging and classifying by LC or Dewey?

7. Develop a new working tool for the department. Do catalogers need a dictionary of some sort, a compilation of catalog card notes, a new chapter in the department manual?

8. Prepare a bibliography. Would a bibliography on water pollution or a listing of the library's phonorecord holdings help users?

9. Construct a thesaurus of words used in two or more indexing or abstracting services. Is there a need in the library for a standard authority list which will aid the researcher in locating related materials in more than one indexing or abstracting source?

10. Prepare a report on a significant development in the department. Is there a new technique, routine, or type of equipment that should be reported to a neighboring library, state convention, or national journal?

11. Test a new in-service training program for clerks. Have a control group learn under the old method and another group under the new program.

12. Prepare a subject heading list. Is there a patron-group that would appreciate a list of subject headings used in the card catalog on a certain topic?

13. Conduct a bibliographic search. Would users want a brief explanation with an annotated bibliography on local zoning laws or other current topic?

14. Visit other libraries in the area. Would the department benefit from a visit and a subsequent report on how other libraries are staffing their CRT terminals, coping with their backlogs, cataloging their nonbooks, or processing their government publications?

15. Investigate the costs of establishing and maintaining different forms of catalogs. Should the library produce a book catalog, or switch to a COM catalog?

16. Write a publication on how to use the card catalog. Would a short explanation on how to use the public card catalog and other of the library's bibliographic tools help patrons?

17. Index a collection of special materials in the library. Has the library received a gift collection of archival materials to which there is no access?

18. Perform a literature search. Peruse the literature for information on how other institutions are answering the concerns of employees who work with video display terminals. What are other libraries doing to help eliminate the eye discomfort and back aches that terminal operators are beginning to complain about? Do the terminals pose a radiation threat to users, as some of the operators in the department fear? If not, what documentation can be found that will alleviate such fears?

As is evident in the listing above, research need not be limited to published reports. A bibliography that helps library patrons find books on a subject can be just as important as a national survey on the same subject. And this kind of research can best be performed by someone familiar with local resources, bibliographic control methods, and patron needs. The point is that any research that improves library services, solves a local problem, or informs patrons is legitimate. If it also relates to a national problem, so much the better.

There are still other activities (perhaps more properly called services rather than research projects) which members of the catalog department can support. For example, catalogers with foreign language abilities might assist patrons in translating journal articles, passages in books, even personal letters. If long translations are involved the service could be placed on a fee basis. Such bibliographic services are proper activities for any catalog department. Reference librarians already serve the public in this way; so can catalogers. Or, a local business may have a small collection of books or documents that needs organizing. Although the company could not afford a full-time professional librarian to oversee the collection, a few hours of counseling, and even some help in establishing the cataloging and classification procedures, would be a real service. The department might even provide a brief training program in basic cataloging for one of the company's secretaries, a service that might mean the difference between a pile of unusable documents and a working collection. Research projects, consulting services, training programs, seminars, and cooperative processing services should be natural byproducts of catalog department activities.

Of course, every cataloger cannot be expected to be continually engaged in major research or service projects. But if encouraged, professionals can compile bibliographies and help gather statistics. At the very least, staff should be urged, while performing their normal duties, to consider alternative ways of performing day-to-day routines. Research need not be a major contribution to the literature to be significant; raw data for use either by others in the library or by a faculty member in some far-off library school are well worth gathering. A major concern among researchers is the lack of such raw data in the form of simple records and statistics.

Selecting a Project

Selecting a research project is not easy; if it is to yield results, the research and researcher must be compatible. A project that suits one cataloger may not suit another. Likewise, a problem that relates to one library may have little meaning to another. To be successful, the research, whether individual or institutional, must fulfill five basic criteria.

1. Is there a need? The first and most obvious criterion is that there be a purpose. In other words, is the research worth doing? Put even more simply--who cares? Unless the problem is a real one, time should not be wasted in solving it.

2. Is the problem solvable? For some problems there are no workable solutions. Sometimes this will not be apparent until the project is well underway. But more often than not, if a solution is available, it will become apparent with study.

3. Are there enough time and resources available to carry the research to its conclusion? More to the point, are the library and the individual willing to spend the time and resources necessary to complete the project? The only way to guarantee success is to set aside a specific time (one or two hours a day, Saturday mornings, or whenever) for the project. A reasonable schedule should be established and followed.

4. Is the librarian qualified to conduct the research? Is he, above all the others in the library, in the school system, or in the company, the individual best qualified to carry out this research? To find the cure for the common cold is a worthwhile research project--there is certainly a need and, we must assume, a solution--but chances are no one in the catalog department will be qualified to undertake it. On the other hand, compiling a bibliography on the common cold could be an excellent undertaking for almost any librarian.

5. How significant is the research? Although most research will concern local problems, to be really significant it should have implications for others. At the very least, the researcher should consider sharing the results with patrons or other institutions in the area.

The Research Report

The ideal research report is impossible to describe. It will vary depending on the nature of the project, the findings, and the audience. A bibliography compiled for library users will obviously have an entirely different format from a report to fellow librarians on how to compile library bibliographies. But there are a few common-sense guidelines that should be followed no matter how simply or how elaborate the research. First of all, the report should be readable and to-the-point, even if this means deleting some of the data. Too many researchers feel that to impress the readers they must include all the facts they can lay their hands on. A bibliography need not include all possible citations, nor should an annual report cover all possible events of the year. If a long report is unavoidable, it should also include a short summary or cover letter explaining the findings as concisely as possible.

In writing the report, the audience should be kept in mind. The report should actually be aimed toward a specific reader. A committee report for the library director, for example, should be written specifically for him, not for the library world at large. If the report has state or national significance, then it must be re-edited for the new audience. Another important point to consider: librarians must be as aware as politicians of conflicts of interest. A report on the efficiency of the catalog department will not be taken seriously if it is simply a device to make the department look good. Finally, the report should not end with the obvious statement that there is a need for further research on the subject. What the writer is saying is that the report is inconclusive and that, therefore, no action need be taken. If there is any doubt as to exactly what course to take, some alternative interpretations, indicating how they relate to the evidence, should be provided.

Encouraging Research

What can the library administration do to encourage research?

1. Create a research atmosphere. If research is not encouraged in the library or in the department, none will be produced.
2. Provide the necessary resources. Professionals should be allowed released-time from assigned duties, and, if necessary, the library should provide an emergency staff that can substitute for catalogers engaged in research. Clerical assistance should be provided, and publication outlets sought.
3. Take notes on needed projects. Clearly the best

source of research needs is the day-to-day problems encountered in the department. When a problem is discovered it should be noted and passed on
to a research-minded cataloger.

4. In the department's recruiting program professionals should be sought who, if not trained in research, are at least sympathetic toward it. The
willingness to engage in research is more important
than a research background.

5. All professional positions should be truly professional. If there is slack time in a cataloger's
duties, he should not be assigned clerical work (unless, of course, that is all he can handle); instead,
he should be steered toward a special project.

6. Members of the department should be encouraged
to prepare themselves for research through formal
course work and informal reading. Through professional study, subject specialization, and research
methodology courses, the cataloger should keep
abreast of research trends and projects both in library science and his subject field.

Mining for Ideas

Perhaps even more important to the development of the
catalog department than research are ideas. Every research
project must, in fact, start with an idea. But good ideas produce other things besides reports, proposals, statistics, and
bibliographies. An idea can result in a change in a marking
procedure, a different card duplication technique, a more logical assignment, or an entirely new set of job-streams. And
like worthwhile research projects, the best ideas come not
from library school professors or even library administrators,
but from the working staff. For whether administrators will
admit it or not, staff members know their specific jobs better
than anyone else. The cataloger, the terminal operator, the
filer, each is experienced and knowledgeable in at least one
aspect of the department's operation. Yet seldom does the
department head tap this resource of in-house experts. Many
department heads seem to think that just because they head
departments they also are the sole possessors of bright ideas.
Not so. Those who do the actual cataloging can also do the
actual thinking, if they are only encouraged. Granted, staff
members will come up with some pretty worthless suggestions,

as the department head often does. But those who do the work are often in the best position to suggest improvements.

The department head must, therefore, encourage ideas, a practice which is not as easy as it sounds. Too many catalogers are willing to accept the status quo; others are just too lazy to think creatively, a process which does take energy. Still others lack self-confidence; they feel they could not possibly have what it takes to think of anything worthwhile or are afraid that the department head will ridicule their suggestions. These fears are real and must be overcome.

The first step, then, is to encourage staff to start thinking--thinking creatively. Some members may already be feeding in ideas, but others may have ideas to submit but, for whatever reason, have not done so. The department head must let everyone know that he is not only open to staff suggestions but that he is actively seeking them. If necessary, he must be specific. He must ask how to prevent cataloging backlogs, why duplicate cards are appearing in the card catalog, what is causing card stock wastage, whether or not morale is slipping, or how to combat whatever else is currently plaguing the department.

When the ideas start rolling in, each must be carefully considered. Many will be pretty bad; but that is to be expected. Any idea that does not measure up should be given back to the originator with a careful explanation of why it will not work. If it has merit at all but is not thought through, the submitter should be asked to re-cast and resubmit it. And he should be encouraged to keep submitting. The next suggestion may be just what the department has been looking for.

At any rate, the department head must not reject a recommendation out of hand. No matter how radical or how unusable it may seem, it should be thoroughly investigated. An idea that seems weak at first can develop into something really productive. Nor should the department head let prejudice toward an individual or toward the way an idea is submitted cause him to reject it. He must listen carefully to everything submitted and appraise each as potentially usable. The submission of a new idea is, at the very least, a signal that at least one person in the department thinks an old one is not working.

If the idea turns out to be worthwhile, it should be followed up immediately. It need not be put into action the day it is received, but someone should at least start working out the details. As the plan unfolds, the staff member who submitted it should be kept informed on the progress. In this way he will know his suggestion is being taken seriously, and that the department head wants more. It is also important to give proper credit. To show appreciation for a good suggestion, if only by way of a "thank you," will not only reward the person, but will encourage others to try a little harder.

Is It a Good Idea?

How does the department head know whether an idea is a good one? How does he know that a bright idea from a bright young cataloger is really a solution to a perplexing problem or perhaps the basis for a research project? He really does not know--that is, until it is tested. An idea is really only a possibility until it is given an opportunity to nurture, to grow, to work.

Questions asked of any idea are: Will it work? Does it yield the desired results? Is this the time to put it into operation? Finally, exactly what will it improve? For to be really worthwhile, the idea must improve one or more conditions. It must improve quality, working conditions, output, use of staff, operations, or equipment. Above all, it must improve cost-efficiency. Some ideas may be good in the abstract, but when put into practice, prove to be of little or no value. And often, a new idea which results in an improvement in one area, detracts from another. By way of elaboration, here are the areas any well-meaning idea can--and should--improve.

1. Increase quality: Some of the ideas received will be aimed at increasing the quality of either output or individual performance. The department head must, however, make sure that any proposal to improve quality does represent an improvement. For instance, a suggestion to purchase heat-sealing book labels which are more secure than the ones used now might, indeed, result in a better quality label. Yet, if the library's book labels are generated by a computer which cannot handle pressure-sensitive materials, the recommendation

will have to be discarded or the labels and the heating device will have to be applied manually at added expense.

2. Increase production: Ideas for increasing productivity will range from a simple suggestion to Xerox six instead of four catalog cards at a time to a detailed recommendation for complete automation of the catalog department. Production recommendations are among the most frequent, yet most complex, the department head will be asked to consider. More often than not, an idea to increase cataloging output also involves more money or more people. But any suggestion that may possibly allow a cataloger or a clerk to accomplish more in less time should be welcomed.

3. Improve use of staff: Closely related to ideas that improve production are those that improve use of department manpower. Recommendations aimed at the improved use of staff will usually increase cataloging production. For this reason, staff should be encouraged continually to examine manpower use. Which jobs should be handled by clerks and which by professionals? Are the filing duties large enough to establish a separate section? Perhaps reference personnel should be in charge of filing into the public catalog? They are constantly using the catalog and could learn a good deal about locating items if they also had to do the filing.

4. Improve working conditions: Many ideas will have to do with library surroundings. Most will be brushed aside as complaints: "I can't work with all this noise." "I can't stand the glare from the computer terminals." "It's too hot in here." "I can only type on an electric typewriter." The department head must be careful, though. What on the surface may appear to be gripes, may nevertheless be the germ of a bona fide idea. An investigation into a clerk's insistence that she must have an electric typewriter may reveal that, in spite of the added expense, electric typewriters will improve the speed and output of all typists.

5. Improve methods and techniques of operation: A cataloger may suggest assigning all nonbooks, regardless of format or subject, to one cataloger instead of dividing them by subject as the department is now doing. Would this improve the overall operation of the department? Perhaps. In any case, all arguments must be examined. While the cataloger would become quite proficient in processing various

nonbooks, he would also need a good understanding of various subject fields as represented by music recordings, incunabula or microfilm, and scientific materials on microfiche.

6. <u>Improve equipment</u>: Here again, ideas can range from a more efficient method of holding an electric eraser to a recommendation to install the latest generation computer. The former is certainly the type the department head will most often hear, and over which he will have at least some jurisdiction. If he does not have the authority to make a decision on a specific suggestion, he should pass it along to someone who does. Ideas for new and more efficient uses of equipment often involve more than one department. Instead of buying a special sign-making machine for the circulation department, someone might suggest that the catalog department's marking typewriter be used. While this may not benefit the catalog department directly, it could provide a more efficient use of equipment for the library as a whole.

7. <u>Cost-cutting</u>: Most ideas, if they have any validity at all, will result not only in increased output, improved quality, and more efficient use of manpower and equipment, but in lower costs. This is really the name of the game. No matter how imaginative, innovative, or efficient a recommendation may be, unless it results in eventual savings--that is, doing more for less money--it will be difficult to sell to the library administration. Conversely, if it can be proven that an idea will save money, it will be given serious consideration--and will probably be adopted.

Chapter 8

ORGANIZATIONAL GROWTH

To forecast accurately how a particular catalog department will look five, ten, or more years from now, everything that could possibly affect its operation must be considered. Certainly there will be technological changes. No doubt the needs of users will also change. There may even be a sudden rise or drop in funding. There may be organizational changes too. A new director, for example, might impose on his staff a completely different managerial philosophy from that previously employed, and as a result add or subtract various functions. It may be impossible to predict accurately what the next few years will bring to a catalog department in any given library, but this does not mean that the department head should not prepare for the future. He may not know specifically when, why, or to what extent his department will change, but he does know it will change.

One way to prepare for the future, whether in times of change or relative stability, is through the continuing analysis of contemporary organizational theories. Granted, theory is sometimes difficult to relate to day-to-day practice, difficult in librarianship as in all fields. Yet even the most practical-minded department head can learn something through this approach. If nothing else, he will identify a few possible ways of structuring or re-structuring his department.

Organizational Groupings

Libraries have grouped cataloging activities in certain traditional ways. Because these groupings are traditional and because they seem to have worked tolerably well for local cataloging needs, little if any thought is ever given to the rationale behind them. The fact is, librarians have always considered the theory of organizational grouping of little practical concern. Even when bottlenecks appear, it seldom occurs to anyone that there might be basic structural flaws in the department's organization. This complacency is bound to be shaken as libraries add new manual and automated techniques which are no longer adaptable to traditional flow-patterns. Centralized processing, networking, and the need to process new and as yet unknown materials will undoubtedly force department heads to look to different combinations of groupings. The head of the catalog department must continually examine and test alternative solutions. At the very least, before a new section is added, a new job-stream developed, or the department reorganized, all possible groupings should be considered, including the following:

By material or service. In most departments at least some duties and responsibilities are divided by material. For example, books are generally assigned to catalogers by subject or type of material, with one cataloger processing all serials, another all music scores, and perhaps another all microforms. A few larger catalog departments divide their cataloging operations by teams of catalogers and support staff. One team will catalog all English language books, another all music scores, another all serials, and so on. In this way the department head takes advantage of the specialized knowledge and skills of the staff, and can more effectively coordinate related operations. Likewise, the department head might group together all activities associated with a particular service. A typing pool that processes all department catalog cards, forms, and correspondence is a good example. The division by service is particularly efficient when equipment such as typewriters or CRT terminals are concentrated in one area.

But there are disadvantages to material and service departmentalization. For one thing, it encourages the duplication of certain operations. Each cataloger, for example, is performing the same cataloging and classification functions as every other cataloger. In addition, there is a danger that catalogers will make decisions without regard to the central administration of the department and without understanding how their decisions will affect other department activities.

By staff specialization. Division by staff specialty is one of the most popular grouping techniques. It is similar to division by material, except that the emphasis is on the individual not the material being processed. Actually, most catalog departments prefer to focus on the cataloger's subject, language, or other specialty rather than on the material itself. Catalogers naturally feel at home in areas with which they have both competence and confidence.

By user. The division of activities by user is evident in departments where catalogers process materials used by special patron-groups (children, for instance). Division by patron-group, like division by product, allows the department head to focus on specialized knowledge of staff members, and, more importantly, allows staff to relate their activities closely to the needs of patrons. However, the pressure to cater to a special group often results in favoritism. While the changing needs of each patron-group is perhaps better served by the user division, it is sometimes difficult to coordinate activities with other sections and departments. If activities are divided by user, the department head must be aware of and make allowances for fluctuations and inconsistencies.

By location. If the library operation is spread over a school district, university campus, or city system at least some department activities will be delegated to branch or department libraries. Even within the main library building certain activities may be assigned by location. For example, the responsibility of filing catalog cards will probably be delegated to department or branch librarians instead of to the central catalog department. It is much more convenient if clerks do not have to travel up a flight of stairs or across town to file their cards. If performed locally such activities are more economically controlled and better adapted to local needs and conditions. Moreover, by dividing activities such as filing cards by location the library will greatly reduce the problem of sharing or even duplicating supervisory responsibilities between the catalog department and the branch librarian.

Much of the cataloging itself can be done in a branch or department library. If there is no one in the catalog department with the music background necessary to catalog phonorecords or music scores, the music library may have to do the processing. Or perhaps the music cataloger will be located in the music library to be close to his tools and materials. Drawbacks of geographic departmentation are that it requires the training of more people in certain skills, increases the difficulty of standardization, and encourages duplication of certain services and resources.

By system or channel. Closely related to division by location is the division by the method in which materials reach the user. Instead of emphasizing the geographic location, consideration is on the channel through which the materials flow. Specifically, then, it is not the fact that a branch is located five or ten miles from the main building that determines the division of labor and responsibility, but that it represents an identifiable means of reaching patrons. Whether books are channeled through interlibrary loan, bookmobile, branch library, or other identifiable system would, therefore, determine the division of labor. However, this concept, while applicable to certain library operations, has not as yet been a real factor in the division of cataloging responsibilities.

By time. The department head may want to assign certain cataloging operations such as filing catalog cards to students or clerks who work those hours in the day when the public catalog is not heavily used. The division of duties by time became popular in industry during World War II when defense plants were open 24 hours, some jobs being best performed at night, others during the day. This concept is being followed today in many automated library systems where certain computer operations are performed during the day and others (usually the longer and more straightforward runs) are carried out at night. Division by time is also evident in circulation and reference departments where duties such as shelving books are best performed by staff who work specific day or evening hours.

By process or equipment. Still another possible division is by process or equipment. Generally clerks who operate unique types of equipment such as labeling machines or computer terminals are grouped together. Thus the marking clerk will be responsible for all library labeling regardless of the nature of the material or the point of origin. The main advantage of concentrating a process or type of equipment in one area is performance efficiency. A specific operation by specialized staff under the supervision of one person using the same facilities and equipment is generally considered a highly efficient method of grouping work. Most libraries, for example, departmentalize their EDP equipment. Instead of

separate computers and in-put equipment for the acquisition
department, circulation department, serials department, and
catalog department, all processing, and most especially the
equipment, will be centered in one operational area. In some
cases, a library will even share equipment with other municipal, campus, or company groups.

By function. A glance at most organizational charts
will show that libraries often divide and sub-divide their departments by function. Functional departmentation is considered a logical arrangement by both administration and staff.
The main advantage of grouping by function is that it brings
together specialized knowledge needed for a particular activity. In larger libraries, for example, certain catalogers will
assign subject headings, others will do descriptive cataloging,
and still others will classify materials.

Unfortunately, division by function, which often divides
organizations into very specialized units, encourages staff to
concentrate on their own interests, disregarding department
needs and, in many instances, the goals of the library as a
whole. The larger the library the more the tendency for
functional grouping and the more the danger that staff members performing these functions will put their own interests
above those of other departments. Like other grouping methods, departmentation by function is really not as clear-cut a
separation as may appear on an organizational chart. What
can be easily defined and separated as searching, original
cataloging, and LC cataloging functions often results in a
good deal of overlapping.

By number. Departmental grouping by numbers is an
elementary method based on the concept of span of authority.
It states that no one can supervise more than a certain number of people. Dividing library operations by number, while
a fundamentally valid concept, does not, however, really affect most cataloging operations. This grouping is perhaps
most apparent in circulation activities where, to be effective,
large numbers of student shelvers must be divided into several small workgroups.

By taskforce. Although the taskforce is in itself relatively new, the concept of establishing a temporary unit to
meet a sudden and unforeseen need has been common in business and industry for some time. The temporary unit, usually

based on a product-oriented division of labor, is established
on the understanding that it will be disbanded when the project is completed. Although catalog departments will be using
the taskforce concept more and more in the future (for example, a temporary re-classification team), its primary use today
is for problem solving. Staff members are appointed to form
a taskforce, usually part-time and always temporary, to investigate and make recommendations on solutions to a specific
problem. The taskforce defines the problem, gathers information, investigates possible solutions, makes recommendations,
and disbands.

Although the above grouping techniques are all theoretically sound, in actual practice it is not that easy. Work
assignments, flow-patterns, and supervisory responsibilities
cannot always be segregated into logical, identifiable units;
and arbitrary decisions to divide a department into neat and
equal parts simply will not work. Individual abilities, eco-
nomics, uncertain department growth, and even personality
conflicts will dictate department organization as much as careful, logical planning. A sudden influx of materials into the
department can throw well-defined flow-patterns out of balance;
consideration for the loyalty of a cataloger may cause the department head to create a special niche instead of recommend-
ing dismissal; and a cataloger's motivations and interests may
determine his assignment even more than his skills or the department head's determination to fit him into a particular
work assignment. A cataloger who is not up to a particular
assignment may be, even with his limitations, the best person
available for the slot. The department head must, therefore,
distribute some of his work to others, or even give him several
unrelated duties he can handle. The result is a somewhat il-
logical distribution of work. There may be another cataloger
who is good at two or three unrelated assignments. Perhaps
he has a strong engineering background, reads Russian, and
is an amateur musician. Should he catalog Russian literature
and phonorecords, as well as scientific serials? The department head would probably do better to use this person's abilities to the utmost than to slavishly follow a preconceived, although quite logical, organizational chart. The organization
of a catalog department is, therefore, a matter of compromise.

But no matter how loosely structured the department,
it is important to establish boundaries between groupings. Uncertainty as to which section or individual is responsible for a

certain task can cause confusion that nullifies even the most apparently logical subdivision. Also important are possible inter- and intra-department conflicts. To establish responsibilities without regard for staff morale is dangerous. Another consideration is the formal versus informal organization. No matter how the department head conceives of the department's formal organization, he must also give some thought to its "informal" structure, that is to say, the changes and modifications in department policy and routines that catalogers and others make daily. These modifications must be taken seriously, not because they contradict established policy and must be stopped, but because they may actually be improvements over those officially prescribed. The department head must not block such deviations if he wants an efficient department. Many catalogers are ingenious in making a department work effectively in spite of cumbersome, outdated procedures. Granted, the informal organization can also harm a department operation. Catalogers have been known to develop their own procedures simply to cover errors, to make work easier for themselves, and for many other reasons which are not necessarily beneficial to the library. The department head must be aware of subtle changes in the department's operation, and either officially incorporate them or eliminate them.

Perhaps most importantly, organizing a department into a preconceived package must not be an end in itself. What is important is to accomplish department objectives as efficiently as possible without regard for how it looks on paper or whether categories conflict. The department head must constantly look to the future, of course. Changes in the relative importance of certain activities will require frequent changes in organizational groupings. A certain division of labor will not last forever. The department head must reserve the right to change, not for the sake of change but for a more effective use of department resources.

Department Structure

How is the soundness of a department to be judged? How does the department head know when the department needs restructuring? To get an idea of the relative health of a catalog department, the following questions should be asked--and answered:

1. Is the department accomplishing its objectives? From time to time, the department head should analyze the operation to discover just how effective it really is.

2. Is the structure of the department properly balanced? Although it is difficult, if not impossible, to achieve a perfectly balanced organization, proportion should be kept in mind when analyzing department needs.

3. Are the resources--personnel, equipment, time, finances--being used as efficiently as possible? The department must not only be properly staffed and equipped but these resources must be used to their fullest.

4. Is there adequate control over records, procedures, and standards? To maintain a sound department, accurate checks must be kept on performance.

5. Are work assignments divided into as small a number of dissimilar functions as possible? To control department operations adequately, tasks should be isolated and subdivided into identifiable units.

6. Are materials flowing through the department in a logical and efficient manner? From time to time, bottlenecks will occur, but they should not be the result of inherent flaws in the organization.

7. Has the scope of authority and responsibility of each departmental position been defined? To establish a position and not define the degree of responsibility involved will eventually lead to frustration and misunderstandings.

8. Is the department chain of command clearly established? Everyone must understand where he or she stands in the formal communications hierarchy.

9. Beyond this, are all channels of communication, both formal and informal, clearly identified? Everyone in the department should have access to everyone else.

10. Is there feedback in the department? To find out whether a department is accomplishing its objectives, there must be an active two-way communications network.

11. Are there opportunities for staff members to improve themselves, both for personal betterment and to fulfill library needs? There must be a chance for advancement and for continuing education. And there must be an active replacement program.

12. How is department morale? Poor morale is the
first sign of a poorly organized department.

The Future

How will the catalog department of the future be organized? Looking at the present accelerated pace of library
development, we can make one significant assumption. In
the catalog department of the future, as in all other areas
of the library (and our society), the key word will be "temporary." To survive, catalog departments will have to continually accommodate new materials, processing systems, technological advances, and managerial concepts. The department
of the future will be problem-oriented. It must, for example,
be able to switch from a functionalized structure to one based
on staff specialization, and then back again, depending on
circumstances. There will continue to be shifts in conventional groupings and a merging of responsibilities. Staff members
will form taskforces and project groups to move from one unit
to another to solve problems, organize operations, and process
materials. Dual and multiple assignments will become common-
place. Libraries will rely on temporary systems and groupings, and staff will be used anywhere in the library that
their talents are required. Paraprofessionals will replace professional librarians in many positions, and machines will take
over many of the routine duties previously performed by support staff. Employees will be differentiated less by rank and
status and more by skills and training. Emphasis will be not
so much on positions as on getting the job done.

There will be greater opportunity for creativity and less
emphasis on routines. Staff will have more opportunities to
influence the duties they perform and will have greater control over their development in the department. There will be
increasingly more room for honest differences in judgments
and opinions, more give and take, and more openness in employee relations. Because of the growing need for collabora-
tion in complex tasks, skills in human interrelations will be
essential at all levels. The department head will become more
of a "coordinator" and "communication link" and less of a
"boss." Much of his work will be in getting staff to work effectively in a department characterized by continuous change
and flexibility. He will need to possess the skills necessary
to coordinate activities, individuals, and groups. The con-

tinuing growth of centralized processing centers will affect the structure of every library's cataloging operation. Where centralization does not answer local needs, networks and consortia will continue to emerge and merge. With advances in computer technology and telecommunications, access points to library collections will extend outside the library to include computer terminals in shopping malls, business centers, college campuses, and other public places. Patrons will someday be able to obtain library services at home, in the office, and in the classroom.

Essential to the catalog department of the future will be the ability to make changes quickly and effectively. The department head formerly had ample time for long-range planning and for implementing new policies and procedures. Likewise, staff could take months, perhaps years, adjusting to a switch in a routine or to a policy change. Not so in the future. Much of the department head's time will be directed toward adapting and helping others adapt. Alvin Toffler coined the term "future shock" to describe the impact of change on people. This shock is as real in the catalog department as it is in every other sector of our society. Planning for and adapting to change will become an essential preoccupation for every librarian. The accelerated rate of change in catalog departments will put more emphasis on innovation and focus more frequently on problem-solving processes. Change, called by writers on management "the central theme of our society" and "the metaphysic of our age," will eventually produce a new kind of catalog department whose survival will depend on its ability to adapt to innovation.

Change and How to Sell It

One of the major managerial responsibilities of the department head will be to plan, initiate, and anticipate change, and when change does occur to introduce--or, to put it bluntly, to sell--it to others. When a change occurs, therefore, the following points should be considered:

1. Carefully plan the change. Unless staff members realize that the change has been carefully researched and is being deliberately executed, they will hesitate to give it their wholehearted support.

2. Introduce the change as an experiment. If a change is presented as a kind of research project in which the department head expects staff to provide feedback, he will be more successful than if he announces an arbitrary decision. This is not only the most diplomatic approach, it is the most practical. Feedback from staff will help de-bug the scheme.

3. No matter how convinced of success, do not force change on the department. If the department head pushes too hard his people will automatically resist.

4. Present changes one at a time. If several changes are to be initiated, it is best to assimilate one before embarking on another. The successful outcome of the first will make the others more acceptable.

5. Be sure that all members of the department clearly understand the change. A careful explanation of exactly what is involved will squash rumors, avoid misunderstandings, and keep morale high during the changeover. A cursory explanation of what may be an important event in a person's working life can be very deflating.

6. Assure each person involved that the proposed change will not adversely affect his security. One of the biggest problems in automating catalog departments has been the fear among personnel that their jobs will be taken over by machines. Any threat to job security is bound to bring resistance from staff.

7. Emphasize the future. In presenting the change do not complain about the past or expound on how bad things are now. To look backward diverts attention from where the department is going.

8. Involve the staff. If members of the department can take a personal interest in a problem and actually contribute to its solution they will not only accept a new policy or procedure but will take pride in its success. One way to do this is to present the change as a personal challenge.

9. Create a problem-solving atmosphere in the department. If change is introduced in a climate of change, it will be accepted. Conversely, nothing is more difficult to fight than the apathetic feeling that the established way is inherently the best.

10. Be patient. Chances are that others in the department will not, at least at first, be as confident about a new idea or the results of a research project as the department head. Condemning them for their lack of understanding or rejecting their criticisms will only cause more resistance, perhaps justifiable resistance. If a change is worthwhile, others will eventually show interest and help get the plan moving.

11. Emphasize physical change. It is much easier for people to accept tangible changes than abstract ideas. The appearance of a new computer may command awe and respect from staff members; the idea of a systems analysis of the cataloging routines, unless properly presented, may evoke confusion and mistrust.

Chapter 9

DEPARTMENT COMMUNICATIONS

The catalog department has at its disposal a variety of communication devices and arrangements. Each has its advantages and disadvantages; each is necessary in a balanced communications program. Some are suitable for internal use only, others reach beyond the department. Some are versatile, others relatively limited. It is necessary, therefore, to maintain a careful inventory of department media and, from time to time, examine their place in the department. Periodic reviews may reveal new uses (and perhaps a few limitations) of present devices, and even uncover some communication possibilities not previously identified.

Forms management. No catalog department can function without forms. If information had to be communicated orally and retained by memory most departments would cease to operate. Just about every data item, statistic, and decision is recorded and communicated on some type of form.

By way of definition, we can say that a form is any printed piece of paper or card that contains constant information and which provides spaces for entering data on a prescribed basis. Typical forms used in the catalog department include book order slips, serials check-in cards, computer in-put workforms, employment applications, and letterheads, to mention only a few examples.

A form, whatever its specific function, is expected to accomplish the following:

1. Speed the communication of information.
2. Speed the collection and interpretation of information.

3. Indicate precisely what information is to be gathered and communicated.
4. Facilitate the making of multiple copies of data items.
5. Eliminate the need for duplicating standard data.
6. Store information for future use.

No matter how simple or how complex a form, the key to its effectiveness as a communication medium lies in its design. Few communications media are so dependent on proper formatting as is the form. Yet designing an effective department form is not easy. One reason is the lack of standards that can apply to every possible form in every catalog department. The most that can be said is that to communicate information quickly and accurately a form must be easy to write, easy to read, and easy to process. Whether selecting a form from a library supply catalog, ordering one from a local printer, or designing a simple sheet to be reproduced on the library's copy machine, these three criteria should apply.

Easy to write

1. Pre-print as much information as possible on the form. The less writing or typing required the more efficient the form.
2. Allow sufficient space for fill-ins, particularly for variable lengths of data. Determine also whether data is to be entered by hand, typewriter, or computer printer.
3. Group all related information together. And if information is to be transferred from one form to another the sequence of items should agree on each sheet.
4. Either arrange the entry of data to reflect the sequence of operation or place the most used items first on the form. Both if possible.
5. Structure the form so that only one entry can be made for each item. The more automatic the entry of data and its interpretation the more effective the form.
6. Prefer "ballot boxes" which reflect alternatives rather than fill-ins that require the writing or typing of data. Fill-ins can be time-consuming to write and awkward to type.

7. Construct the form in a way that will avoid constant adjusting of the typewriter. Fill-ins should be spaced so they can be quickly lined up vertically and horizontally and so that writing and typing proceeds from left to right and from top to bottom.

Easy to read

1. Place the department's name prominently above all forms that leave the department.
2. Print a title at the top of every form. A brief, descriptive title is necessary for identification, filing, and control.
3. Assign a title that will describe its function. It should be concise yet indicate the form's purpose.
4. Make captions precise. Captions and headings should indicate clearly what information goes where.
5. Be concise. Where appropriate, use incomplete phrases.
6. Use appropriate wordings, and do not use abbreviations if they will be mis-interpreted.
7. To help in identification, use various type faces, colors, heavy and thin lines, and shaded areas. For instance, use different colored papers in multi-order forms to help identify various copies.

Easy to process

1. Strive for uniformity. All forms used in the same process should be of the same type, design, and size.
2. Begin with the least flexible item, designing everything else around it. The filing title, for example, should be placed prominently at the top, with other items printed below.
3. Consider standardization in terms of both internal and external department use. For example, book order forms should conform to publisher needs, serve as a notification slip, serve as a temporary slip in the card catalog, and meet vendor requirements for ordering cards.
4. Make all forms standard sizes: $8\frac{1}{2}$ by 11 inches, 3 by 5, and so on. Standardization makes forms easy and economical to print, process, and file.
5. Pay attention to the location of special features on

the forms. Perforated edges, fastenings, punched holes, and folds should be appropriately placed.
6. Leave adequate margins. Margins aid in stapling, in handling, and in appearance.
7. Consider carefully the type and weight of paper stock. For example, a routing slip made of lightweight paper will bend when placed in a book.

Information slips. Communications in the catalog department can be simple or complex, formal or informal. One simple, informal but exceedingly important communication device found in just about all catalog departments is the information slip, or, as it is often called, the flyer or flag. Small departments may have one or two multi-purpose slips, and larger ones will develop several slips of various sizes, types, and colors. The primary function of the information slip is to convey information quickly and accurately about the processing, treatment, and destination of a book or other material. The technique most often used is to cut long, thin strips of paper (usually six to ten inches long and one to four inches wide) made of sturdy stock, on which are listed several words or phrases: "added copy," "rush," "bind," "rare book," and so on. To indicate the action desired, a staff member either checks or circles the appropriate word or phrase. Space can also be provided for additional instructions. After a book arrives in the catalog department (or, in some cases, before its arrival) an information slip, appropriately checked, is inserted. The slip remains with the book as it proceeds through the various processing steps.

The department head may want to make several different flags, including one listing type of material such as "added copy," "added volume," and "replacement"; perhaps a marking slip to indicate "cut pages," "change call number," "gift plate," "tip in errata sheet"; and still another slip for the bindery specifying "commercial bind," "do not bind," "make pockets," and so on. Larger departments will want a location slip listing department, branch, and other locations, and perhaps a special notification slip with space to list the patron, staff member, or branch library to be notified after the book has been processed. Most libraries will also have a brightly colored "rush" slip. Like the notification slip, it should provide space for noting to whom the book is to be "rushed." In addition, the department should develop slips for special purposes, for example, a reclassification flag providing space for new call number and new location.

Bulletin boards. One of the most popular communication media in the library is the bulletin board. It is accessible, quickly scanned, and if kept up-to-date a fast method of transmitting both official messages and social announcements.

The bulletin board is ideal for carrying brief messages to staff quickly; it is not, however, a medium for detailed information. It is appropriate for displaying department schedules and special library events, carrying motivational announcements, and calling attention to another medium--for example, a journal article on the latest in automated cataloging or an item in the library newsletter on a new building addition. Other examples of the type of communications appropriate for the bulletin board are notices of the promotion, transfer, and recognition of staff members; schedule changes and notices of meetings, conferences, and conventions; information on job openings; and announcements of staff activities. The board can also include photos and announcements of outside activities.

To categorize the messages, the catalog department bulletin board should be divided into at least two sections: one for official staff announcements, the other for unofficial news items, with a member of the staff appointed to control the official board. His assignment would be to see that only approved messages appear and to remove all out-dated notices. No item should be kept longer than necessary for full coverage, yet it is important to avoid a regular schedule. If a weekly schedule is established, staff will soon recognize the pattern and look at the board only once a week. If the catalog department is not large enough to have its own board, one should be shared with other technical service departments or perhaps the library will maintain one large board for the entire staff.

Newsletter. No doubt the library will have a newsletter. Its purpose will be to carry interesting and significant news items to the staff. It is not, however, a gossip sheet. It is a local newspaper, issued on a regular basis, which communicates information about the library, its policies, programs, plans, and personnel.

Administrators like the newsletter because it is a relatively fast, informal, and inexpensive way of transmitting in-

formation to staff members. Staff members like it because it
contains information about co-workers and the library not
found in the more official library media. Its most unique features are its flexibility in the type of information it contains
and the wide range of employees it reaches. It is a medium
that reaches all library staff, their families and friends, and
is often passed on to other libraries.

Every department in the library including the catalog
department should have a "reporter" who submits copy.
Each month, a day or two before the deadline, the department head should meet briefly with the department representative to relay news items compiled during the month. Items
should include significant changes in the department, promotions and transfers, and brief reports on staff trips and vaca-
tions.

Memos. No matter how well an idea is explained orally,
chances are that unless it is put on paper it will not be considered official and therefore not taken seriously. This goes
for ideas sent up the administrative ladder and down. A
department head's detailed explanation to the library director
about a revolutionary plan to streamline the department's
terminal operations will only result in a request to "give me
a memo on it." It is one thing, however, to ramble on en-
thusiastically about a bright idea and quite another to document it succinctly on paper.

A memo should be used whenever the sender wishes to
do one or more of the following:

1. Transmit in as precise a method as possible information to another staff member.
2. Provide a permanent record of a policy or decision.
3. Confirm as a matter of record an agreement made
   in a phone conversation, interview, meeting, or
   other oral medium.
4. Communicate exactly the same information to several
   staff members.

If the library does not supply standard memo forms, the
department head should have some made for department use.
The sheets should be headed with the name of the library
and department, the words "To," "From," and "Subject" listed
at the top, and a space provided for the date.

The sender must clearly indicate to whom the memo is addressed, and everyone receiving an information copy should be listed at the bottom. Memos may be either routed or personal copies sent to each staff member. Although department policy memos will be published in at least one official medium (usually in the department manual) those messages that need emphasizing should be circulated to each member of the department.

It is not, however, the format of the memo that makes it an economical communication tool and that contributes most to its ease of use; it is the content of the message and how it is stated. To be taken seriously, the memo must say something. The message should be stated in direct unqualified terms, by using precise and concrete words. The sender should never "back in" to his message, but start out with the important point, omitting tiresome preliminaries. Above all, every memo should meet a specific need and be aimed at specific readers.

Monthly and annual reports. The head of the department will be expected to produce a number of reports, including monthly reports. In his monthly report, designed to keep the administration informed on month-to-month activities within the department, the department head should present a clear picture of department activities during the previous month, with activities distinguished from accomplishments and the significance of each accomplishment related to immediate and long-range department objectives. The report should be in narrative form, subdivided if necessary by topic headings and accompanied by monthly statistics. Above all, the department head should not sugar-coat or hide facts; nor should he try to use the report as a propaganda tool to enhance his position in the library. The purpose of the monthly report, as with all library reports, is to communicate facts.

The department head will also be expected to contribute to the library's annual report. He may be asked to write the section devoted specifically to the catalog department or the director may prefer to incorporate all the statements from contributors into one general document. Some directors require only statistics, others expect their department heads to interpret, evaluate, and analyze, perhaps even add recommendations for the coming year. In any case, all information requested should be included with nothing held back in the hope that time will cover up a particularly knotty problem. The point is that the library director should be told about worsening situations before they get out of hand. Certainly he will need to know, if not through the official annual report at least in an accompanying unofficial memo, how the department's problems, particularly bottlenecks and backlogs, are affecting other library operations.

For a detailed report, it is best to use topic headings, for example, personnel changes, automation, staff accomplishments, recommendations, and so on. Another report-writing technique is to pick a central theme, either a need (for example, a budget increase) or an accomplishment (the elimination of a long-standing backlog) and carry it through the narrative. Whatever the approach, the department head should never attempt to include every possible event of the year, but select the more important items and detail them as succinctly as possible.

Statistics. So far we have been examining primarily internal communications. But communications extend outside the department, too. Members of the department will communicate to patrons, to co-workers in other departments, and to the library administration. The department head, in particular, will send and receive both official and unofficial communications. One of the most informative official communications will be the department's statistics. They are, in fact, the method by which most people inside and outside the library will come to know what and how the department is doing.

Statistics have other purposes, too. They show the growth rate of the collection, point up trends, and are the most reliable method available for comparing local cataloging output with that of other institutions. For this reason, department statistics are essential both for the library's annual report and for filling out innumerable questionnaires that various government and private organizations send to libraries. Department statistics also help control department operations. Specifically, statistics will aid in determining what is professional and what is nonprofessional work, in assessing flow-patterns, in spotting bottlenecks, and in monitoring the performances of individuals and the department as a whole.

Each member of the department should keep a detailed record of what he has processed, and submit this record to

the department head at the end of each month for computing
department totals. At the end of the fiscal year, the year's
statistics are submitted to the library administration. The
specific items included will depend on the complexity of the
operation and how the library intends to use its statistics.
At least the following items of information should be tallied:

1. Total number of titles cataloged.
2. Total number of physical volumes cataloged.
3. Total number of titles and/or volumes withdrawn.
4. Total number of titles and/or volumes recataloged
   and reclassified.
5. Added copies and added volumes (or this can be
   included in the total cataloged volumes).

In smaller libraries, the above categories are fairly
straightforward, but in larger, more complex operations they
are not. The department head may want to break down the
titles cataloged by form or type of material: books, periodicals, analytics, music scores, maps, microfilms, etc. Likewise, volumes should be divided by type: volumes, reels,
sheets, discs, etc. The library may also want a breakdown
by purchases, gifts, exchanges, and other specific sources.
Many libraries will also subdivide by department library, by
language, and by percentage of original cataloging and cataloging with LC copy (in other words, the percentage cataloged by professionals and that cataloged by nonprofessionals).
If the library belongs to a network, the number of titles cataloged using MARC and member-library records should also
be recorded. The number of titles and volumes withdrawn
can be categorized by form as well as by reason for withdrawal:
lost, worn, out of date, superseded.

Still other possible categories include volumes transferred, items accessioned, volumes reinstated, titles briefly
cataloged, cards and card sets typed, terminal hits, time
spent in other duties such as filing and revising, and total
items processed. Normally, however, statistics should be
kept to a minimum. Some may be kept exclusively for department use; others, perhaps more selective, passed on to the
administration for their needs. Unfortunately, statistical reporting, like many other cataloging operations, has never
been standardized. Each library has its own methods and
breakdowns. Until all institutions can agree on a uniform
reporting system and a standard method of tabulation, each

department head will have to judge for himself exactly what it is he and others need in the way of statistical communications.

The letter. All department heads must communicate by letter--to prospective staff members, to suppliers and vendors, to network headquarters, to federal and state agencies, to other librarians. Whenever details must be discussed, facts explained, prices requested, or titles listed, a letter is necessary. Above all, a letter establishes a tangible record which can be used for later reference by both sender and receiver.

To write an intelligible letter, the department head must first decide what he wants to say, and how. He should decide the subject of the letter and its purpose, how he will present the subject, and who will read the letter; he may even want to prepare an outline. At the very least, he should jot down the main ideas giving special attention to the beginning and ending sentences.

As for its format, a good business letter usually contains these elements: heading, inside address, salutation, body, complimentary close, signature, and signature identification. In writing a heading, the department head should always check for correct name, title, and address. The person's name should be stated in the salutation, and if the sender is on a first-name basis, the first name should be used: "Dear Bill." The impersonal "Dear Sir, Madam, or Ms." should be a last resort.

Also important is a friendly closing. "Sincerely yours" is preferred to the more stilted "Yours very truly." The close should be followed by a personal signature above the typed name and title of the signer. Where applicable, the initials of the department head and typist should be added and an indication made of the number of enclosures and distribution of copies.

In larger libraries, the mechanics of letter-writing are taken care of by the typist. The content, however, is the responsibility of the writer; obtaining an organized, clear, and friendly communication cannot be delegated. The following points (which apply to just about any written communication) should help.

1. Present an orderly communication. Tell what the letter is all about in the first paragraph; use the middle to advance and explain the message logically and with an orderly flow of ideas; and close quickly on a friendly note. Depending on the letter's purpose, the closing might contain a request for action, a summary of the main points, or a show of appreciation.

2. Use a conversational tone. Use short sentences, familiar words, and write directly and forthrightly. Try to avoid the stiffness typical of so many business letters.

3. Avoid gobbledygook. Do not use hackneyed phrases or stereotyped expressions. Examples to avoid: "at your earliest convenience," "avail yourself of this opportunity," "I beg to remain...."

4. Be specific. A well-written business letter provides necessary information briefly. Wordiness is the chief characteristic of faulty letter-writing.

5. Include all necessary facts and ideas. Omitting important points is just as annoying to the reader as is wordiness. If the reader must write asking for more information and the department head must reply again, a good deal of valuable time will be wasted, and both parties will become irritated.

6. Keep the letter reader-centered. Involve the reader by using familiar words and by relating the reader's experience and background to the subject. Another reader-centering technique is to use the person's name at least once in the body of the letter.

7. Be tactful and courteous. In written communications where words can be easily misinterpreted, the department head should avoid phrases which might antagonize or embarrass the reader, such as "You failed to ..." or "You claimed that...."

8. Write positively. A positive, optimistic tone will do much to stimulate a favorable reaction from the reader. Avoid negative words (error, neglect, dissatisfaction) unless, of course, the reader is to be left with a negative picture.

9. Strive for an attractive page. No matter how few errors, how correct the English, how concise the language, or how brilliant the presentation, if the letter has strikeovers, irregular spacing, ragged margins, and a messy appearance, it will be received differently than intended.

10. Re-read for errors. Obvious mistakes in grammar, spelling, and punctuation can be a major distraction to the reader and will reflect on both the department head and the library.

11. Make sure the letter is sent out immediately. If research must be gathered, a short interim letter should be written explaining the situation and promising complete information as soon as possible. Sitting on a letter only invites the person on the other end to procrastinate.

Attitude surveys. One of the more recent additions to the department head's arsenal of communication media is the attitude survey. Its purpose is to discover the opinions and underlying feelings of staff members about either specific working conditions or about their working environment in general. Attitude surveys can be administered by the department head, by the library personnel office, or by an outside consultant firm. The thinking behind the attitude survey is that staff know better than the administration the conditions under which they work and what their working conditions ought to be. They are closest to their jobs and therefore their opinions on ways to improve are valuable.

Attitude surveys are used, among other things, to measure how staff view policy changes, especially changes brought about by new technology and departmental reorganization; if carefully structured, an attitude survey can uncover potential problem areas before they surface. Attitude surveys can be used also to uncover reasons for lowered morale, high turnover, and substandard production. They are especially valuable in evaluating breakdowns in communication, and they can suggest new communication channels. Finally, attitude surveys provide excellent opportunities for staff members to discuss privately their personal concerns with the department head.

But conducting and evaluating a survey is not a simple undertaking. For one thing, the information gleaned tends to be subjective and therefore difficult to identify and analyze. Gaining the confidence of staff can be another stumbling block. So is the tendency for administrators to fail to follow through after the results of a survey have been tabulated. For these and other reasons it is important that the department head not rely solely on a survey (or on any other single communication tool) to assess staff opinions, but employ as many media and methods as possible.

To be successful, the attitude survey must receive the cooperation of everyone in the department. One of the best ways to gain staff cooperation is to form a committee of employees that would help prepare, distribute, and collect questionnaires, and that would review the data, collate the answers, write a report summarizing the results, and offer recommendations for action. After receiving the committee's report, the department head should meet with all members of the department to explain the results and to outline the actions to be taken. Regardless of who administers the survey--department head, committee, personnel office, outside consultant--staff members should have as much input as possible. Also, it is essential that the findings be shared with the division head and library director.

Questions should be structured so that they are readily understood and quickly and easily answered: yes-or-no, multiple-choice, and ballot-box seem to work the best. Ballot-box questions are especially popular, with each question requiring a check on one of four or five boxes headed something like "Very Low," "Low," "Average," "High," "Very High." Survey questions, if they are to be taken seriously, should be relevant to the needs and concerns of the staff and should focus on general problems, not on trivial grievances. Typical ballot-box and yes-or-no questions used to evaluate a catalog department's communications network might include these: "Does your supervisor welcome ideas from others?" "Do you work in a friendly environment?" "Would you like to participate more in department planning?" "Do you receive enough information to adequately do your job?" Typical open-ended survey questions might include these: "What suggestions do you have to improve department meetings?" "How can cooperation with other departments in the library be improved?" "How could your work be made more effective?"

Chapter 10

ORAL COMMUNICATIONS

Just about every communication medium, whether written, oral, visual, or nonverbal has a purpose in the catalog department; each has its strengths. The chief value of a written communication is that it provides a record of what was transmitted; multi-copies can even be made and distributed to others. A written communication also offers the sender a chance to carefully and logically state his message, edit and revise, re-read and study.

Even nonverbal communications--body movements, gestures, symbols, sounds of various kinds--can communicate; silence too can convey meaning. Nonverbal communication can provide feedback, encourage oral or written communication, reveal friendliness or hostility, and signal that a certain channel is open or closed. Through nonverbal communications staff members can decide such things as whether or not to communicate, who speaks first, and what to say and what not to say.

Nonverbal communications can also act as a barrier. Facial expressions (a stern look, poker-face, yawn, or lack of eye contact), voice intonations (whispering, stuttering, or angry voice), appearance (formal dress or long hair), and even such environmental stimuli as a closed office door can bar communications.

The most popular and most used--and most often mis-used--means of transmitting information in the catalog department is orally. Oral communication is a fast, spontaneous means of communication whereby the speaker can receive instant feedback and the listener can judge the mood and feelings of the speaker. Oral communication can take place on a personal, one-to-one basis; it is also the prime means of transmitting information in meetings, conferences, and group discussions.

The interview. Whenever the department head talks to a member of his staff for any length of time and for any specific reason, whether to solve a problem or exchange information, he is conducting an interview. The successful department head will find himself continually in interview situations. We have already examined a few, including employment and problem-solving interviews. There are many others, formal and informal. Certainly during the department head's tenure he will be involved in counseling interviews, disciplinary interviews, appraisal interviews, exit interviews, and perhaps the most frequent variety, just plain gripe interviews. Regardless of what type, an interview, in order to accomplish its purpose, must be carefully planned and executed.

First of all, the stage must be set. A private interview must be private. Ideally, it should be held in a private office, with comfortable chairs and surroundings, and in an office that is not only out of earshot but, if possible, out of view of others. Above all, the department head's manner should encourage a relaxed atmosphere.

Techniques the department head can use to provide a relaxed atmosphere include the following:

1. Start off on a friendly, informal basis. If possible, offer a cup of tea or coffee. Begin with a few general remarks; ask about a mutual interest. Although the department head does not want to give the impression that he is straining to be relaxed, he must try to ensure that participants begin in an easy frame of mind.
2. Do not be impatient. A hurried interview gives the impression that the interviewer considers his time too valuable for such an unimportant activity.
3. Do not permit interruptions. A telephone call, a knock on the door, a book dropped on the floor, or other loud noises can break the mood of a conversation, which can be difficult to recapture. Continual interruptions may persuade the interviewee that he is not the center of attention.
4. Create an air of confidentiality. A proper atmos-

phere cannot be established if the speaker believes that what he is saying will not be kept confidential. He may want to discuss a very personal matter or perhaps register a complaint. If he must be guarded, hold back information, or deal in vague generalities, the interview will lead nowhere. The department head must not only say that the meeting is in strict confidence; he must mean it.

5. Be concerned. If the interview is worth having it is worth everyone's total interest. If the person feels that the department head is really not interested, that he is skeptical, and that this is just something both must somehow get through he will feel that the subject and, more importantly, he himself are being rejected.

6. Accept the other person as a person. Accept him for what he is and for what he presents. He is neither a stereotype nor an object. He is someone who must be taken seriously, just as he must take the department head seriously.

7. Never prejudge, nor even post-judge. The department head should never give the impression that he is there to pass judgment or evaluate. If he can make the speaker understand that he is capable of doing his own evaluating a good working relationship will develop.

8. Take a positive attitude. Look for good points, look for solutions, look for the future. Create the idea that whatever the problem, the interviewer and interviewee working together will find the solution. End the discussion on a positive note, and with the conviction that improvement is imminent.

If there is one key to a successful interview, it is good listening. By listening carefully everyone learns. Moreover, the more the department head listens the more the speaker is motivated to unload facts that will help in reaching a final decision. Good listening also indicates that the interviewer is really interested in what is being said. The speaker will appreciate the interest and be encouraged to listen himself. Even if there is a good deal of disagreement, the fact that each is willing to listen to the other's views will encourage understanding.

Allowing the speaker to "tell all" without interruption

lets him relieve himself of his feelings and perhaps some hostilities. It is therapy for the speaker as well as a source of information for the department head. Careful listening also helps the listener understand how the person really feels about the subject. Understanding comes not only through words, but by observing gestures and emotions, listening between the lines, and paying attention to the tone of voice. Quietly listening to the other person may even help him see his own problems better. If he is allowed to talk out his problem, he may come closer to the solution than if the department head continually interrupts and interjects ideas.

Once all the information has been gathered, the session should be ended as quickly and as politely as possible. If there is action to be taken, it should be made clear when it will be taken and by whom. Any promises made must be kept. If necessary, the conversation should be restated in another medium. In most interview situations, the follow-up will be just as important as the interview itself.

Department meetings. More than any other device, the catalog department meeting, if properly planned and intelligently conducted, can mold a department into a cohesive and efficiently functioning organization. By department meetings we do not mean the old-fashioned kind where the department head stands on a podium to announce that all the clerks must clean their typewriters once a week, or demand that Miss Smith stop talking to Miss Brown. Nor is this the place to pass down dicta from the director on coffee breaks and work schedules. The meetings discussed here are those in which the department head (who is not only the head of the department but a member of it) and other staff members work together to establish a harmonious working relationship.

The prime purpose of the catalog department meeting, then, is to improve department operations in an atmosphere of cooperation and understanding. Specifically, meetings provide opportunities to solve mutual problems, make decisions, discuss plans, and collect and communicate information. Some library directors feel that staff meetings, especially at the department level, are a waste of time. They are not. Even if they only provide for stimulating discussions and a chance to air problems, catalog department meetings are worth the time and effort; they are vital to the management of the catalog department.

The first step is to prepare for the meeting, including seeing that the meeting room is available and set up properly for group participation. Ideally, the library should have a special area set aside for staff meetings. It should be well lighted, properly ventilated, and free from visual and noise distractions. Participants should be able to hear and see each other without straining. Gestures and facial expressions help convey meaning. If the group is small enough, one large table (preferably round) is best. For large departments, a u-shaped arrangement of tables works well. Ashtrays, blackboards, easels, pencils, note pads, and any other aids should be in place and ready for use, or participants should be asked to bring their own. In addition, the department head should collect any reports, memos, or other materials required for the meeting.

A definite time should be set aside for meetings: the last Friday of every month, the first and third Monday, depending on department needs. The question of exactly how often to meet should be decided by the staff itself, not dictated by the department head. To eliminate the feeling that department meetings are an added burden, they should be held during regular work hours, preferably early in the day. Regularly scheduled meetings, should include all full-time staff, nonprofessionals as well as professionals.

Definite scheduling does not, of course, rule out special meetings. From time to time, the head of the department will need to arrange for an inter-departmental meeting; also he will want to call meetings just for his professionals, terminal operators, the marking section, or other groups within the department. But when a special meeting is called, everyone should know why. Scheduling a meeting without informing participants why they are being called together can evoke fears, rumors or attitudes which will be unproductive.

The department head should pre-plan, prepare, and distribute an agenda (topics to be covered, their sequence, and time allotted for the meeting, and so on) in advance of each meeting--and should ask for additional items to be covered. He should also prepare a more detailed outline for himself. Enough time should be allotted to accomplish all objectives. If the meeting must run two or more hours, a recess should be scheduled.

In preparing the agenda, brief announcements should be placed at the beginning, the more complex and controversial items left for the end. To throw out a controversial question at the beginning can turn the entire period into a haranguing session in which many agenda items will not be considered or dealt with. Also, by saving controversial items for the end, the session can be effectively cut off before arguing gets heated and unproductive; and participants will have something to chew on afterward.

During the meeting a member of the department should take notes. The results of each session should be circulated to department members and to others in the library, certainly to the technical services librarian and the library director. The notes should be kept as a permanent record to which staff can refer as the need arises.

If possible, refreshments should be served at the meetings, at least coffee and other drinks. Refreshments not only help build morale but "refresh" as well. Before adjourning, the department head should summarize all major points discussed and clearly state any conclusions and agreements reached, as well as all disagreements. Finally, he should announce the next meeting.

Committees. Many libraries do a great deal of their policy making and fact finding through committees and task forces. Committee centered organizations are, indeed, becoming more and more popular. A committee may be permanent or temporary (ad hoc). The latter is formed to carry out a specific task and then disbanded when the job is done. Committees may be made up of professionals and/or nonprofessionals from various departments within the library, or can be limited to catalog department staff. The make-up will, of course, depend on the nature of the committee's charge. The department head or library director may, for example, form a committee to examine the feasibility of automating the department, to plan a new building addition, to search for a new serials cataloger, to arrange a going-away party for a typist, or for a variety of other tasks.

There are many good reasons for the committee approach, not least the old chestnut: "Two (or more!) heads are better than one." This is particularly true if the heads represent a cross-section of interests and opinions. Since they represent the combined judgment of several individuals, committee solutions are often more objective than individual ones. The process of simply discussing divergent opinions on a problem will often pinpoint the weaknesses or strengths of various proposed solutions. Long-term solutions are particularly suited to committee deliberations.

The committee approach is, therefore, a good way to coordinate different viewpoints in the library. Through committees, administrators can judge how people feel about particular aspects of a problem. This is especially true for problems that have many possible solutions. The committee is also a means of preventing hasty decisions. Although committees have been criticized for wasting time and delaying important decisions, there are times when delay, if accompanied by careful deliberation, is desirable.

Many department heads, especially in larger libraries, use committees to keep themselves informed on various aspects of their departments' operations. Committees can gather and communicate information and thus save valuable time and energy. As long as the use of an information-gathering committee is not abused--which it too often is--this can be a valuable device in supporting a library's communications program.

Also, committee decisions are bound to carry more weight and will be better accepted by the staff than decisions handed down through the chain-of-command. This is especially true if the committee is well-balanced and represents varying points-of-view. Morale is also involved. The more people involved in the decision-making process, either directly or indirectly, the more the staff will feel a part of the organization.

Still another important by-product is the knowledge gained by members through participation in committee work. Committee participation is particularly good training for catalogers who often get little chance to interact with other librarians. It is also a good opportunity for staff to appreciate each other's strengths and weaknesses, and to encourage interdepartmental coordination.

Then why isn't the committee approach used more often? More to the point, why don't department heads use it to better advantage? First, consider the nature of most committee

decisions. Too often, a committee report is either a weak
compromise or, at the other extreme, a highly personalized
declaration by the chairman or a particularly active minority
on the committee. The poor quality of many decisions is the
result of the committee make-up. For one thing, committee
members are often selected because they represent certain
departments or interests (or, more recently, certain minorities), not because they are qualified to solve a specific problem. Not only is the credibility of many decisions in doubt,
so is the accountability. When several people are responsible
for a particular decision or action, the responsibility is dif-
fused--no one person feels accountable. Thus the committee
is likely to take more risks than the individual. This may be
either good or bad, depending on the decision itself. Poor
decisions also result because committees seem often to be
working under one handicap or another: members with in-
sufficient time for the project, an impending decision date,
lack of motivation, poor leadership. Social pressures and the
dominance of one or more members can also adversely affect
a decision.

Anyone who has been a committee member knows the
amount of time wasted in irrelevant discussions, fruitless
arguments, and meaningless report-writing. Even an effi-
ciently-run committee wastes a certain amount of time. And
when the committee has finally finished its work, it too often
finds it lacks the authority to implement the decision, and
those with the authority either cannot or will not carry it
through.

Despite these criticisms, committees can function effectively if properly handled. It is important to remember
that committees are ideal for certain functions but inappropriate for others. For handling day-to-day administrative
decisions a committee is ineffectual and time-consuming. Yet
they work well for special long-range decision-making situations. Specifically, committees function best in any situation
where the library needs advice on a particularly complex
problem, most especially for interdepartment and department
problems that require detailed investigation. Many cataloging
matters benefit from the committee approach. For example,
an inquiry into the pros and cons of the divided catalog
would be a good committee assignment. In a question of this
kind, not only cataloging but reference and other library
functions are affected. There are opinions to sample,

literature searches to make, libraries to query, findings to assemble, and decisions to make--all of which can be handled effectively through a committee.

The size of the committee will depend, at least to some extent, on the specific task at hand. For most, five members is about right. But the optimum size will vary according to conditions. Generally, though, anything below four really is not much of a committee (three of anything inevitably leaves and odd man out); and a group of more than seven is unwieldy and nearly always ends in splinter groups, one of which does all the talking (and working).

Whenever possible, the department head or whoever is doing the selecting should choose a balanced committee whose members will complement and communicate with each other, and who are interested in and have some knowledge of the task. Ideally, the committee should include a task leader and a social leader, some intelligent followers who will contribute as well as follow, one or two communicators, a good compromiser, and at least one technical expert on the subject. A fairly well-balanced committee can usually absorb at least one "difficult" member (i.e., someone who talks too much or is short on problem-solving ability).

Before the first meeting, the chairman should analyze the members of the group. He should have some idea about their interests, attitudes, and, most especially, their relationships to each other. An important consideration in selecting committee members is to make sure that no one feels (or is!) threatened by participation. This is done by establishing a relaxed, friendly, and cooperative atmosphere. Animosities have no place in a committee meeting--nor in any library situation, for that matter. This is not to say that strong personalities should be weeded out or that feelings should be stifled, only that petty differences and rank-pulling are taboo. If it is evident to everyone that antagonisms do exist, it is not inappropriate for the chairman to give a brief "let's-all-pull-together" speech before getting down to business. And remember that the purpose of the committee is not to provide a vehicle for a participant's (or chairman's) ego trip. Hopefully, the prestige of each member will be enhanced by participation, but not at the expense of the others or to the detriment of the project.

An agenda, listing the major subjects to be covered, should be prepared for the first meeting, and an estimate made of the time needed to carry out each point. The chairman should determine how much group participation he wants at the first meeting, and then outline the questions he wants to raise and the material he wants to offer for consideration. Finally, he should look ahead to task assignments and future meetings.

Should committee votes be taken? If so, should the chairman insist on unanimity or will a simple majority do? Certainly a consensus is important to any committee action-- important, also, to the democratic process. The chairman may want to call a vote to end a prolonged discussion or to keep participants involved. Unanimity is usually difficult, if not impossible, to achieve, and insistence on absolute agreement on every point can result in long, involved discussions, ill feeling among participants, or, at best, compromise rather than bold, imaginative action. Thus, while unanimity should definitely be sought on important issues, if the committee is to be kept moving and effective decisions reached, the chairman should be prepared to settle for a simple majority with, if necessary, a minority report.

The committee chairman should send members a clear statement of the problem in advance of the first meeting, and include a tentative agenda listing date and time of the meeting. If possible, he should indicate how long the first meeting will last, and set a time when everyone can attend. In addition, he should search the literature for writings on the subject and make the literature available to the members. At the first meeting, the problem should be stated and defined, its history summarized, a possible agenda discussed, and either formal (Roberts' rules) or informal rules of order adopted.

A regular procedure for subsequent meetings should be established. Each session should begin with a welcome to members and an introduction of visitors. Then the minutes of the last meeting can be read and approved, or, if formal minutes are not being taken, the chairman should summarize the last meeting himself. Unfinished business should be discussed; new business taken up; new assignments made and tasks delegated; results of the meeting summarized. The meeting should end with a discussion of plans for the next one.

During discussions it is the duty of the chairman to guide the flow of discussions; encourage participation by everyone; draw out reluctant members; keep the discussion on the subject; see that a few members do not dominate the conversation; show appreciation for all contributions; maintain good humor and a relaxed atmosphere; clarify questions and procedures; avoid personality clashes; bring the discussions to a clear and definite conclusion; and finally, make sure that a permanent record is made of the results of the meeting.

Participants have certain responsibilities, too. Each should attend all meetings and keep the interests of his constituents in mind. Anyone who cannot attend should inform the chairman before the meeting. Beyond this, all members should be punctual and arrive in the right frame of mind; participate intelligently in all discussions; refrain from irrelevant haggling; leave personal prejudices outside; prepare by reading up on the subject under consideration; digest any materials circulated before the meeting; conscientiously carry out all tasks assigned by the chairman.

Telephone. The telephone is one of the most convenient and flexible person-to-person media available for communicating inside and outside the library. Certainly the telephone is time-saving. It is much quicker for a department head to telephone someone than to see him personally or to write a letter or memo. In addition, the telephone can provide the intimate contact of a personal communication while allowing the caller to jot down questions and comments to keep in front of him while talking. Still another advantage is that the parties can talk back and forth, something that is impossible in a written communication. And if the person is unavailable, the caller can leave a message or call back later.

To use the department telephone to best advantage does mean learning a few basic courtesies. First off, the department head must make sure that all calls coming into the department are answered promptly; in other words, make sure that someone is available to answer every phone in the department. A long wait does little to improve the department's image. Every incoming call should be answered with an identifying statement of the department and the person answering. If the call must be transferred to someone else, the caller should be asked courteously to wait a moment until the

right person is reached. If there is a delay, the caller
should be notified that it may take a minute or two until the
call is transferred, and then be thanked in advance for waiting. If the staff member is occupied, the caller should be
told that the party is busy at the moment and would like to
call back later. If there is a question to look up, a book to
trace, or a shelflist to consult, the staff member can say that
he will call back when the information is located, and he
should give an approximate time the call will be returned:
five minutes, two hours, nine o'clock tomorrow morning.

The department head must show the same concern and
courtesy in placing a call as in receiving one. Before calling,
he should learn as much as he can about both the subject of
his call and the person he is contacting, and he should anticipate any questions that may arise. He might even want to
jot down the important points to be stressed so he can concentrate on the conversation instead of on what he wants to
say next. After he has reached his party, whether inside
the library or out, he should immediately identify himself and
then get to the point. If the conversation will be lengthy,
common courtesy dictates that he ask if the party has the
time to talk. If his party is busy at the moment, the department head should ask if he can call back at a more convenient
time.

All telephone conversations should be carried on in a
friendly, relaxed voice. The telephone is a cold electronic
device and if no warmth is added the communication will be
cold and formal; smiles and other facial expressions cannot
be communicated over the phone. A casual remark made in
jest can be interpreted differently when the receiver cannot
see the accompanying facial expressions.

Department grapevine. Two prominent characteristics
of the grapevine are its speed of transmission and its selec-
tivity. Information not only travels fast but is able to reach
certain people unerringly while somehow skipping others. At
times it can be discriminating, at other times it will include
an entire department or building.

Like every other communication medium, the grapevine
has its weaknesses. Facts are not always accurate or reliable. Usually, too, information is fragmentary. Nor does
the department head have the same control over the grapevine

that he perhaps should have. Yet when all else fails, it is
often the only means of communicating between the department head and his staff and between units within the department.

The grapevine often functions, for better or worse,
when all other channels have been blocked. When nothing
else is available, it may be the only way the department head
has of securing feedback. And when he does not communicate (or, worse yet, communicates misinformation) the grapevine is always there to fill the void.

The grapevine acts as a safety valve: it allows staff
to blow off steam. Although a staff member may not be able
to tell off his supervisor he can still transfer his frustrations
to the grapevine. Finally, the grapevine can serve as a
means of gratifying a staff member's need for recognition; it
can even act as an outlet for his creative needs.

The department head must, therefore, accept and deal
with the grapevine positively, and not think of it as strictly
a negative medium. If he listens carefully and is sensitive
to what he hears, he will learn a good deal not found in any
other medium; but if ignored, the grapevine can spread false
rumors, damage morale, and even lead to irresponsible actions.

Although neither the department head nor any other
staff member can control the grapevine in the same way other
media can be controlled, it can and should be influenced.
The department head must, for example, make sure that the
grapevine does not distort facts or interfere with formal department communications. Whenever possible, he must integrate the grapevine with the more formal internal media and
use it to spread significant items of information and receive
feedback. When a false rumor is uncovered, he must counter
with facts. Most important, the department head must keep
his staff informed on all department and library plans through
the bulletin board, memos, newsletter, staff meetings, and
other formal media.

Communication Blocks

Selecting the proper communications medium for the
message is not enough. The department head must see that

nothing or no one interferes with communications sent and
received in the department. Whether conducting a meeting,
writing a report, or holding an interview, he must make sure
all messages (policy statements, opinions, reprimands, con-
gratulations, statistics, or whatever) convey the precise information intended. In other words, he must make sure no
blocks exist. Communication blocks can take many forms,
and they are not always easy to identify.

Distrust of the communicator. One communication block
is the receiver's distrust of the sender. This is particularly evident in communications between junior and senior clerks
and between the department head and his catalogers. Does
the department head, for example, automatically go on the defensive when a junior cataloger suggests an improvement?
Is his first thought, "Is he implying that I don't know my
job?" Does the typist reading the department head's memo
on the conservation of supplies wonder, "Is he trying to save
money on pencils because he has overspent the budget
again?" Does a clerk, when the library director enters the
department, instinctively think, "What have I done now?"
The visit may simply be the director's way of communicating
his appreciation for what he considers an efficient department, yet the defensive clerk will receive a totally different
message.

Poorly expressed communication. Jargon, ill-chosen
words, vague implications, and abstract terms can undermine
the good intentions of any message. The problem of semantics
is found in all areas of the library, but nowhere more so
than in the catalog department. The cataloger is told that
he must catalog a book immediately. Does this mean he should
catalog it as soon as he has finished what he is doing?
Does it mean get it out today? Or what about: "The quality
of your filing must improve"? Improve how and by how
much? Even such common words as "cooperation" and "objectives" have different meanings to the library director, department head, cataloger, clerk, and student assistant.

Different frame-of-reference. Even the backgrounds
of sender and receiver can act as a barrier. Both previous
experience and the nature of the group with which a person
presently identifies will affect how a communication is sent
and interpreted. A staff member's background is particularly
apparent in the in-service training program. Words such as

"serial" (a breakfast food?) or "tracing" (according to Webster: "a mechanical copy by marking on thin paper over the original") may have different meanings for the new typist and the supervisor. Unless information is communicated in a manner that will take into consideration the typist's frame-of-reference, the training program will fail. In addition, the library director, division head, and department head must keep in mind differences between reference groups. If the gulf between groups becomes too great, as it often does between the library administration and the clerical staff, the department head must assume the responsibility of interpreting and translating memos and other communications into language which will be understood by everyone.

Inappropriate channels. Blocks will also occur if messages are sent by the wrong medium. Written communications, for example, are particularly appropriate for policy decisions, yet with oral communications the sender can explain, answer questions, get feedback, and judge reactions. The communication must always be compatible with the medium. A personal reprimand should not be posted on the bulletin board; nor should the department head announce that he has just become a father (or mother) at a specially-called meeting. One message may call for a personal interview, another for a memo, still another for a short meeting.

Unfortunately, many department heads tend to overload a favorite medium. If a meeting is called for every possible communication, time will not only be wasted but staff will soon become dulled and indifferent to meetings. They will either begin to ignore all communications or try to select and filter-out those they consider unworthy of attention, perhaps not giving attention to the really important ones. The department head should be particularly alert to messages that pass through his office. It is not only his responsibility to translate communications that pass back and forth between the director and members of the department but in some cases he will have to re-channel certain ones into more appropriate media.

Emotional involvement. The insecure, angry, worried, frustrated, or fearful cataloger will send and interpret a communication differently than the cheerful, confident one. A sarcastic request from the circulation librarian to change a book which has been improperly classified will undoubtedly meet with an overreaction from the defensive cataloger. And certainly the cataloger's out-of-hand rejection of the request will, in turn, create still more barriers to block further communications between departments.

Premature evaluation; or, "I know it all." Catalogers, like everyone else, resent change. Rightly or wrongly, most feel that they know, better than anyone else, how to do their jobs, and they resist any interference. They tend, therefore, to ignore information that conflicts with what they already "know." Many times, all a cataloger needs to hear is one sentence--"Why don't we computerize our cataloging operation?"--that conflicts with his preconceived ideas, and everything that follows is rejected, out of hand. Indeed, it is impossible to discount previous experience. The department head, for instance, may announce at a department meeting that staff members who work most efficiently will receive the biggest raises. Yet through experience they "know" that raises and promotions are given not on quality and quantity of work, but on seniority. Or, what happens when a memo on a procedural change is circulated to the staff, then a few days later another appears which modifies or even reverses the original decision? Clearly, the result will be delayed action on future memos, perhaps even complete disregard of them. If staff have learned through experience that the department head is constantly changing his mind, they will, understandably, discount his messages.

The organizational structure. The library itself can be a block to effective communications. The channels through which information passes, especially if they are traditionally conceived and rigidly imposed, can discourage if not prevent the exchange of information. If a clerk's recommendation for improving the labeling process must pass in writing through the marking section chief, to the head of the department, on to the technical services librarian, up to the director of the library, and back down, there is little chance of it being sent, let alone implemented. If the library simply does not have effective communication mechanisms or if the process is haphazard and erratic, the flow of information will be stifled.

Motives of the communicator. What are the motives behind a communication: to divide the staff, to make the department head look good, to discredit a cataloger, to block a promotion? Is the communication simply another way of pleasing the library director? Is it an attempt to "cover-up" instead of communicate information? A communication will fail if it tries to divide or threaten the staff, implies that someone is ignorant or lazy, or is simply a propaganda ploy.

Lack of motivation. Lack of interest in the subject of a message can also act as a barrier between sender and receiver. This is evident in the staff member who fails to read the bulletin board or who quickly glances over a memo because he has "more important things" on his mind. To get a message across, the department head may have to use attention-catching devices and emphasize those aspects that will benefit the receiver. For a complete understanding of a message, concentration and self-involvement are essential.

Lack of knowledge. To fully assimilate a communication, the staff member must have at least some understanding of the subject. The department head may have to provide background materials, discussion time, and follow-up. Whether dealing with staff or the public, the department head cannot always assume that his audience has adequate background information to understand what is being transmitted. Before transmitting, the person's knowledge of the subject must be determined and the message cast accordingly.

Failure to communicate. As obvious as it may sound, for a message to be sent and received there must be a communication. The deliberate withholding of information, the assumption that everybody already knows (or that a certain person need not know), and just plain procrastination are still other very real barriers to the communication of information. The withholding of information, for whatever reason, is in itself a communication--although, to be sure, a negative one.

What can be done, then, to insure effective communications in the catalog department? Certainly the above blocks must be avoided. But some positive steps must be taken, as well. When the department head, or anyone else in the department, writes a memo, conducts a meeting, or posts a notice, he should consider the following:

1. Know what is to be communicated. If the communicator does not know precisely what he is going to say, neither will anyone else. If in doubt, he

should try writing it out. If it cannot be written, it cannot be expressed in any medium.

2. Keep the message simple. The sender should not communicate jargon.

3. Emphasize the benefits. If the department head is trying to communicate an idea, it should be expressed in terms of the benefits it will bring.

4. Do not exaggerate. In his communications, the department head must not oversell. If optimism turns to pessimism, future communications will be ignored.

5. Anticipate reactions. If the communicator thinks there will be objections or negative reactions, he should bring out possible objections in his communication so that they will be understood by everyone.

6. Be alert to symbolic meanings both in transmitting and receiving communications. If a communication is met with unexpected resistance, the sender should look below the surface.

7. Realize that differences in viewpoint can cause a message to be lost or confused. This is a particularly important consideration in a catalog department staffed with professionals, clerks, and student assistants of different backgrounds and education.

8. Timing is important. Staff members will react best to a communication when they are motivated, when the message is not competing with another stimulus, when it is not preceded by rumors, and when those with the need-to-know hear it first.

9. Reinforce the communication with action. If the department head has a reputation for not following words with action, communications will be ignored-- and rightly so.

10. Give reasons. A policy statement that radically changes a procedure must carry with it (or be followed by) detailed reasons. The department head should not simply insist that all clerks file into the card catalog between the hours of 8:00 and 9:15 a.m. He must explain why.

11. Be clear and precise. To get a message across, the sender should organize, itemize, underscore, illustrate, associate, relate, and simplify.

12. Repeat, review, and retell important communications several times, and in several ways. To guarantee successful communications, different media may have to be used.

13. The number of items in a given communication should be kept to a minimum. Too much detail or too many facts will result in a smothered message. For important communications, it is better to give too little information than too much.

14. Likewise, do not hide an important message among routine ones. To insure that certain messages are not lost and that others are not over-emphasized, important items should be separated from routine messages.

15. Keep the message out in the open. The department head should not try to sneak an unpleasant communication by his people by sugar-coating it.

16. Select the appropriate medium, and make sure a favorite one is not over-used. It is not only important what is communicated, but how.

17. Be sure the communication comes from the appropriate source. Both the personality of the communicator and his position in the library are important. A cataloger should not receive a policy change via a student assistant.

18. Keep communication channels open at all times. As part of "middle management" it is the department head's responsibility to keep both upward and downward messages flowing freely.

19. Finally, a successful communication is the result of good feedback. With each message, opportunities should be provided for comments and reactions.

Chapter 11

DEPARTMENT TOOLS

Without proper tools the department head cannot possibly
manage his department, nor can his staff carry out their assignments. By department tools we do not mean pencils,
electric erasers, and typewriters, as necessary as these may
be to cataloging operations. The tools we will examine in
this chapter are, for the most part, software tools: the department manual, job description, plus various managerial
concepts such as systems analysis and MBO. Although designed to accomplish many of the same management objectives
as the communication media and methods discussed in the two
previous chapters, the department tools presented here are
intended primarily as aids in organizing and controlling department activities rather than in supporting department communications.

The Reference Shelf

Catalog department personnel must have direct access
to at least three separate reference shelves. Each cataloger
should have his own desk reference collection, the use of a
sizable collection of tools shelved in the department, and access to the library's general reference collection. The individual desk collection should contain those tools continually
used by each cataloger. Items found on the cataloger's desk
should include: one or two foreign language dictionaries
most frequently consulted, the Dewey classification schedule
(or the individual LC schedules most relevant to the cataloger's
subject field), Sears List of Subject Headings (the LC subject
heading list is too cumbersome for desk use), a Cutter table,
a copy of the filing rules, the latest edition of AACR, the
department manual, and perhaps one or two specialized refer-

ence works most often consulted by the cataloger. If the cataloger is working with an automated catalog, he will also need the coding manuals supplied by the computer center or bibliographic network.

Catalogers will also need an extensive department reference collection. Exactly how extensive will depend on the size of the department and available funding. There should be sufficient copies of the LC or Dewey classification schedules, plus various information bulletins such as LC's Cataloging Service Bulletin and newsletters and bulletins from the library's bibliographic network. The department will need a complete collection of foreign language dictionaries and the important biographical dictionaries, who's who's, specialized subject dictionaries, a comprehensive gazetteer, at least one good atlas, the U.S. Government Manual, a comprehensive almanac, and such important yearbooks as the Yearbook of International Organizations.

If the general reference collection is located near the catalog department, it may be convenient to house many of the frequently-used tools there instead of duplicating expensive items in the catalog department. Tools that could be shared with the public include: the National Union Catalog and other foreign and domestic union listings, the Union List of Serials, CBI, BNB, Monthly Catalog, PW, Books in Print, and the larger and more expensive encyclopedias. Many libraries establish a separate bibliography room close to the technical services area in which are shelved indexes and bibliographies for use both by the public and staff. But whether the reference tools are on the cataloger's desk, in the department collection, or in a general bibliography room, they must be accessible to department staff at all times.

An important responsibility of the department head is, therefore, to seek the advice of staff on what they need at their elbows and what they can consult in the reference department. If a cataloger insists that a Spanish dictionary he is using is inadequate, it is up to the department head to see that he gets a more satisfactory tool. Tools produced both by and for the department must be carefully prepared and intelligently used. While it may be a relatively simple matter to select a dictionary that will satisfy department needs, it is not so easy to construct a suitable job description or department manual.

The Job Description

The job description, discussed briefly in Chapter 5, is a basic department tool. Its purpose is to set down on paper the characteristics, duties, responsibilities, and department relations of a specific cataloging job. It is a picture of one of the department's operations. Descriptions vary, of course, from library to library and from job to job. Some are quite specific; others, particularly those for professional positions, need not be. Unlike most other tools, however, the job description continues to evoke controversy. One cataloger will say that without a written job description he does not really know what his duties include; another will complain that his job description does not give him enough flexibility. One department head will claim that the job description is necessary for making job assignments; another will insist that it limits his freedom in assigning work. But the fact remains, a properly designed job description is a basic and necessary tool in the management of a catalog department.

A job description has many uses. The personnel office will use the descriptions to establish a departmental as well as an institution-wide job grading and salary structure; and the department head will use them for salary recommendations. Job descriptions can also be used in the recruitment program, both in determining the people to be recruited and as a basis for establishing requirements that applicants can consider. After the new employee arrives, the job description will be used in the orientation program to remind the newcomer (and his supervisor) of his duties. Still later, it will be used in settling misunderstandings and disagreements regarding work assignments. If, for example, a typist complains that she is performing a task for which she was not hired, the department head and typist can sit down with the job description to review exactly what the duties include. In fact, the job description should be before the department head in reviewing any job-related complaint. Too often, without something specific on paper, a particular job will look quite different to the typist, department head, and library director.

The department head can use the job description as a checklist in the evaluation program, especially if the annual evaluation is considered a progress report, as it should be. Has the cataloger been carrying out his assignments as described in the job description? If not, comparing his performance with his duties and responsibilities as listed in the description is a particularly helpful way to eliminate subjective factors.

The job description can also be used in any decision regarding the promotion or transfer of a staff member. Do the duties of a terminal operator in the acquisition department qualify her for transfer into a cataloging vacancy? To find out, the department head can look at her present job description. Does the quality and quantity of an operator's work merit the transfer? Again, the department head can look at the job description for statements on minimum requirements.

In various ways, the job description is an important communications instrument. With the description in hand, the director can tell how members of the catalog department are performing, and thus how well the department is carrying out its responsibilities. This is an excellent way to get an operational picture of the department. In addition, periodic reviews of the descriptions should help clarify duties within the department, facilitate reassignment of responsibilities, and improve the department's organizational structure. Whenever there is a reassignment of duties the description must be changed.

How, then, is a job description constructed? The first step is to gather material about the position to be described. The head of the department should know the duties and responsibilities of each person under him. If he does not, he should sit down with each staff member to discuss the job. The best way to discover what a specific job is all about is to ask the person who is performing it. It is important, however, not to describe what the typist or cataloger is doing, but what he or she is supposed to be doing. There may be a difference. This discussion will, incidentally, teach both the department head and the employee something about the job.

After the department head has talked the position over with the person, he should check with the immediate supervisor to clarify misunderstandings and ambiguities. If the department head is the immediate supervisor, then it is best to recheck with a co-worker to make sure that nothing has been overlooked. The job holder may be new and not understand all of his duties; or, he may be an older employee who performs his duties automatically without really thinking about them.

The next step is to gather all pertinent notes and write out the description, using a standard job description form. It is usually best to use one kind for clerical jobs and another for professional positions. If the library does not have standard forms, then the department head can format his own to fit department needs. A typical job description for a clerical position would list: job title, date, duties and responsibilities, required qualifications (general, skills, and education) and any additional desirable qualifications.

The main part of the form will be that which defines and describes the duties of the job. In listing these duties, action verbs (types, labels, records, operates, inputs, etc.) should be used in short sentences. Examples: "Collects books and periodicals for binding." "Sorts and files catalog cards in various catalogs." "Types headings on catalog cards." Duties should be listed in order of importance, with those tasks which are only occasionally performed either omitted altogether or prefaced with qualifying statements such as "usually performs" or "may perform." For many jobs, the number of tasks will be too numerous to list. It is really unnecessary to list all the tasks the catalog clerk could conceivably be asked to perform. Therefore, the possibility of tasks other than those listed on the form should be indicated, if only to protect the department from future misunderstandings. One way to do this is to state the last descriptor simply as, "Performs other tasks as required."

The section on qualifications can be subdivided into skills, academic preparation, and perhaps even physical and personality qualifications. Under general qualifications, qualities such as dependability, ability to work with others, cooperativeness, and sense of responsibility can be listed. If a bindery clerk is expected to lift books on and off shelves and pack them into boxes, if a book marker must write legibly, or if a catalog clerk is expected to work with the public, it should be included in the qualifications. If a clerk is to type 60 words per minute, it should be listed. If accuracy is important, then a phrase such as "Typing speed of 60 wpm with accuracy" should be noted. If the library personnel office gives all clerical applicants a typing or other test, a specific score or percentile expected of the job holder can be listed.

As for academic qualifications, the form should indicate

whether the department wants someone with a high school diploma, two years of college, two years typing, a 3.0 grade point average. It is best to set qualifications a little higher than the job actually requires. While a high school sophomore could mark books, no less than a high school graduate should actually be required. To make sure that qualified people are not ruled out, the phrase "or with equivalent experience" can be listed after the education requirement. Another possible category would be "Additional desirable qualifications." Here would be listed specific college courses, foreign language ability, or previous library experience.

Still another heading often included on the job description is "Training period," that is, the length of time needed to complete the initial in-service training. This information tells the employee how much training is involved, something of the relative difficulty of the job, and perhaps even the length of the probationary period, which, incidentally, should also mean a step up on the wage scale. Also, somewhere in the job description should be a reference to whom the individual reports and what his supervisory responsibilities are, if any. This can be a special heading designated as "Organizational relationships" or "Administrative responsibilities," or it can be included under "Duties and responsibilities." In the latter case the list of duties can begin with statements such as "Under the supervision of the chief typist ..." or "With a minimum of supervision by the Department Head, the cataloger...."

After the description has been written it should be taken to the employee for review. The job should be once again described to see that it fits what was written, and any inaccuracies changed. Finally, after the final draft has been neatly typed, it should be sent to the division head for review. After the library administration has checked it, copies should be made for the employee, department head, division head, and library director. One should also be placed in the individual's personnel folder.

As with the jobs themselves, job descriptions for professional positions will differ from those written for clericals and paraprofessionals. A professional description places more emphasis on the duties and responsibilities, less on how to carry them out. The professional description is less a detailed description of a specific job than an explanation of

overall responsibilities and an indication of the individual's
relation to others in the library. There is also less concern
with present duties and more emphasis on the future and what
the professional should strive to achieve.

The format, too, may differ. There may be headings
such as "Responsibilities" and "Formal education," with less
emphasis on specific skills. It may even be more convenient
to write the descriptions in paragraph form, instead of in
traditional short sentences. The uses to which the professional job descriptions are put will also differ. Professional
descriptions are used less for salary adjustments, more consideration being given to professional activities both inside
and outside the library. In many libraries, the professional
librarian himself prepares the description with only minor
input from the department head. In still other libraries, job
description preparation is a committee assignment.

Exactly how specific a particular professional job description should be will depend on several factors. The more
senior the position, for example, the more leeway allowed the
individual to create his own job. Likewise, the smaller the
department the more the cataloger should be allowed to change
the position to suit his talents. And certainly the leadership
philosophy of the department head will affect the job description. If he favors a bureaucratic organizational structure the
description will be more precise.

To aid in developing a job description program, here
are a few more points to consider:

1. Keep the descriptions up to date. An out-dated
   job description, which can cause misunderstandings,
   is worse than none at all. Set a specific date when
   all descriptions are to be reviewed. They must be
   up-dated whenever the context of the job is
   changed.
2. Make the descriptions as complete as possible yet
   not over-detailed. Be particularly careful to distinguish between primary and secondary duties.
   Emphasize those factors that are relatively important.
3. Be as objective and as impartial as possible. Personal feelings about the job holder must not affect
   the description of the job. The department head

must resist the temptation to upgrade a job in hopes
of getting the holder a salary raise. He must apply
the same criteria and the same standards to each
job in the department. Once again, it is the job
that is being described not the individual.

4. Give special consideration to the job titles; they
should clearly define the job. In larger departments where jobs are relatively specialized, staff
members should not be designated simply as cataloger or typist. If the cataloger catalogs serials,
then he is a serials cataloger. Thus, for clarification more than one-word titles may sometimes have
to be used.

5. Although the format of the job description should
be uniform, there will be variations within the sub-
sections. It may be wise, therefore, to type forms
individually, including all headings and subheadings,
in order to conform to the amount of material included under each.

6. Finally, while job descriptions will not solve all job-
related problems and misunderstandings, they will
at least put the duties and responsibilities on paper
and, therefore, out in the open where they can be
examined both by the job-holders and the administration.

The Department Manual

The department manual is a basic working tool, perhaps
the department's most important tool. Its purpose is to codi-
fy all department procedures. The department manual forms
the basis of the in-service training program, and is a major
reference tool for the staff. It is imperative, therefore, that
a good deal of thought be given to its design. Characteristics of a good department manual are:

1. Complete coverage. All information necessary to
carry out department duties and responsibilities
should be included. All questions not answered
in AACR and the department's other working tools
should be answered here.

2. Easy to use. It is important to assure ease of use
through logical chapter and section design, intelligent organization of headings, a good index and

table of contents, appropriate illustrations, systematic page identification, and logical organization.
3. Easy to read. This is accomplished by presenting
the material logically and clearly, and by using
short paragraphs and sentences, concrete words instead of abstract words, and active instead of
passive voice.
4. Easy to revise. This is done by providing a loose-
leaf format and using a page numbering system that
will allow for additions and deletions.

Format. The size of the manual should be 8½ x 11
inches to accommodate standard size paper. This size is also
convenient for material produced on office duplication machines and for standard size letters and forms which should
be incorporated. To permit easy revision, a loose-leaf binder
of some sort should be used. With a loose-leaf binder, sections can be duplicated and distributed selectively to staff.
The standard three-ring notebook is satisfactory, although
there are other kinds that will serve the purpose. The only
prerequisite is that the material can be easily inserted and
removed and that the binder permit pages to open flat for
convenient use. The department head may want to consider
a specific colored binder either to match or contrast with other library manuals. For added convenience, colored pages
can be used for special inserts or sections. But whether
white or tinted, the paper must be good quality so that materials can be easily read without strain, and so that pen or
pencil notations can be added. Also, the paper should be extra strength to take the abuse it will undoubtedly receive.
Supports may be necessary to protect the holes from tearing
in the binder.

Arrangement. A typical catalog department manual will
include the following: 1) title page; 2) letter of transmittal;
3) preface; 4) table of contents; 5) body; 6) appendices; 7)
index.

1. Title page. This should list editor, title, edition
and imprint.

2. Letter of transmittal. The letter of transmittal,
signed by the department head, is the official statement of
presentation. Written in usual letter format, it sets the tone
of the manual, acknowledges the help of contributors, and
contains a brief statement on the purpose of the manual.

3. Preface. Similar to and often a substitute for the letter of transmittal, the preface (or, in some manuals, the introduction) should include a brief explanation for users, an indication of the scope of the manual, and a statement on updating procedures.

4. Table of contents. Because the manual will have to be continually updated it is essential that the table of contents present, in a logical manner, the major subject areas broken down into subchapters and sections. Yet the contents must be flexible enough to allow for additions without continual revision. The table of contents should show readers at a glance the major divisions and subdivisions.

5. Body. The contents should be subdivided into chapters and, if necessary, into two or more physical volumes--one volume for professional duties, the other for clerical routines. The first chapter should be an introduction which contains a brief history of the department, an explanation of the organization of the department (with an organizational chart), and an overall explanation of the work flow through the department, perhaps in flow-chart format. In addition, it is a good idea to include a brief overview of the flow of materials through the entire technical services division.

Each department will, of course, have a different organizational structure and evolve a different set of routines. Thus each will require a different format for its manual. Typical topics--and, therefore, typical chapter headings-- are: general cataloging and classification procedures, recataloging and reclassification routines, serial cataloging routines, rush book routines, statistics, and cataloging special materials. Topics for the clerical section might include chapters on typing routines, book preparation, withdrawals, filing routines, card reproduction, added copies and volumes, and, if the library is automated, there will be chapters on coding, inputting, and other data processing procedures. It is important to include reproductions of forms and working records such as catalog cards, order forms, and routing slips. A simple reproduction of a catalog card indicating correct spacings is worth a thousand words to a neophyte typist. Illustrations and forms that cannot be integrated into the main body should be placed in the appendix.

6. Appendix. After the initial training period, new

employees will undoubtedly refer to the appendix more than to
any other section of the manual. The appendix should include such items as a bibliography of professional reading
materials, a list of abbreviations used by the library, a Cutter table (that is, if it is an abbreviated one such as LC's),
a lettering and numbering guide for the marking section, a
list of location symbols, reproductions of the more important
LC transliteration tables, and copies of pertinent LC, vendor,
network, and other service bulletins.

7. Index. An index should be prepared. It should
be as thorough as possible, anticipating the needs of users.
Cross-references should be used, of course. Theoretically,
the index should be re-issued each time material is added or
deleted from the manual; practically, this just is not feasible.
The department head will have to use his own judgment on
how often to replace the index. To maintain continuity between revisions, important words should be penciled in the
index of each manual. To provide room for interpolation of
new subjects, entries should be double (or triple) spaced, or
one side of each index page can be left blank.

Revising the manual. The manual should be organized
so that it can be periodically updated and revised. If the
manual is well thought out staff will be able to insert additions and changes without destroying the logical interrelations.
One way to do this is to number inserts with sub-letters or
sub-numbers. If, for example, material is inserted after page
25, the inserts can be numbered 25a, 25b, or 25.1, 25.2,
etc. To keep track of the revisions, each should be dated.

The department head should keep a master copy of the
manual which contains all revisions. From time to time, staff
members will want to check back over previous changes.
Also kept in this master copy will be official memos that initiated the manual revisions and that contain approvals of the
policy changes. These memos should be dated and numbered
in accordance with the manual numbering system.

Some libraries attach a revision notice with each set of
revisions sent to manual holders. Included on the notice
should be date and revision number, the effective date of
each revision, listings of pages to be removed and pages to
be inserted, brief explanation of the revisions, and the department head's signature.

The revisions and a revision notice should be distributed to each holder of a manual. Manuals can be issued to each full-time member of the department; or several persons can share a manual with various sections duplicated and distributed to catalogers and clerks on a need-to-know basis. In the latter case, the department head must keep track of each section of the basic manual and issue revisions that apply to the various sections.

Procedure. The department head should prepare an outline, breaking down the manual into sections and chapters. He should select an editor (or act as editor himself) and an editorial committee. Each committee member should be selected on the basis of: 1) knowledge of specific cataloging routines; 2) ability to visualize these routines in relation to the total library operation; 3) understanding of logical relations of cataloging procedures; and, 4) ability to express himself clearly in terms understood by readers. Each member should be assigned the responsibility for one or more of the topic chapters. To maintain continuity of operations, committee members should not only prepare the instructional materials for the new manual but should also be responsible for future revisions.

Naturally, chapter assignments will relate to duties. But each committee member should also consult others in the department. Staff members can even be asked to write out descriptions of their routines to be submitted to the committee for revision. The editor or a committee member can do the editing and proofreading, or committee members can proofread each other's chapters. One person should be responsible for indexing the manual, another for distribution control. Then the committee should establish a timetable for writing assignments, training and planning sessions, first draft, editing the first draft, second draft, final editorial review, indexing, proofreading, duplication and assembly, and distribution.

Points to remember:

1. Arrange material in logical order so that related information is found together.
2. Use precise and concrete words, not abstract words. And illustrate whenever possible.
3. Be alert to details. Write the manual so that there

is no question about procedures and so that the
newcomer can easily understand and follow each
routine.

4. But do not over-detail. Too much detail provides
   no room for individual variation and will not allow
   for minor changes without complete rewriting.
5. Anticipate future revisions and additions.
6. Before adding a new procedure into the manual,
   test it out to discover and correct unforeseen problems.
7. Take advantage of auxiliary sources, particularly
   publications from the Library of Congress and, if
   the library is part of a network, publications distributed by network headquarters.

The Budget

The budget is both a method of obtaining department
funds and a tool for implementing department goals. Most
funds, of course, are fixed and remain at a fairly constant
level, affected as much by inflation, funding sources, and
other outside factors as they are by department needs. The
department head will have little to say, for example, about
funding new building facilities, computer hardware, and most
other capital expenditures. He should, however, have a good
deal to say about funding the department's day-to-day staffing, equipment, and supply needs.

Library budget procedures are as varied as the budgets they produce. In smaller libraries that exist as single
budget units there may be no formal guidelines at all. Often
the entire process is in the hands of the director with staff
members and supervisors involved only in a brief memo or an
informal conversation. Larger institutions, on the other hand,
often have highly structured procedures with the various departments asked to submit detailed budget statements, which
in turn are joined together to form larger budgeting units until there is one budget for the library and finally a master
budget for the parent institution.

To make budget preparation an orderly process, most
library directors issue budget calendars describing the tasks
involved, the staff members who are to participate, and the
dates on which each task is to be completed. The process

itself usually begins with a meeting of library administrators
(designated in some libraries as the "Budget Committee") to
formulate budget policies and to anticipate funding needs and
resources. Each department head is then asked to prepare
a budget for his or her area of responsibility, guided by the
procedures outlined by the director or budget committee. The
department head submits his budget up the administrative
ladder or directly to the budget committee where the department budgets are discussed (and usually revised) and a master budget prepared.

Library budgets are sometimes based on a specific plan--
for example, the PPBS or MBO approaches which will be discussed later in the chapter or on some version of Zero Based
Budgeting (ZBB). Zero Based Budgeting, like PPBS and
MBO, is a systems approach to budgeting in which each department head is required to justify every expenditure from
point zero. To use ZBB the department head asks himself:
"What would happen if the programs in the budget were to
receive no funds at all?" He must then justify, to himself
and to the library administration, each of his budget requests
based on this assumption of a zero budget.

A more realistic version of ZBB is to start not from a
zero base but from a base that provides only minimum department services. In this case, the budget is first calculated
on an austerity level, then on a business-as-usual level, and
finally on a projected improved level.

A more traditional approach, however, is for the library
director to ask the department heads to list new budget items
in priority order; that is, according to the importance of
each item in supporting the department's goals. At the top
of the list would be essential items followed by requests that
are necessary for the improvement of department operations
but not so essential that the department could not function,
and ending with those requests which would be desirable but
which could be postponed or even eliminated. Priority lists
are most often used when unanticipated revenues (a bond issue, the elimination of a library program, a larger than usual
legislative allocation) suddenly become available.

Whatever the procedure, the first step in preparing a
department budget is for the department head to review last
year's budget, even if the budget process has changed. A

review gives perspective. Next, the department head re-
searches and writes out his budget requests, taking into consideration the following points.

1. Research all requests. When requesting equipment,
furniture, and supply expenditures, the department head
should check carefully through library supply catalogs for
specifications, prices, and any other information that might
help in the purchasing process. Even if the items are ordered from a different source, this information lets the reader
know exactly what the department needs; it shows also that
the department head knows himself what is needed.

2. Consider the purchasing policies of the library and
its parent institution. To prepare a realistic budget, the department head must know such things as whether his requests
must be put out on bid, if the library is restricted to a particular supply source, if requests must conform to specific
library-wide specifications, and if the library receives educational discounts or discounts for purchasing in bulk. All
this can be learned from the library budget director or the
central purchasing office.

3. Calculate support items and support staff. To request a typist without also requesting a desk, chair, typewriter, and supplies would be of little value to the department. Likewise, in requesting a cataloger, the department
head must also consider the impact the new professional position will have on the department's support staff.

4. Accompany budget requests with a clear statement
of justification. Justifications can range from a series of
complaints from the terminal operators to a technological
breakthrough. In the case of equipment, the department
head should state specific reasons for replacement--obsoles-
cence, broken beyond repair, etc. The department head
should also use established standards and guidelines such as
square feet per employee or specifications set up by the
American Library Association or other professional organization. This information can be included either in a narrative
or as footnotes.

5. Where possible, break budget requests down to
costs per unit of output--for example, dollars and cents per
card set. Costs-per-unit give a more realistic picture than

mere dollar or unit requests. Simply wanting staff additions
and new equipment is not enough.

6. Don't become overly concerned with the numbers
game. Although unit measurements and statistics are both
informative and impressive in a budget request, quality is
more important than quantitative results and should be emphasized. Whether a typist or a typewriter, request quality.

7. Don't overbudget; that is to say, don't ask for
more than is needed. The department head should give a
realistic picture based on needs and then let the director
make the final budget decisions based on the evidence provided.

8. Involve everyone in the budget process. Just as
the director should involve all the department heads in preparing the library budget, the department head must assume
that each person in the department knows best the needs of
his or her area of responsibility.

9. Think of the budget as a year-round project, not
as a once-a-year crisis. The department head should maintain a budget file where day-to-day budget needs can be de-
posited. As suggestions come in from staff members and
from department head's observations he should jot down figures and facts on a memo pad and slip it into his "budget
folder." At budget-preparation time he need only pull the
file, arrange his notes, and begin researching and writing.

10. Include a summary in narrative form. In the narrative the department head should justify any changes from
the norm, including major increases (and decreases) in the
budget. Mention should also be made of long-term needs
that relate to future budget periods and an explanation given
of budget needs that are not being met, and why. The narrative can also call attention to sources of additional information and offer any other data that the reader might need to
evaluate the requests.

The Consultant

Perhaps no single concept has so transformed the catalog department as the unprecedented proliferation of outside

services. Few of these outside services have proliferated
more than the consultant.   If the library director wants to
automate the catalog department he will call in an consultant;
if he is planning a new library addition he will seek advice
from a building consultant; and even if the library is only
looking for a new card duplicating machine a consultant may
be part of the package. Many library-supply houses, vendors,
and networks provide consultant service to libraries using
their equipment or services. These consultants either visit
clients on a regular basis or are "on call." Often they are
professional librarians who, although not directly employed
by the company, are retained on a special basis. True, it
is sometimes difficult to know where the consultant begins
and the salesman leaves off. But even if his real-life job is
selling catalog card cabinets, as with any department tool, it
is how he is used that counts, not his motives.

Advantages of a consultant are obvious. A specialist
who has served many clients and has dealt with situations
that other librarians encounter will have a wealth of experience upon which to draw. Because he enters the library
without preconceived notions or prejudices, he can look at a
local situation objectively and with a fresh viewpoint. Also,
because the consultant usually devotes full-time to a relatively specialized field, his knowledge of this field is, theoretically at least, superior to that of the average librarian. In
addition, the consultant can offer a variety of services. He
will make recommendations, install equipment and programs,
train staff, and provide follow-up.

Yet many librarians look upon consultants with suspi-
cion, if not hostility. When the library director brings the
consultant into the department, a noticeable chill may de-
scend. "Will he replace me with a computer?" "Will he finger
me as the bottleneck?" Complaints of catalogers are well
known: "He offered us theory but no practical suggestions."
"He came here to do the boss's dirty work." "All he did was
pick our brains, gather a few statistics from the annual report, and incorporate it all into his fancy prepackaged formula."
"Sure he gained some more consultant experience, but he left
us with a lot of recommendations that no catalog department
could possibly afford to implement." Unfortunately, there is
as much truth as fiction in such complaints. But justified or
not, unless everyone in the department, including the department head, does everything possible to assist the consultant

in his work, the department itself must share responsibility
for less than satisfactory results.

Whoever does the selecting must make sure that the
consultant knows his business; that is, that he (or his firm)
is experienced, is familiar with similar libraries, and has a
good reputation. Unfortunately, all a library consultant needs
to go into business today is a calling card and a letterhead.
The best way to verify the reliability of a consultant is to
check with other libraries that have used his services, and
carefully review reports he has made for others. If the library has no one in mind, a reputable organization (ALA, for
example) should be asked to send a list of accredited consultants. In most cases, it is best to get estimates from at
least two or three persons or firms, and then select the one
whose services (and fees) best suit local needs. After the
consultant has been selected, the following points should be
stressed.

1. Let the consultant know exactly what is expected
of him. If, for example, the department wants to improve
its card reproduction process, he should be told this as precisely as possible. Does the catalog department need a specific recommendation, a detailed report, a list of alternatives,
a plan of action?

2. By the same token, staff members should be honest
with him. The consultant should be given a clear picture
(both written and oral) of department procedures. Members
of the department should discuss openly and honestly both
personnel conflicts and operational problems, and anything
else that will help him in his assignment. The picture should
not be distorted in any way.

3. Prepare the staff. Both support staff and professionals should be told exactly why the consultant is coming
and what he is expected to accomplish.

4. Introduce him to every member of the department
involved in the operation he is surveying. And everyone
must have a chance to talk with him confidentially.

5. Establish a point of contact in the department
(either the department head or another professional) to promote an efficient line of communication between the consultant

and the department. He should not be allowed to wander around on his own, reporting to no one in the department.

6. If the library is contracting with a firm of consultants, the department head must make sure he deals only with one person--the person in charge. There may be more than one consultant in the library at a time, and getting feedback from all of them can be confusing.

7. To keep up with developments of the survey, periodic progress reports should be required. These can be simply weekly informal briefings. Also, the final report should be fully discussed before the consultant leaves the library. It is almost impossible to straighten out inconsistencies and jumbled facts after the consultant has left.

8. Finally, agree on costs. Whoever is responsible for paying the bills should have a clear idea of the fees, whether they are on a per-diem or fixed-charge basis.

Management by Objectives

Typical of the more innovative management concepts (that is to say, tools) found in libraries today is "management by objectives" (MBO), or as the technique is sometimes called, "goal analysis," "management by results," and "appraisal by results." All such goal and objective techniques use the same basic rationale: the establishment of goals (long range targets) and objectives (specific outcomes desired) that make possible the measurement of future success.

To manage by objectives: 1) all members of the catalog department must have a common understanding of the approach; 2) everyone from the library director to the student assistant must be committed to the program; and, 3) all must have a desire to make it succeed. Given these three prerequisites, most departments that operate under this management system have claimed measurable improvements.

To implement MBO, the broad goals of the library must first be determined. More specifically, the department head must determine the goals of his department. This is accomplished through discussions with the library director, division head, and members of the department. Clearly, too, department goals must be compatible with the goals of other library units. Ideally, department heads should reach agreement on all library goals. Each goal should represent a basic statement of intent; and to be true goals, each should be timeless and non-specific in nature.

From these goals are evolved the specific objectives which will describe what the department must achieve to realize its long-range goals. It is important that the entire staff be involved in setting department objectives. One way to do this is to have each member of the department submit a list of objectives toward which the department should work. Then, at a department meeting, the objectives can be compiled and rated, and the relative importance of each discussed. Since the objectives will represent a plan for promoting the original goals, they must be realistic, specific, measurable, and, even if difficult, not impossible to achieve. In addition, a time limitation should be placed on each.

Once the objectives have been listed and discussed, staff can begin sorting, adding, and deleting. All duplications, redundancies, and abstractions should be eliminated. The group may also want to list alternative objectives based on projections of available time, money, and personnel. Then, once again, the list should be rated and those objectives thrown out which the group feels are unobtainable or unworthy of immediate attention. Next, for each of the objectives the question should be asked: If we achieve this objective will we have helped to achieve our goal? To determine periodically the progress toward accomplishing these objectives, the department head simply measures the discrepancies between them and department performance. Although the timetable may have to be re-adjusted from time to time, the department will be continually operating under both a rational and a measurable plan-of-action.

By way of example, we will assume that the department's goal is "to provide bibliographic access for all users to all materials in the library." After discussing the goal, staff members formulate several objectives including, "to eliminate all cataloging backlogs in the department within six months." Since this statement meets the criteria of specificity, measurability, and, presumably, attainability, it is a legitimate objective. To discover the department's relative progress one need only look at the shelves to see how much of the backlog remains. If at any time, and for any reason (lack of funds, a sudden influx of books, a flu epidemic), it is found that the objective is unattainable, it can be restructured. The point is that the department have both a commendable goal and obtainable objectives to which the department can commit itself and against which the department head can measure progress.

By way of review, here are eight do's and don'ts for the department head to keep in mind when implementing MBO:

1. Do provide a thorough orientation. To help insure staff cooperation, the department head should carefully explain the MBO program to everyone in the department before implementation.

2. Don't impose objectives on the department. Even more important, the department head must take seriously all suggestions from staff and discuss each one thoroughly.

3. Do proceed slowly. The department head might even want to start with a "pilot project" in one unit of the department before involving everyone.

4. Don't be inflexible. The department head must be ready to make changes in the program, including restructuring the objectives and altering the timetable.

5. Do give feedback. To hold the commitment of everyone in the department, staff members must be kept continually informed of the progress, or lack of it.

6. Don't get bogged down in techniques and details. The department head must emphasize goals and objectives, not the details of the program, and he must never allow MBO to become an end in itself.

7. Do secure agreement among other departments in the library. Everyone in the library must be committed to the catalog department's MBO program and support its goals and objectives.

8. Don't use MBO by itself. MBO is a tool to be used along with all other departmental tools. In any case, Management By Objectives will only be as effective as the leadership provided by the department head.

Systems Analysis

Systems analysis, as much an art as a scientific method, can be defined as "the systematic examination of alternative actions related to the accomplishment of desired objectives." It is a problem-solving, decision-making, information-gathering tool which can be used to analyze library work situations of all sorts. The more complex the situation the more useful the tool.

Success in applying systems analysis to a particular cataloging program will depend on the analyst's ability to 1) define the situation being analyzed; 2) divide and subdivide it into identifiable segments; 3) analyze and compare possible interrelationships; 4) uncover alternative solutions; and, finally, 5) restructure the operation to meet stated objectives.

If, for example, the department head wants to analyze a particular typing routine, he first defines the routine and its objectives. This is done by examining the job description, department manual, monthly statistics, and any other information relating to the job in question. He then interviews one or two typists, and perhaps the chief typist. After he has gathered sufficient data, he carefully and systematically breaks down the typing routine into sequential steps, noting the relationships of each. It is particularly important to make each step as explicit as possible, listing the functions and their relationships to each other. Or, to better visualize the routine, he can construct a flow chart. Flow-charting is simply charting the flow-patterns of an operation by the use of variously shaped boxes, triangles, and circles, all connected by lines denoting the directions of the work-flow. The shape of each box indicates the type of action or operation represented at that step. For example, circles usually indicate the start or end of an operation, rectangles denote action of some sort, diamonds represent the entrance and exit of material along the flow sequence, rounded boxes are decision points, and so on. For further clarification, inside each box is written a brief explanation of that particular step.

After the flow sequences are put on paper, either in narrative or flow-chart format, the department head analyzes and evaluates the sequence of the entire routine, studies the interrelationships of each operation, and determines the how and why of each step, examining possible alternatives. He must assess and compare resource costs and benefits associated with each alternative, being careful to make both quantitative and qualitative comparisons. Hopefully, alternatives will evolve that will more effectively and more efficiently fulfill department objectives. At the very least, a careful systems analysis will show that the original routine is, as far as can be determined, the best possible way to reach the stated objective.

Actually, systems analysis can be as complex or simple, as formal or informal, as structured or unstructured as the librarian cares to make it. Perhaps one of the most complex techniques developed in recent years is PERT (Program Evaluation and Review Technique). PERT was originally a computer technique designed by the U.S. Navy for use in its missile program. Today, both pen-and-paper and computer PERTing are being used by government, industry, and educational institutions as a planning tool. Specifically, it is used to determine and schedule the time necessary for accomplishing various tasks. Given a desired outcome or completed event (the move into a new building, elimination of a cataloging backlog, organization of a workshop), the PERT planner traces backward through all the steps necessary to reach the final goal. This is usually done in a flow-chart type diagram. He examines the many steps involved and their interrelationships, comparing his diagram with the final outcome. After his analysis, he can then re-deploy resources and reassign time allocations. He may switch certain people from one work group to another, or allow one group more time than another. As might be expected, PERT and other systems techniques have become particularly popular in budgeting procedures.

Industry and government have also found PPBS (Planning, Programming, Budgeting System), originally developed by the Rand Corporation, useful in planning, especially fiscal planning. The PPB system consists of: 1) organizing a program budget in terms of explicitly stated long-range objectives; 2) developing plans to meet the objectives; 3) listing alternative ways of achieving these objectives; 4) rigorously analyzing each alternative to select the most appropriate; and, 5) establishing means for measuring the resources used and the results achieved which can be fed back into the planning exercise. By portraying cataloging activities as a system,

PPBS can serve to integrate the processing of library materials with financial administration and depict the effects of all the component variables of a cataloging operation. Thus, if properly conducted, PPBS, like all systems tools, can provide libraries with a complete basis for rational choice. Also like all systems approaches, it is basically the application of common sense.

The Delphi Technique

With change accelerating in most cataloging operations, the need to predict trends and events five or ten years into the future becomes increasingly important. Indeed, prediction-making is a fundamental part of department planning. Particularly important is the ability to narrow down the dates and circumstances of events that will affect department operations. At what point in time will library acquisitions reach 10,000 titles a year? When will the catalog department grow out of its present quarters? When should the department automate? These are among the questions every department head must face at some time or other.

One managerial tool developed by social scientists to help predict such future events is the Delphi technique. Principally an intuitive forecasting technique, Delphi is used in libraries today to predict approximately when an event will occur or an idea will be put into practice.

A typical Delphi study goes something like this: A listing of future events (for example: When will all libraries in the community be serviced by a central automated processing system?) is sent to several local experts. Although these "experts" should all be familiar with the field, it is also important that they possess expertise in different areas. In fact, they need not all be professional librarians. Without consulting the others, each is asked to predict when the events will occur. Participants are also invited to explain and defend their predictions. The results are tabulated and the outcome returned to the experts who, after examining all the written comments, indicate their revised predictions. The tabulated results represent the final compromise or median prediction.

This is not the sure-fire, scientific tool that most de-

partment heads might hope to use in long-range planning, but
there is no such thing as a fool-proof prediction-making tool,
and the Delphi technique may come as close as any. As a
trial run, the department head could write out a few projections and send the list to members of his department, asking
them to estimate the probable time of occurrence for each.
Then, following the above formula, he can develop a few
guesstimates that will, perhaps, aid in the department's long-
range planning.

Accountability

Whatever tool or system is used to make a decision,
gather information, or organize a routine, the results must
contribute to the catalog department's accountability. Accountability is the determination of how well the department
is doing, what it does, and whether it is doing exactly what
it should. Simply put, accountability is doing what is supposed to be done. It is, in other words, the raison d'être
of the department manual, MBO, Delphi, budget, all of the
department's other tools, techniques, methods, systems, and
activities. It means that the department agrees to perform
specific services for which it will be held answerable according to agreed-upon terms. Furthermore, each service must
be performed within an established time-period and with a
stipulated use of resources and performance standards. To
fulfill a service, clear and complete records must be kept,
and the information made available for outside review.

By way of example, the cataloging department, through
a systems or other careful analysis, determines that it can
catalog a specific number of phonorecords during the fiscal
year with a cataloger and supportive staff working a given
number of hours per day and according to agreed-upon standards of bibliographic control (i.e., following AACR2, using
an accession numbering system, and so on). Careful statistics are kept and, at the end of the year, are reviewed to determine the degree of success. All parties (library director,
department head, catalogers, clerks, and, indirectly at least,
library patrons) must understand and agree upon what is expected and what is not expected. If the number of phonorecords cataloged during the year does not meet the specified
standards the department must provide a convincing explanation for the failure. The agreement also obligates the library

director (or any other reviewer) by establishing the criteria for his expectations. He cannot whimsically change the requirements by demanding a more detailed classification system or insisting that additional added entries be made for each title cataloged.

Actually, the accountability principle is found today, in one form or another, in all catalog departments. In contracting for an outside service, for example, the department head will apply some variation of the accountability principle. He will insist that the various firms or supply houses submit bids specifying the exact services they will provide, the costs, and delivery time. And he will hold them accountable for the results. To be sure, this "bidding" is usually done through a simple review of library supply catalogs. Nonetheless, this is accountability in action.

Advantages of accountability are obvious. Accountability increases participation in decision-making for everyone affected by cataloging activities. It forces librarians to examine their goals and their methods of achieving these goals. Accountability enables the department to show what it is doing with its dollars and forces it to refine its techniques for measuring and judging what it is doing.

But there are potential dangers, too. Accountability may force the department to pursue those goals which are most easily attained, most simply stated, or most accurately measured. It also renders the department more susceptible to outside pressures. In addition, it may encourage the department to use resources in ways which are not really desirable, or which cause staff to refrain from attempting the creative and innovative. Accountability may result in opposition from staff who see it as a challenge to standard practices and a sign that their work is constantly being evaluated. Administrators may resist, too, if they find that additional monies will be required to accomplish certain activities or that they must drastically reorder library priorities.

But whether we like it or not, accountability is being demanded from both public and private institutions today. The clear implication for the catalog department is that everyone in and outside the department wants to know and must be told how and why library holdings are being organized and controlled. The user wants to know why it takes so long for a book to reach the shelves; the director wants statistics on whether or not the newly established regional network really catalogs books more economically than local processing methods previously employed; the division head wants information on whether the catalog department has the resources necessary to eliminate its backlogs; and the library board wants an accounting of the ways the department is spending its allocations. With taxpayers and, in turn, administrators becoming more and more insistent on getting their "money's worth," the catalog department, as well as every other library unit, must be prepared to justify its methods of operation. For each activity performed, the department must, using whatever approach is considered most appropriate, establish reasonable goals, keep clear and precise records, and be accountable for the results.

Accountability does not mean the same thing to everyone, of course; and it places different obligations on different groups. To the taxpayer accountability means paying for results, not promises; to the catalog department it means specifying in advance desired outcomes; to staff members it means becoming involved in the decision-making process; and to the library director it means reordering strategies and personnel. Finally, to everyone concerned accountability means keeping informed on what can and cannot be done in the way of bibliographic control in given situations, and why.

Chapter 12

THE COMPUTER

The biggest and most expensive tool used by the catalog department is the computer. Yet most staff members never see it. Some may not know it exists. Even so, a computer will probably be responsible for the catalog cards the department buys, the order and billing slips that accompany the books, and even the catalogs, indexes, subject headings lists, and other tools used by the department to catalog the materials the library receives. If the library is part of a corporate, municipal, state, or federal system, the department's personnel records, not to mention paychecks, will be controlled by a computer. Granted, staff could care less whether their catalog cards (or paychecks) are produced by a computer or by some other tool, as long as the cards (and checks) arrive on time and are reasonably free from error. But what happens if the library buys or leases its own computer? How is a complex tool like this to be used? Actually, staff members will have little to say about its use. After the department has gone online, the department head and everyone else will be told precisely what to do with the computer and how to do it. They will have less to say about how to use this, the department's largest and most important tool, than any other tool in the library. The really important decisions come before the computer is installed--and these are vital decisions.

Someone will have to decide, for example, whether the department really needs a computer, what kind--latest generation, minicomputer, microcomputer--and what is expected of it. It is at this point, when first considering whether and how to automate, that the real hard-nosed questions must be asked, and intelligent answers received. If the library director and department head fail to make the right decisions, either through poor judgment or by default, the catalog department and the library will suffer irreparable damage. Although it is not the purpose of this book to present a detailed description of automated cataloging (there have been many good books written on the subject, including several listed in the bibliography), a few guidelines on selecting an appropriate system should be noted.

1. Will the proposed system be compatible with MARC and with computer-based bibliographic systems and networks now in operation? Will it interface with present and possible future acquisition, circulation, and serials automated systems? If not, it should not be adopted. With the present emphasis on networking and centralized processing, this is no time for a catalog department to go out on its own private (and expensive) limb.

2. Make sure the library has its own computer specialist on board. If the specialist is not already familiar with the cataloging operation, he should spend several months studying and perhaps even working in the department before the library embarks on an automation program.

3. Although the catalog department must have at least one specialist on call who is both a librarian and a systems person, the library must be wary of building its own in-house automation staff. Instead, the administration should have an independent company come in, plan and organize a turnkey system, train staff, and then leave. The catalog department wants the best possible installation with a specialist handy to see that the system continues to run smoothly; it does not need an expensive automation staff playing games at the library's expense, and at the expense of library patrons.

4. Know exactly what is expected of the computer. Do not accept anything less; just as important, do not accept anything more. The catalog department must not get talked into services it neither wants nor needs. The computer can do just about anything it is told to do, but in most cases more expensively than manual operations.

5. Clean up all records before automating. The cliché "garbage in, garbage out" is nowhere more appropriate than in automating a cataloging operation. If the library director considers it too expensive to up-date, revise, and correct catalog cards and other department records, then it is also too expensive to automate them.

6. Look to the future. Even though the library may not want (or cannot afford) a fully automated library system, neither can it afford to box itself in. If the catalog department is automated only half-way, it must be sure it can go all the way when the time comes.

7. Insist on a realistic timetable. The department head should sit down with the systems analyst and map out each step in the process, estimating time lag for each major operation. He should also make sure that on-going operations will interface smoothly with the new computer. There will be miscalculations, but they should be minor and honest ones. One of the most persistent criticisms of automated cataloging systems is the time it takes to establish, de-bug, and fully operate an installation.

8. Do not discontinue the manual operations the minute the first catalog cards come tumbling out of the computer. Both systems should be used until everyone is absolutely sure that the new operation is completely de-bugged and performing exactly the way it should.

Bibliographic Networks

The high cost of setting up and maintaining an in-house automated cataloging system has encouraged many libraries eager to take advantage of the latest in computer technology to form computer-based library cooperatives, called systems, utilities, consortia, or networks. For the catalog department, the chief advantage of joining a computer-based network is the opportunity it offers members to share cataloging information.

A typical library cooperative works something like this: Member libraries contribute cataloging to be stored in a central computer which other members can then search and visually display the results of their searches on local cathode ray tube (CRT) terminals. A library can modify the cataloging displayed on its terminals and by signaling the central computer receive cataloging products (catalog cards, printouts, magnetic tapes, microforms) formatted to its specifications. Many networks also provide interlibrary loan, acquisitions, serials check-in, and other bibliographic services.

A network can be limited to a specific type of library (medical libraries, for example) or it can include all types; a network can be local, statewide, regional, or national. Presently, some of the largest computer-based networks include WLN (Washington Library Network), RLIN (Research Libraries Information Network), and OCLC Online Computer Library Center (formally the Ohio College Library Center). Under the OCLC automated umbrella are the regional networks of NELINET (New England Library Network), SOLINET (Southeastern Library Network), AMIGOS, among others. Someday it may be possible for all computer-based networks to join together to form one national system. Until then any library or group of libraries considering membership in a library cooperative must select from one of the existing systems. An important responsibility for the department head will be to evaluate competing networks and to assist the library administration in selecting the one system best suited to the library's needs.

First, the department head must learn all he can about the network being considered and the services it provides; equally important, he must learn the network's future plans. Few if any networks are presently offering all the bibliographic services they hope to provide. On the other hand, most offer many more services than the typical small or medium-size library will need or want.

Specifically, then, what does the network have to offer, now and in the future? Can the library receive, and does it want, hard copy, spine labels, or circulation cards produced at a printer attached to the terminal? What local modifications can the library receive on its catalog cards--juvenile subject headings, call numbers formatted to its specifications, special notes, holding statements? How quickly will the library receive cards from the processing center? Will they arrive in alphabetical order, in call number order, or how? Can the library receive history tapes with which to produce book or microform catalogs? Will the tapes interface with the library's vendor tapes or with its own minicomputers or microcomputers for circulation and other local applications?

What searching capabilities can the network provide--author, title, author-title, call number, ISBN (International Standard Book Number), ISSN (International Standard Serial Number)? Can the computer conduct subject searches, including searches using combinations of subject descriptors?

The department head will want to learn how the network monitors the quality of input and its success at eliminating duplications. Will, for example, a MARC record or a record that is in accordance with the latest AACR bump an older record?

What start-up services does the network provide? Will it take care of terminal installations and advise on workflow adjustments and help with profile changes? Does the network offer training sessions, workbooks, manuals, a hot-line to answer questions?

The service contract should be scrutinized. Will services cover paper clips in the keyboard as well as blow circuits, and is there a local troubleshooter on call to take care of terminal malfunctions? Certainly the department head will want to check with libraries already in the system for information on such things as response time, down time, systems failure, and liaison service.

What about governance? Will the library be accepting standards and following decisions made by the network management or by an advisory committee made up of participating libraries? How much input will the library have in the management of the cooperative and in developing future services? Does the network have the capacity to grow and develop, to link up with other networks, and to continue the same level of service as more and more institutions join the system?

How much control will the library have over its own records once they have entered the data base? Can the library, for example, make its cataloging available to other libraries in the area or can only institutions that belong to the network have access to the library's machine-readable records?

How large is the data base? Will the library be paying for more software and hardware capabilities than it can possibly use and will it be supporting a data base of which it uses only a small percent of the records; or is the data base so small that the number of terminal hits will make participation impractical?

Finally, what are the estimated costs? Are there annual fees or are costs based on the amount of transactions, number of terminals, card sets ordered, terminal time, or a combination of these? And will the library be charged for spurious searches, unwanted responses, "zilch" cards, programming errors?

Staffing

Libraries that have installed computers, joined computer-based networks, or otherwise automated part or all of their cataloging operations have also had to change many of their work assignments. Automation has not meant, as librarians once hoped, a reduction in personnel (except where automation has caused a tightening of workflow patterns and a more efficient use of personnel); instead, the chief staffing changes have been an increase in the responsibilities of support staff, changes in job descriptions, and a reclassification of positions. Adjustments in department assignments have had to be made, new skills learned, and added demands placed on staff.

To make effective use of the computer, department heads have had to merge many of their cataloging, searching, and inputting functions. Staff members who work at the terminals, especially in libraries that belong to computer-based networks, have often had to assume several different bibliographic functions, including searching the data base, verification of call numbers, completion of cataloging copy, selection of entries and subject headings, and checking the copy of contributing libraries against the local standards and practices. A large percentage of what was once considered original cataloging is now being handled at computer terminals by support staff who must be knowledgeable in MARC formats, the latest cataloging code, and local cataloging practices.

Automation has also caused the reorganization of many catalog departments, usually the creation of a separate unit within the department or a separate department within the technical service division. In larger libraries, this unit is usually staffed by terminal operators who add records to the data base, paraprofessionals who search and update the copy of contributing network libraries, and a professional or an experienced paraprofessional to supervise; in many smaller libraries, however, professionals work at the terminals, inputting as they catalog.

Work schedules have also had to be changed, both to make maximum use of expensive terminal time and because response time is usually slowest during peak periods of use. In many cases, terminals have had to be staffed from 6:00 a.m. to 6:00 p.m. or later, and on weekends.

Another important staffing change has been the use of terminals by staff members in combination with other duties. Unlike typists who spend up to eight hours a day at their typewriters or paraprofessionals who can spend all day searching various bibliographic tools, few employees can be expected to concentrate at the terminals for more than four or five hours a day or for more than two or three hours at a stretch. This means that those who add records to the data base must also be trained in a variety of manual operations.

Just as significant is the need for libraries to follow the latest cataloging codes and adhere to rigid formatting standards. A catalog department that belongs to a computer-based network in which each member relies on every other member for its cataloging can no longer take short-cuts in the processing of either books or nonbooks; nor can errors be tolerated. The department head must continually stress accuracy and insist that everyone working at the terminals follow minutely the formatting procedures set up by the network or utility, procedures that are becoming more complex as the networking-state-of-the-art develops. This in turn requires a dedicated and highly trained staff.

Training

The same techniques used to train staff in the department's manual routines (see Chapter 5) should be used to instruct staff in performing the various terminal operations. There will, however, be a shift in the emphasis and scope of the training. For example, a good deal of training will be carried out away from the library, especially if the library has joined a bibliographic network or if an outside firm has installed a turnkey system. Also, regardless of who is responsible for the training, everyone in the department will need to receive a basic orientation which would include an explanation of the terminology of library automation, a description of the capabilities and limitations of the new system, and demonstrations of the terminals, printers, and other equipment.

The department head must make sure that everyone under-stands what the system will do and how it will affect the work of the department. All library employees, even those not di-rectly involved with computer operations, should be allowed time off to attend orientation sessions and to read manuals, reports, newsletters, and other related documentation. During the planning stages, the department head will want to use every communication medium at his disposal--memos, progress reports, group orientations, committee assignments, training sessions--to keep his staff informed of the latest developments in the system. There is bound to be confusion and appre-hension among staff, which means that everyone in the depart-ment should be encouraged to ask questions and voice con-cerns.

Once the library has gone online, the training of cata-logers, searchers, terminal operators, and others who work di-rectly with the equipment should be the responsibility of the immediate supervisors who, in turn, will have been trained by the bibliographic utility or vendor. It is important also that one staff member be put in charge of the system and over-see the training of all library staff. In a large integrated system this person would be a professional systems librarian from outside the catalog department; in smaller libraries, the head of the catalog department or other department head might be asked to oversee the system. Because computer hardware and software are continually changing and being up-dated, training will be an on-going process, involving a variety of methods and techniques, always reinforced with hands-on experience.

COM Catalogs

Many libraries that have access to a data processing center have switched, or at least are considering the switch, from their traditional card catalogs to computer-produced microfilm or microfiche catalogs, known as COM (computer-output-microform) catalogs. Besides the availability of a com-puter, other reasons libraries have given for initiating COM catalogs include membership in a network that has the ability to produce COM catalogs; reclassification from Dewey to the Library of Congress classification system and using the re-classification project as an opportunity to begin a microform catalog; and closing the card catalog and choosing a COM cat-alog as the replacement.

Whatever the reason, a COM catalog does offer several advantages over the traditional card catalog. Once the library's holdings are in machine-readable form, for example, the computer is able to duplicate all kinds of microform catalogs, indexes, and bibliographies, which means greater use by patrons. Updating and correcting cataloging records is easier and quicker with the aid of a computer. Finally, as with other types of automated catalogs, a COM catalog allows the library to consolidate many of its bibliographic activities (acquisitions, interlibrary loan, serials check-in, circulation) onto one machine-readable file.

At the present time, however, hardware and software costs make COM catalogs available only to a few larger library systems, mainly those who already have their holdings stored on computer tapes, disks, or drums. If a library does not have its holdings in machine-readable form it will have to either contact a commercial firm to set up a turnkey automated system, join a network that has COM capabilities, or arrange with the library's own municipal, campus, or business center to do the work.

Once a COM catalog has been decided upon, the department head should stipulate what information he would like included on the records. Should all the information now contained on the catalog cards be replicated, or would a less detailed (and less expensive) abridged version be acceptable to patrons and to librarians? Could users do without full illustration and imprint statements, size, and notes? Or would a compromise be acceptable, with a complete bibliographic record for the shelflist microform and with the other files containing only main entry, title, edition statement, publisher and date, call number, and holdings? Partial records are usually more than adequate to interface with an automated circulation and acquisition system.

Will the library want to include all its holdings in one union catalog or should it publish several indexes for different users and types of materials? It could, for example, issue a main catalog for monographs and several separate microform files for technical reports, serials, maps, and A-V materials, and even produce "browsing lists." The COM catalog, in other words, offers the library a chance to rethink completely its record formats and its methods of bibliographic access.

How many microform sets should be produced, and how should they be distributed? All branch and department libraries will want at least one set (with supplements) and a viewing machine. Sets should also be sent to interested libraries in the area and to institutions belonging to the library's consortium or network. The department head should also have a voice in the selection of fiche holders, viewers, and carrels.

What about the method and frequency of updating the COM catalogs? Monthly cumulations are best, but a much more economical arrangement would be to issue cumulated monthly or bimonthly supplements, with full cumulations produced annually or semiannually. Above all, the department head must look to the future. He must make sure that the COM system is flexible enough to integrate with other foreseeable library automation projects, including an online catalog.

Online Catalog

One of the basic differences between an online public access catalog (OPAC) and a COM catalog is that the online catalog provides direct interaction between user and the catalog. The data base is the catalog, which means, among other things, that access to the records is instantaneous. There is, for example, no waiting for the appearance of the latest microfiche supplement or for catalog cards to be produced and filed. Also, accessibility to records is potentially much more flexible than with other catalogs. Besides searching records through the traditional access points of main and added entries, title, subject, and series, users have access by call numbers and by ISBN/ISSN and LC card numbers; and with Boolean search capabilities, records can be located by keywords and searches can be qualified by publisher, date, language, and other parameters.

Besides considering many of the same criteria necessary for selecting other computer-based systems, there are specific factors that the department head should look at when deciding upon an online catalog. If the terminals are to be used by patrons with a minimum of assistance from librarians, an essential prerequisite would be that the system be user friendly. The arrangement of the keyboard and the clarity of the screen are, therefore, important considerations; also, search instructions should be easy to follow and users should be able to quickly and simply institute a search and then move through the system with a minimum of confusion.

Because the online catalog provides users with direct access, response and down time, number and location of terminals, and availability of at least a temporary backup must all be considered. As with a COM catalog, the decision of whether to use full or brief record formats is an important factor, as would be the decision of whether or not users can and should have access through the terminals to all the materials, book and nonbook, housed in the library. If at all possible, an online catalog should interface with the library's other automated files. Eventually, users should be provided access to serials holdings and receive acquisition information on in-process items. Ideally, the system should also provide users with circulation-status information and even be able to handle inter-library loan requests.

The most important consideration is, of course, costs, which up to now have made online systems possible for only a very few libraries. However, if the system is fully integrated, as it should be, costs could be spread among several of the library's bibliographic services and not represent solely a catalog department budget item. Costs would have to include not only initial hardware, software, and site preparation, but provide for maintenance, staffing, training, and supply needs that would continue on into the foreseeable future.

Retrospective Conversion

A major concern in automating a catalog department is a procedure called retrospective conversion (recon or retrocon, for short), which is the conversion of a library's holdings from the old catalog cards to machine-readable form. In developing a conversion program, the department head must decide, among other things, exactly how much of the old cataloging information to include on the new records and what new data to add. Ideally, the machine-readable records should contain full MARC format and complete AACR2 cataloging. This allows the library to exchange records with other data bases and to make full use of bibliographic utilities and vendors. If the library has been using brief or minimal-level cataloging for its nonbooks or other selected materials, the department head has the choice of either upgrading the present minimal-level cataloging during the conversion process or keeping the machine-readable records in brief formats for local use only. Of course, if the library is a member of a bibliographic network, it should conform to network standards.

A decision will have to be made on whether to do the conversion locally or to contract with an outside source to do the work. The answer will depend on several factors, including staffing requirements, number and type of records involved, fullness and quality of the old cataloging, available time and funding, and accessibility to a bibliographic utility. If the library is a member of a computer-based network (OCLC, for instance), it can use the network's data base. The library simply matches its records against those in the data base, editing where necessary, and produces machine-readable records. For those records where no matches are found, the library would have to enter the records manually, just as it would for future incoming materials not found in the data base. The library could also input all its records directly into the data base, editing and updating as it went along. One of the least expensive but most time-consuming methods is to convert records "on-the-fly"; in other words, to convert a record only when the item is returned to the circulation department or when the catalog cards or book has been pulled for some reason.

The library can also contract with a vendor or other outside source to do the conversion. In this case, the library would send its shelflist or other hard copy to the vendor for matching (or direct inputting) or prepare a tape containing ISBN/ISSN or LC card numbers which the vendor would match against its data base. Direct, or manual, inputting, either by the library or by an outside source, would be the most expensive alternative and is usually done only when the records require a good deal of editing or are brief or otherwise unique.

After a conversion method has been selected, the department head will have to access the impact of the project on the department's regular activities and determine the time and resources needed to complete the conversion. If the work is to be performed locally, the project will have to be coordinated with the department's other operations and provisions will have to be made for personnel to match and enter

records and to perform the various related activities, such
as searching for missing cards and books. At this point,
the department head might also want to consider weeding the
collection. Certainly he will want to establish minimum standards and set up quality control methods or make sure that
whoever has contracted to do the converting has developed a
consistent control method, including the establishment of cross-
references in the bibliographic file. If the library is a member of a network, the authority control, like the fullness of
the cataloging, should follow network standards and be based
on the network's files.

As with all management decisions, the most important
considerations will be future considerations. Whether the library is converting its old records into machine-readable
form, joining a computer-based network, moving to a COM
catalog, preparing for an online catalog, or a combination of
the above, the department head must continually look to the
future and to unforeseen technological developments. In
other words, whatever the library's latest approach to bibliographic access might be, it will be far from final.

SELECT BIBLIOGRAPHY

Allerton Park Institute, 24th, 1978. Supervision of Employees
  in Libraries. Urbana-Champaign: University of Illinois
  Graduate School of Library Science, 1979.

American Library Association. Library Administration Division.
  Personnel Organization and Procedure: A Manual Sug-
  gested for Use in Academic Libraries. 2d ed. Chicago:
  American Library Association, 1968.

_____. _____. Personnel Organization and Procedure:
  A Manual Suggested for Use in Public Libraries. 2d ed.
  Chicago: American Library Association, 1968.

Argyris, Chris. Personality and Organization. New York:
  Harper & Row, 1957.

Bailey, Martha J. Supervisory and Middle Managers in Libraries. Metuchen, N.J.: Scarecrow Press, 1981.

Bakewell, K. G. B. Management Principles and Practices:
  A Guide to Information Sources. Detroit: Gale Research
  Co., 1977.

Bartlett, Alton C., and Thomas A. Kayser, eds. Changing
  Organizational Behavior. Englewood Cliffs, N.J.: Prentice-
  Hall, 1973.

Beach, Dale S. Personnel: The Management of People at
  Work. 4th ed. New York: Macmillan, 1980.

Bennis, Warren G. Changing Organizations. New York:
  McGraw-Hill, 1966.

Boaz, Martha, ed. Current Concepts in Library Management.
  Littleton, Colo.: Libraries Unlimited, 1979.

Boss, Richard W. The Library Manager's Guide to Automation. White Plains, N.Y.: Knowledge Industry Publications, 1984.

Broadwell, Martin M. The New Supervisor. 3d ed. Reading, Mass.: Addison-Wesley, 1984.

Chapman, Edward A. Library Systems Analysis Guidelines. New York: Wiley, 1970.

Chen, Ching-chih. Library Management Without Bias. Greenwich, Conn.: Jai Press, 1980.

Cohen, Elaine. Automation, Space Management, and Productivity: A Guide for Libraries. New York: R. R. Bowker, 1981.

Conroy, Barbara. Library Staff Development and Continuing Education: Principles and Practices. Littleton, Colo.: Libraries Unlimited, 1978.

Corbin, John B. Managing the Library Automation Project. Phoenix, Ariz.: Oryx Press, 1985.

_____. A Technical Services Manual for Small Libraries. Metuchen, N.J.: Scarecrow Press, 1971.

Davis, Keith. Human Behavior at Work: Organizational Behavior. 7th ed. New York: McGraw-Hill, 1985.

Dougherty, Richard M., and Fred J. Heinritz. Scientific Management of Library Operations. 2d ed. Metuchen, N.J.: Scarecrow Press, 1982.

Drucker, Peter F. Management: Tasks, Responsibilities, Practices. New York: Harper & Row, 1974.

_____. Managing for Results. New York: Harper & Row, 1964.

_____. Managing in Turbulent Times. New York: Harper & Row, 1980.

Dunkin, Paul S. Cataloging U.S.A. Chicago: American Library Association, 1969.

Dunn, J. D., and Elvis C. Stephens. Management of Personnel. New York: McGraw-Hill, 1972.

Emery, Richard. Staff Communication in Libraries. Hamden, Conn.: Linnet Books, 1975.

Evans, G. Edward. Management Techniques for Librarians. 2d ed. New York: Academic Press, 1983.

Fallon, William K. Effective Communication on the Job. 3d ed. New York: AMACOM, 1981.

Godden, Irene P., ed. Library Technical Services: Operations and Management. Orlando, Fla.: Academic Press, 1984.

Gore, Daniel; Joseph Kimbrough; and Peter Spyers-Duran, eds. Requiem for the Card Catalog: Management Issues in Automated Cataloging. Westport, Conn.: Greenwood Press, 1979.

Hayes, Robert M., and Joseph Becker. Handbook of Data Processing for Libraries. 2d ed. Los Angeles: Melville Pub. Co., 1974.

Herzberg, Frederick. Work and the Nature of Man. New York: New American Library, 1973.

Hickey, Doralyn J. Problems in Organizing Library Collections. New York: R. R. Bowker, 1972.

Kemper, Robert E. Library Management: Behavior-Based Personnel Systems: A Framework for Analysis. Littleton, Colo.: Libraries Unlimited, 1971.

Koontz, Harold, and Cyril O'Donnel. Essentials of Management. 3d ed. New York: McGraw-Hill, 1982.

_____. Management: A Book of Readings. 5th ed. New York: McGraw-Hill, 1980.

Lee, Sul H., ed. Emerging Trends in Library Organization. Ann Arbor, Mich.: Pierian Press, 1978.

Likert, Rensis. The Human Organization. New York: McGraw-Hill, 1976.

_____. New Patterns of Management. New York: McGraw-Hill, 1961.

Lipsett, Laurence L.; Frank P. Rodgers; and Harold M. Kentner. Personnel Selection and Recruitment. Boston: Allyn & Bacon, 1964.

Lowell, Mildred H. The Management of Libraries and Information Centers. 4 vols. Metuchen, N.J.: Scarecrow Press, 1968-71.

McClure, Charles R., and Alan R. Samuels. Strategies for Library Administration: Concepts and Approaches. Littleton, Colo.: Libraries Unlimited, 1982.

McGarry, K. J. Communication, Knowledge and the Librarian. Hamden, Conn.: Linnet Books, 1975.

McGregor, Douglas. The Human Side of Enterprise. New York: McGraw-Hill, 1960.

_____. The Professional Manager. New York: McGraw-Hill, 1967.

Marchant, Maurice P. Participative Management in Academic Libraries. Westport, Conn.: Greenwood Press, 1976.

Markuson, Barbara E., and Blanche Woolls. Networks for Networkers: Critical Issues in Cooperative Library Development. New York: Neal-Schuman, 1980.

Martin, Lowell A. Organizational Structure of Libraries. Metuchen, N.J.: Scarecrow Press, 1984.

Maslow, Abraham H. Motivation and Personality. 2d ed. New York: Harper & Row, 1970.

Matthews, Joseph R., ed. A Reader on Choosing an Automated Library System. Chicago: American Library Association, 1983.

Moore, Franklin. Management, Organization and Practice. New York: Harper & Row, 1964.

Plate, Kenneth H. Management Personnel in Libraries: A

Theoretical Model for Analysis. Rockaway, N.J.: American Faculty Press, 1970.

Reynolds, Dennis. Library Automation: Issues and Applications. New York: R. R. Bowker, 1985.

Ricking, Myrl, and Robert E. Booth. Personnel Utilization in Libraries: A Systems Approach. Chicago: American Library Association, 1974.

Riggs, Donald E., ed. Library Leadership: Visualizing the Future. Phoenix, Ariz.: Oryx Press, 1982.

Rogers, Rutherford D., and David C. Weber. University Library Administration. New York: H. W. Wilson Co., 1971.

Saffady, William. Introduction to Automation for Librarians. Chicago: American Library Association, 1983.

Sager, Donald J. Participatory Management in Libraries. Metuchen, N.J.: Scarecrow Press, 1982.

Sartain, Aaron Q., and Alton W. Baker. The Supervisor and the Job. 3d ed. New York: McGraw-Hill, 1978.

Sayles, Leonard R. Managerial Behavior. New York: McGraw-Hill, 1964.

Scott, William G. Organization Theory. Homewood, Ill.: R. D. Irwin, 1972.

Shields, Gerald R., and Gordon J. Burke, eds. Budgeting for Accountability in Libraries: A Selection of Readings. Metuchen, N.J.: Scarecrow Press, 1974.

Shimmon, Ross, ed. A Reader in Library Management. Hamden, Conn.: Linnet Books, 1976.

Sigband, Norman B. Communication for Management and Business. 2d ed. Glenview, Ill.: Scott, Foresman, 1976.

Stevens, Norman D. Communication Throughout Libraries. Metuchen, N.J.: Scarecrow Press, 1983.

Stone, Elizabeth W. Factors Related to the Professional

Development of Librarians. Metuchen, N.J.: Scarecrow Press, 1969.

_____, ed. New Directions in Staff Development. Micro-Workshop on Staff Development, Detroit, 1970. Chicago: American Library Association, 1971.

Studies in Library Management. 6 vol. Hamden, Conn.: Linnet Books, 1972-80.

Stueart, Robert D., and John T. Eastlick. Library Management. 2d ed. Littleton, Colo.: Libraries Unlimited, 1981.

Thomas, John M., and Warren G. Bennis. The Management of Change and Conflict: Selected Readings. Middlesex, Eng.: Penguin Books, 1972.

Toffler, Alvin. Future Shock. New York: Bantam Books, 1971.

_____. The Third Wave. New York: Morrow, 1980.

Woods, Lawrence A., and Nolan F. Pope. The Librarian's Guide to Microcomputer Technology and Applications. White Plains, N.Y.: Knowledge Industry Publications, 1983.

Wynar, Bohdan S. Introduction to Cataloging and Classification. 7th ed. Littleton, Colo.: Libraries Unlimited, 1985.

INDEX